Learning to Dream Again

Learning to Dream Again

REDISCOVERING THE HEART OF GOD

Samuel Wells

WILLIAM B. EERDMANS PUBLISHING COMPANY

GRAND RAPIDS, MICHIGAN / CAMBRIDGE, U.K.

Published 2013 by
Wm. B. Eerdmans Publishing Co.
2140 Oak Industrial Drive N.E., Grand Rapids, Michigan 49505 /
P.O. Box 163, Cambridge CB3 9PU U.K.

Printed in the United States of America

19 18 17 16 15 14 13   7 6 5 4 3 2 1

Library of Congress Cataloging-in-Publication Data

Wells, Samuel, 1965-
Learning to dream again: rediscovering the heart of God / Samuel Wells.
pages   cm
Includes bibliographical references and index.
ISBN 978-0-8028-6871-8 (pbk.: alk. paper)
1. Christian life. I. Title.

BV4510.3.W43 2013

248.4 — dc23

2013001753

www.eerdmans.com

For Richard Brodhead

Contents

Contents

Preface

I had the very great privilege of serving for seven years as Dean of the Chapel at Duke University, and as a professor at Duke Divinity School; this book is made up of reflections that were written during my time there. I have a sense of gratitude for those seven years of plenty, a gratitude that will never cease.

I am thankful for being given space to think. At Duke I always knew that I was employed to think, meditate, and pray deeply about the sources and nature and purposes of our common life, and to set that common life in the perspective of the kingdom of God. What a vibrant life. What remarkable conversation partners. What an invigorating task. What a dream.

And in various settings around America, sometimes in England, and occasionally elsewhere, there were audiences, classes, and congregations willing to listen to and evaluate arguments and proposals. When I heard ideas that needed wider airing, or putting into personal or institutional practice, I had extraordinary colleagues whose dedication and skills left me in awe. When we got it right, there were few better feelings in all the world. And when I got it wrong, I had people to tell me the truth.

I am deeply thankful for the generosity, rigor, research, insight, challenge, and companionship of Rebekah Eklund, who did most of the work of turning disparate thoughts into a coherent and cogent manuscript. She is the embodiment of the phrase "There is no limit to what can be achieved so long as you don't mind who gets the credit." I can never thank her enough. I am likewise grateful for Adrienne Koch and Dave Allen, whose devoted work as my communications assistants gave me time and space to think, and who often knew my head and my heart better than I did. I am also indebted to Marsá McNutt, who, with characteristic generosity of heart, provided the index.

I want to thank those who never let me forget that wisdom is founded in worship: Meghan Feldmeyer, Rodney Wynkoop, David Arcus, Bruce Puckett, Allan Friedman, Christy Lohr Sapp, Beth Gettys Sturkey, Bob Parkins, Adam Hollowell, Kori Jones, and Keith Daniel.

If I think of what it means to dream, I think immediately of my wife Jo, who has shared with me so many dreams, and with whom, together with our children, I am thankful to continue to dream. There would be no book like this without her support and encouragement and example. If I think of what it means to learn — to love, to live, to think, to read, to feel, or to dream — I think first of Stanley Hauerwas, from whom I have learned more than I can begin to describe or imagine. The ideas found in these pages have also been enriched by conversations with Richard Hays, Ellen Davis, Norman Wirzba, Ray Barfield, Tony Galanos, Greg Jones, Marcia Owen, Blair Sheppard, John Inge, Rick Simpson, Stuart Goddard, Michael Northcott, and Walter Brueggemann. I owe the title, and much besides, to Graham James, who is the gentle counselor named in the final essay of the book.

One person who epitomizes all that is good about Duke University is President Richard Brodhead. He deeply understood all that I sought to do at Duke; he grasped, engaged, and sometimes challenged my ideas, my vision, my faith, and my practice. It was he who invited me to come to Duke — and thus gave me permission to dream. In gratitude, for who he is and what he embodies, this book is dedicated to him.

Introduction

I have three things to say before I begin in earnest. I offer a word about the form of the book, and the way I seek to communicate in these pages. I then move to the theme of the book, and the underlying motivation that guided its composition. Finally I give a brief overview of the book's contents, including an explanation of the title and the shape of the chapters.

Form

In 490 B.C., the Athenians defeated the Persians in the battle of Marathon. According to legend, the Athenian messenger Pheidippides was sent to bring the news of victory to the Athenian assembly. He ran the whole way, a good twenty-six miles, without stopping. He arrived, breathless, and proclaimed, "We won!" He promptly collapsed and died.

When I prepare sermons, addresses, essays, papers, or even books, I want them to be like Pheidippides' announcement. I want them to tell of great news, wondrous news, news on which the lives of my hearers depend. I want them to announce news that shapes the destiny of peoples, news that I'd run twenty-six miles to share. I want them to proclaim news that has involved my whole being to discover, news that takes every drop of my energy to communicate, news that I would be

1

happy to constitute my dying breath on earth. So it has to be the best I've ever done, because the news is even better now than it was when I last preached, or spoke, or wrote. It has to be something in which I'm personally invested, or else I can't demand the attention of my listeners or readers. It has to be good news, otherwise why would I be so eager to tell it or write it? It has to be something my listeners or readers don't already know, otherwise it's not really news. It has to be something that's about life and death, otherwise it's not worth being the last thing I ever say or write. And the way I communicate it, the way it captivates the whole of my being, the way it seeks to transfix the reader or listener, the way it's something I can't keep from singing, expresses almost as much as the news itself.

That's what this book sets out to be. It is made up of short pieces, designed to be read and pondered singly, but grouped into chapters of particular themes or styles. Each of the pieces is an argument, and each of them pursues that argument in four modes — although of course they differ in the degree to which they employ those four respective modes.[1]

The first mode concerns the conceptual, the intellectual, the mental, the cerebral. The first thing I'm looking for is that what I say is interesting. That's not so much about arousing simple curiosity. It's more about addressing a question that most people in the church and elsewhere would rather avoid, or maybe ask in a vague way and never answer. I assume my readers and listeners are largely people who've heard the gospel many times, but who have privately always been bothered by the anomalies, incongruities, and big unanswered questions no one seems to talk about; and that there are also people new to faith, who want to know this is for real, and not just a place of escape from the searching questions of their lives. So as I survey passages of Scripture, I'm looking for something that grasps me that I've never seen before, some symmetry or correspondence with God's gift of sal-

---

1. These are developments of ideas first expressed in Samuel Wells, *Be Not Afraid: Facing Fear with Faith* (Grand Rapids: Brazos, 2011), xiii-xiv. For a fuller account of this framework, see "The Power of Preaching," *Clergy Journal*, November/December 2011, 4-6.

vation, some neat parallel or satisfying resonance — something that makes a story or section a perfect crystallization of a crucial aspect of the gospel. As an argument, each piece in this book takes something problematic and resolves it by a mixture of logic, information, evidence, and persuasion. An argument can usually, in fact almost always, be summarized in a single succinct sentence. If it can't, it often doesn't deserve the name argument at all.

The second mode concerns the nonverbal, the visceral, the primal: the realm of the gut. True believing is about the gut. It's about things you can't give an explanation for; you just know. It's about experiences and commitments that go so deep they sear your soul, and when someone treads on them or abuses them you don't just feel angry or hurt — you feel sick. The vitality of most of the pieces in this book is in the interplay between the head and the gut. It must always be both. The intention is to knock the wind out of you like a punch in the stomach, and then pour a shower over your head that makes you feel fresher than you've ever felt. You should feel alive, and in touch with your body and soul. But, like a short story, the satisfaction only comes if you've been aching in your gut and the piece names that ache and describes it in a compelling way.

The third mode, less important than the first two, is the realm of feeling, emotion, and interpersonal imagination: in short, the heart. There is a role for speaking to the heart, provided that it takes its place behind, and serves the purpose of, speaking to the head and gut. The great danger of a story or illustration directed to the heart, without concern for head or gut, is sentimentality. I try to be rigorous in the employment of moving or emotionally engaging material; that means making sure it is tightly moored to the cerebral argument or firmly rooted in visceral, primal, human reality. The same, not quite so dogmatically, goes for humor. I try to avoid using humor to ingratiate myself to a readership or audience or congregation; I use it even less to avoid a difficult theme by artful or ironic distraction. Yet humor harnessed to argument or to nonverbal, gut-level human experience can be compelling. This is also true of song. Popular and hymnic songs lie so deep in the collective and personal memory that they are close to the unconscious, and the unearthing of them is often a helpful connection with the heart.

The fourth mode is the practical, concrete domain of the hand. A readership or audience or congregation doesn't always need a take-away. Sometimes it is enough either to be simply lost in wonder, love, and praise, or to be confronted with the pathos that there is nothing to do. But as a writer and preacher I usually need to be able to answer the question, "So what?" That must almost never be the first question. I try only to dwell on the hand if I've done a thorough job on head, gut, and heart. Only by proving to people that I know the heart of God, and know the human heart, and love both, do I hope to gain the authority to show them what God wants them to do. Likewise when I'm discussing major public issues, I need to have gained people's trust in advance. Several of the pieces in this book address controversial subjects, such as abortion and torture — but they are surrounded by essays that are straightforwardly about the love of God.

Theme

The nature of most of my writing and thinking has always been reflection on context. Almost all the essays in this book took shape during my time at Duke University, where I served for seven years as Dean of the Chapel. One of the greatest privileges I had at Duke was to be invited to teach undergraduates for one course each year. The course was in public policy and was called "Ethics in an Unjust World." I used to tell the students I called it "Everything I was cross about when I was nineteen." I assumed that the students were distressed about the unfairness and injustice and suffering in the world. I exposed them to helpful texts, challenging site visits, provocative interviews, and interactive lectures. I sought to pass on to them such wisdom as I've gleaned in the previous twenty-five years about how to address social disadvantage. I would then invite them to spend the rest of their lives going deeper and doing better than I had.

At the start of the semester I used to ask the whole class, "How many of you have done an extended service project, like a mission trip or summer internship for a nonprofit?" Of the 150 or so students I had in class over those years, almost every hand went up. And then I would

4

ask, "And how many of you have done a ten- or fifteen-page class paper reflecting on the experience?" No hands — or maybe one or two each year, at most.

Think about what this exercise tells us about the way we organize our lives today. We have a tremendous thirst for experience. The students in my class hadn't just done amazing service projects — they'd done them in every imaginable part of the world. Their résumés were bulging with experience. Meanwhile they'd done a lot of study. They'd taken courses in a dazzling range of subjects from some of the great professors of today and tomorrow, and read great works from yesterday and today. But where in a modern research university — or anywhere else — does all this knowledge and experience percolate into *wisdom*? Could it possibly be that we're anxious about wisdom, so we avoid the moment of truth by simply accumulating more and more knowledge and experience? Is that why we're always in such a hurry — lest anyone call us to account for a wisdom we fear we don't have?

Another question I ask the class is, "Have you ever heard a school or college administrator or professor say, 'We're here to help you discover your deepest passion, and then to show you ways you can pursue that passion wherever it may lead'?" Whenever I ask undergraduates that, they giggle and roll their eyes and say they've heard that speech forty times. So then I ask, "Have you ever heard someone say, 'Some passions are good passions to follow; and some not so good. We're here to inspire and cultivate good passions in you and help you discover ways to turn your transitory desires into lifelong loves, to explore your passing passions until you find your true vocation'?" "No," they say. "I've never heard that speech."

This book sets out to offer different versions of "that speech" — to stimulate its readers to inspire and cultivate good passions, and to help them discover ways to turn their transitory desires into lifelong loves. That's what the ministry of Duke Chapel, under my leadership, has sought to do. That's what my ministry, at Duke and elsewhere, has been about.

It's a ministry that's swimming against a tide. It feels like we're all embarked on a gigantic displacement activity, and knowledge and experience are among the items we voraciously accumulate on the way.

Another item for which there's a vaunted quest is technical skill. "Bureaucracy" is the name for a society that has elevated technique over purpose — that has become better and quicker and more efficient at getting things done, but slower and more reluctant and less articulate about explaining why. Sometimes the word "leadership" suggests that where we're going doesn't matter so long as we have the drive and charisma to get us there quickly. In wider society there seems to be no limit to the power of the words "freedom" and "choice." It's as if the only things that matter are that we have lots of options and no one to tell us what to do. But what's the point of having choice if we never develop the ability to make good choices?

Leadership, technique, choice, experience, knowledge. They all have their place. They're all ways of finding or applying something more fundamental than any of them. And that fundamental thing is *wisdom*. What is knowledge if it's never translated into wisdom? What is experience if it's never distilled into wisdom? What's the use of technique and leadership if there's no wisdom behind their application?

So why *is* wisdom so out of fashion? Somehow it sounds pretentious and archaic. No one wants to give the impression they're sitting cross-legged under a eucalyptus tree uttering epigrams and nodding their head slowly all the time. And yet wisdom also seems elusive: it's not something that's as easily taught as algebra or as readily researched as the prevalence of recidivism among teenagers released from prison over the last three years. It also smells a little bit of privilege and elitism. There's a lingering suspicion that the ancient Greeks talked a lot about it, but they assumed that a wise person was always a man, always had enough wealth to be largely at leisure, and always had slaves to see to his every need. Such things are rightly out of fashion these days. At the same time, talk of wisdom sounds judgmental — tied to outmoded hierarchies and discredited authority: it's one thing to point to facts and demonstrate skills — but who are you to tell me what's wise and what's not? Perhaps most of all, in a world where almost everything we buy promises to give us a shortcut or make our life easier, wisdom sounds just plain *hard* — too demanding, and humorless, and time-consuming to hang around with for long.

So what is Christian wisdom? This book sets out to shape a theological imagination around three themes. Those themes are earthy humility, shameful suffering, and effervescent joy.

The first phrase is earthy humility. We are bodies. Our power is finite, our reach is bounded, our flourishing is fragile, our mortality is unavoidable. We have minds, and those minds can think way beyond our limitations; but those minds are part of our bodies. Our bodies are not clumsy obstacles to our dreams. Instead, any wisdom we find will come out of the harmony of our minds and our bodies, the synthesis of theory and practice, the combination of ideals and realities.

But we're not the only bodies, now or in time. There have been many people before, and they've asked questions as big as ours, and found truth as deep as we have. Their wisdom is the template for ours. That's what the Scriptures are to Christians — the wisdom of those who have encountered God. Our willingness to read Scripture and to be read by Scripture is a sign of our humility that we take our place as small players in a huge story, the general shape of which can't be determined or ruined by us. Scripture isn't a constellation of disembodied ideals: it's an earthy series of pragmatic instances of fragile human encounters with ultimate reality, distilled and percolated over time into wisdom.

Look at the palms of your hands, and take the pulse of your touch; look at your smile in the mirror; listen to your breathing, and inhabit your silence; measure your step; and hear the pace and tenderness of the words you speak. These are the places where your wisdom dwells, and where others will sense it. This is where earthy humility resides.

The second phrase is shameful suffering. There's no avoiding suffering in life. It's so integral to life that a whole religion, Buddhism, has been constructed to address it. A great deal of suffering is the flip side of love. If we didn't love, if we hadn't allowed our whole being to be wrapped up in the lives of others, we wouldn't be so beset by suffering. But we've chosen not to be islands. And so when one part of the body suffers, the body as a whole feels the pain. Yet suffering is inextricably tied up with wisdom. At the end of Sophocles' *Antigone*, with the characteristic Greek pile of corpses and blood disclosing that once again some good kids had made some poor choices with tragic results, Creon is the one figure still standing. And he's described as a man who through suffering had become wise.[2] That's not what suffering is for, but it's the most common way in which we seek to redeem suffering. If you're in a place of intense suffering right now, you'll be facing this reality: Do I let it make me bitter, do I try to suppress it and defeat it — or do I let it make my soul grow and give me wisdom?

But don't miss the sense of shame. We avoid and fear shame maybe even more than we do suffering. Shame strips us of our defenses against our fragile mortality. We have no justice to call on, no public esteem to hope for, no leg to stand on. Just feel that blush that engulfs your whole body. Shame is nakedness in the face of ridicule, vulnerability in the face of blame, and guilt without excuse. If wisdom is going to speak from the depths, it must pierce our pride and reach our shame.

The third phrase is effervescent joy. Think about the moment when you're carried to heaven singing a hymn, or when a very special person comes around the corner at the arrivals lane at the airport and you race toward that person with outstretched arms, or when you open your eyes and realize you wouldn't rather be anywhere else in the world. We can get overly sentimental about the wisdom of children, but children sometimes articulate a joy that no one else can name. Suffering isn't the whole reality of the human lot. There's also ecstasy. There's also worship. To worship is to say "All the reality I've ever known is swallowed up in you; I've been walking my life into a headwind and now I want to turn around and be swept off the ground by your Spirit."

That handing over of control, that letting-go of one's ultimate destiny, is a central part of wisdom. It's the realization that there's immense power in the universe, but it can't be acquired, only received as a gift. Prayer is the moment we tap into that immense power. But it's effervescent because there's always more; it's always overflowing, you can't ever put the lid on it. Wisdom isn't something you can nail down

2. Sophocles, *The Theban Plays: Oedipus the King, Oedipus at Colonus, Antigone,* trans. Ruth Fainlight and Robert J. Littman (Baltimore: Johns Hopkins University Press, 2009), 188. At the very end, the chorus says, "The mighty boasts of haughty men/bring down the punishment of mighty blows — /from which at last, in old age, wisdom comes."

— it's something that bursts out of reduction and rolls away the stone of compression.

Earthy humility, shameful suffering, effervescent joy. This is the shape of wisdom.

In the first century the dominant philosophy was Greek. The Greeks focused their quest for human fulfillment on one thing above all: what they called *sophia*, and we call wisdom. When Saint Paul wrote to Christians in Greece, he said this age-old quest for wisdom had met its destiny in Jesus Christ. Jesus was everything *sophia* was searching for. And what was the wisdom Jesus brought?

Jesus brought the wisdom of incarnation. Jesus inhabited a human body, and made the truth of God visible in tangible form. He blessed the ordinary and the mundane, the created world and the people in it. He spent time in the mountains, on the sea, in the desert, and on the plain. He expressed the wisdom of the country and the discourse of the marketplace. You could call this the wisdom of incarnation: earthy humility.

But Jesus also brought the wisdom of the cross. The cross wasn't just excruciating, slow, agonizing torture. It was utter, wholesale, and merciless shame. It was the way Romans exposed rebellious peasants and recalcitrant slaves and made a fool of them, showing what became of those who thought they knew better than the emperor's idea of peace. We think nothing of displaying crosses on altars, hillsides, and churches, and even around our necks. But never forget that the cross is the symbol of utter shame, so much so that Greeks couldn't comprehend how you could call someone savior if his death was so unspeakably embarrassing. Just for a moment, allow Jesus to speak wisdom from your places of embarrassment and humiliation. Jesus spoke wisdom from the two most terrifying places imaginable. You could call this the wisdom of the cross: shameful suffering.

And Jesus also brought the wisdom of resurrection and the sending of the Holy Spirit. Jesus embodied a life that death couldn't contain, a power that was like wind and fire, a bubbling, overflowing delight that inspired worship and felt like a torrent of cleansing water into which you longed to jump. This was the wisdom of beyond and above and ecstasy and forever. You could call this the wisdom of resurrection and Pentecost: effervescent joy.

So this is the secret of wisdom: Jesus. Jesus wasn't a wandering sage who sat cross-legged and uttered epigrams; he wasn't a distant genius who was so wrapped up in his research that he only had time for opaque monosyllables; he wasn't a member of a privileged elite who demanded leisure to converse and contemplate with others like himself. Jesus' life is the shape of wisdom. It has ordinary, homespun, pragmatic, earthy humility. It has delicately wrought and painstakingly etched consolations chiseled from shameful suffering. It has delight beyond words, and power beyond imagining, bathed in effervescent joy.

Paul has a phrase that draws all this wisdom together and names where it resides. He calls it "the mind of Christ." But here's the astonishing part. He says, "*We have* the mind of Christ" (1 Corinthians 2:16). Not "We've seen it," or "We've heard it," or "We read it somewhere," or "We thought about it for a while," or "We need to get around to it someday," or "We respect it," or "We admire it," or "We like it": "We *have* it." We *have* it. We *have* the mind of Christ. We've been *given* this wisdom.

So this is our test when we're yearning for wisdom — when we're unsure whom to trust and how to follow and where to dwell. This is the church's test in the face of new technologies, environmental challenges, political turbulence, and internal quarrels. This is your test today, if you're caught in the headlights of overwhelming knowledge, contradictory experience, and paralyzing choice. Am I patiently walking with Jesus' earthy humility? Am I blushing and aching with Jesus' shameful suffering? Am I dancing and wondering with Jesus' effervescent joy? Am I denying that I have truly been given the mind of Christ?

Contents

I have entitled this book *Learning to Dream Again* for three reasons. The first is that the notion of "dreaming" synthesizes much of what I said above about the head, the gut, the heart. Dreaming is intriguing because it is on the boundary between what we already know and what we have never fully seen. Dreams place before us familiar images in extraordinary contexts, or extraordinary images in familiar contexts. But dreaming is also disturbing, because it shakes our sense of normal, respectable, and predictable with an inrush of possible, playful, and poetical. I intend for the essays in this volume to do all these things. The notion of "learning to dream" is provocative because it seems an oxymoron — dreaming seems involuntary, beyond control, the realm of the unconscious. But Christian hope is a matter of discipline more than simple self-expression. Hope is about learning to dream — provided one remembers that the dream comes not so much out of one's own unconscious, but out of God's. Hope is first learning God's dream, and then living it.

The second dimension of the title lies in the little word "again." Duke Chapel in general and its dean in particular are the focus of many projections; but the most recurring is that, at a time of considerable loss of confidence among mainline denominations, many people look to a place like Duke Chapel and in particular its regular preacher to be a location of restoring hope, a form of worship, music, architecture, and preaching immune from the inflation of liturgical currency and the dilution of homiletical substance. Like "home," "again" is a word prone to sentimental or nostalgic manipulation. Was there ever a time, after all, when faith and hope and love were what they should be? Nonetheless, "again" identifies the spirit in which much, perhaps most, of my ministry as Dean of Duke Chapel was interpreted. There is an abiding sense that people have participated in something beautiful, true, and good; they are looking for conviction and inspiration to rediscover that, even if they themselves may have changed, God and the kingdom of God fundamentally haven't.

The third dimension of the title is much simpler, and is explained in the final section of the final chapter of the book. At a low point in my ministry, a person of wisdom gave me some kind and perceptive counsel; and from that moment, it may be no exaggeration to say, came the vocation to write, the sojourn at Duke, and the occasion for putting together the contents of this volume. My dream for this book is that it might have the same depth of effect on its readers as that conversation did on me.

The six themes that gather around the general structure of "learning . . . again" are by no means exhaustive. The book begins and ends with chapters concerning what we might call the wisdom of the gut. Here I consider questions of identity and grief, and troubling contexts such as 9/11. Chapter 4 offers six examples of how Old and New Testament texts may speak into and shape contemporary questions. Such reading of Scripture undergirds the approach of the book as a whole. Chapters 2 and 3 are a pair: chapter 2 seeks theological understanding of some great cultural forces — arts, science, medicine, sport — while chapter 3 considers some of the great ethical issues of our time — torture, abortion, taxation, justice, hunger. Such themes are viewed from a different perspective in chapter 5, where questions of marriage and divorce, death, and envy are addressed less as ethical issues than as pastoral challenges.

My hope is that the reader finds in this book wisdom drawn from earthy humility, shameful suffering, and effervescent joy. I would like to believe it presents a faithful rendering of the mind of Christ. I trust that it will stimulate a healthy balance of learning and dreaming. And that it may stir its readers to learn to dream again.

CHAPTER 1

Learning to Love Again

All the meditations in this chapter are reflections on love. They are works of theology — that is, they dwell on the love of God — but they hint at and provoke consideration of ethics — human love. What is it like for God to love? Is love the very heart of God, or is love an attribute of a God whose character is definitely grounded somewhere else? What does it mean to say "nothing can separate us from God's love"? Are there any limits to God's love? How can God truly love us if God truly knows us? What does it mean to wrap our whole identity up in God's love? These are the questions with which this chapter wrestles.

Talking about love, one risks the twin dangers of platitude and sentimentality. To avoid platitude, I seek in what follows to point out that contemporary culture invests heavily in commitments and constructions that will work even if love is absent — indeed, that offer a security more reliable than love. Thus love is dangerous, and not straightforward, normal, or obvious. To avoid sentimentality, I repeatedly stress that God's love is crazy, illogical, and a matter of pure grace. It requires stubbornness and sacrifice, ferocity and persistence. There is nothing sentimental about it.

Love to the Loveless Shown That They May Lovely Be

The thing about prejudice is that there's just a tiny sliver of truth in it, otherwise it wouldn't be so infuriating. If there weren't, you could just dismiss it as stupid. But prejudice takes a tiny insight and makes it into a colossal generalization that obscures the complexity, texture, and goodness of its object.

Many, perhaps most, Christians have a prejudice about the Old Testament. One version is the abiding idea that the God of the Old Testament is a God of war and revenge while the God of the New Testament is a God of peace and love. Another version is that the Old Testament is largely made up of prophecies of Jesus' coming, and now that Jesus has come it is used largely to demonstrate that Jesus was part of God's plan all along. Yet another version says that the Old Testament is full of arcane laws and commands and that these are exactly the kinds of strictures that the gospel releases us from. There's a sliver of truth in all these prejudices, which is why they're still around long after they should have been put to bed. But Hosea 11 shows how impoverished all these perceptions of the Old Testament really are. In fact, if you were to advise a newcomer to Christianity how to read the Old Testament, you'd best skip Genesis, Exodus, and the rest, and start there.

My mother died slowly while I was a teenager. One of the saddest things in my life is that when my mother knew she was going to die, she carefully organized a few things for people after she'd gone. What she did for me was to buy a present for my twenty-first birthday and write me a letter that I would open on that day. She let my father and me know the location of the present and the card so we knew how to find them. The sad thing was that, around a year before I turned twenty-one, while my father and I were out of town on vacation, my father's house was burgled and the twenty-first birthday present and its letter were among the things that were stolen. So I never read the letter and I never found out what the present was. I've always wondered. I've always somehow assumed that letter would have explained all the mysteries of my mother's life and that the present would have displayed all her hopes for my life.

Just imagine if that were your story and you really did find that letter many years later. Wouldn't you hold it reverently in two hands, as if blessed by its wondrous existence, its miraculous reappearance in your life after all those years? Wouldn't you have butterflies in your stomach hoping it wouldn't tell you a secret you wished you'd never known or turn out to be very ordinary and prosaic? Wouldn't you expect reading it to be one of the most revealing moments of your life, a moment when timeless wisdom and personal passion met on a single page? That's the state of mind we need to be in when we read the words of the prophet Hosea in Hosea chapter 11.

What Hosea gives us in chapter 11 is a letter from God saying to Israel, "This is what it's been like over all these centuries to have a child like you." And this is an amazing thing in many ways. Step back and reflect for a moment on the ways we talk about having children in our culture. We understand, first of all, how many people long to have children. We feel sympathetic when a friend, especially a female friend, is single, and realize singleness doesn't just mean not having a spouse but can even more acutely mean not having the experience of bearing and raising children. We try to say the right thing when a couple don't seem to be having children, carefully wanting to affirm career and financial concerns and occasionally mumbling letters like *IVF* or words like "adoption" if we feel there's enough trust and understanding between us. A profound yearning for children is something we seldom question. Then twenty or so years later we anticipate good news of college acceptance letters and graduations and proud-hearted parents not wanting to take the credit but selflessly paying the bills for education and experience and a start in life and a lot to look forward to.

But in between, do we really give one another space to identify and explain what being a parent is really like? It seems parents are all desperate to show one another what good parents they are, by the faultless manners of their children in public, by their exemplary school results, by the designer quality of their athletic prowess, and by their success in convincing the grandparents of their unswerving virtue. But where and when do we say how much a parent shouts, how much a parent weeps, how much a parent feels isolated and alone and a failure and a fool?

Some while ago I sat down with a friend and he told me what it had really been like with his teenage son. How his son lied to him. How his son wasted his brains and couldn't get into the rhythm of junior high school. How he started taking various substances. How he stole money from his parents. How it felt like his son was beyond his reach – tremendous fun and good company about one day in five, but far away most of the time, and sometimes a complete demon. I said to my friend, "How much was your sense of failure part of you and your wife splitting up, now that you look back?" He shook his head, adamantly, but when he opened his mouth to deny it, no words came out. And then we reached that moment you sometimes get between two men with a pint of beer in their hands when, however well you know each other, you're not really allowed to do tears, so you put down your drink and tell a joke instead. "Why did God tell Abraham to sacrifice Isaac when he was twelve years old?" my friend asked me. I shrugged my shoulders. "Because if he'd waited until he was thirteen, it wouldn't have been a sacrifice." This is a man who's had more professional recognition than most of us could dream of, but deep down his experience of being a parent had unraveled every fragile and unresolved quality of his character and exposed every tiny inconsistency in his soul, leaving him with the self-esteem of a mashed potato.

This is the kind of story Hosea records God telling about what it was like to be Israel's parent all those years. But it's not a simple tale of woe. It comes in four distinct parts, and I want to look at each of those four parts because they give a profound shape to the story. The story starts in the past, moves into the present, and finishes in the future, and offers us a model of how we might tell our own stories in a similar way.

Let's look at what God says about the past. "When Israel was a child, I *loved* him" (Hosea 11:1, emphasis added). A tiny child can call out the deepest feelings of pride and protection and heart-bursting wonder and joy. Feel God's chest filling with emotion as you ponder these words: "It was I who taught Ephraim to walk" (11:3). (Ephraim is another name for the northern kingdom that split from Judah after the death of Solomon.) "I took them up in my arms" (11:3). It's like a video recording of a child's first steps.

> I led them with cords of human kindness,
>   with bands of love. (11:4)

God is making an analogy between the reins you put on a child as she's learning to potter around on her own two feet and the demonstrations of love God made to Israel that kept Israel steady on its feet in the early days.

> I was to them like those
>> who lift infants to their cheeks.
> I bent down to them and fed them. (11:4)

You can feel God stroking Israel's soft skin and getting out the little spoon and trying to put some liquidized food in Israel's mouth as it sits in its high chair. What a tender scene.

But then the picture shifts to Israel's present. And suddenly the mood changes, and it's like we're in the bar and my friend is telling me about what his son got up to when he was supposed to be at junior high school. You can see God hunched forward, head in hands, saying these words. "The more I called them, the more they went from me . . . they kept offering incense to idols . . . they have refused to return to me. . . . My people are bent on turning away from me." And God is under no illusions that turning a blind eye will make such things go away by themselves. This delinquency has consequences. The people are already facing — or are going to face — exile, conquest, slavery, and civil war. God is devastated to see the way the intimacy of parent and infant child has got to this terrible state.

And then we come to the third picture, the most poignant one of all. We're given the awesome privilege of a window into the heart of God. And in that heart we see an all-night struggle between sober, realistic pragmatism; passionate, wild fury; and overwhelming, tender compassion. God says,

> How can I give you up, Ephraim?
>> How can I hand you over, O Israel? . . .
> My heart recoils within me;
>> my compassion grows warm and tender. (11:8)

How many parents know what such inconsolable soul-searching feels like? But God emerges from it with a firm conviction.

17

I will *not* execute my fierce anger;
    I will *not* again destroy Ephraim;
for I am God and no mortal,
    the Holy One in your midst,
      and I will *not* come in wrath. (11:9, emphasis added)

This is God's present tense, as the Old Testament most acutely describes it. Torn between wrath and mercy, knowing that mercy will cost not less than everything.

And finally we get a glimpse into God and Israel's future. God will be like a lion, who will roar, and God's children, Israel, will come trembling from the four corners to which they had dispersed, and be reunited with one another, with their homes, and with God (11:10-11). Israel will be as timid and tentative as cooing doves in the face of the mighty roar of God. There's no question Israel's return will be God's doing. But like the prodigal son returning to the father, Israel will come back from exile and be reunited in God's home and in God's heart.

I wonder if there's a word of hope for you in this story. I wonder if you know what it means to have a child, or maybe another person you love, follow a self-destructive path that hurts the child, hurts those around the child, and maybe hurts you more than the child ever seems able to comprehend. No doubt your own positive or negative experience of being a child or a parent shapes the way you hear this story. I wonder where you are in this story right now. Are you thinking back to the beautiful, tender times? Or maybe you're right in the thick of the terrible tormented times. Or perhaps you're experiencing the sleepless nights and restless torment of not knowing whether to follow wrath or mercy, whether to try yet another one last chance or to say you've had it with the person and there's no way back. I wonder if there's consolation in God's words of reunion in the future — not a reunion maybe you can envisage right now, but one that God will bring as irresistibly as a roaring lion.

I want to take you back to that lost letter that my mother wrote me when I was a teenager. I've come to believe that in fact I have read that letter. I don't mean that the letter wasn't really stolen or that it miraculously appeared. I mean that Hosea 11 is that lost letter. Hosea 11 is what my mother wanted to tell me with her dying words. Not that she'd been a patient parent and I'd been her wayward child. Not that I would one day have to experience what it means to be a parent whose child breaks his or her heart. Not even that Hosea is every parent's story. None of those things. What matters about Hosea 11 is precisely that it's *God's* story. And in that story it turns out I'm not the long-suffering parent. I'm the destructive child. Hosea isn't a generalized picture of the woes of parenthood. It's a poem and a prayer and a promise from God that says, "You're my beloved child and you've wandered and strayed and I'm in pieces, but one day you'll be reunited with me, although you'll never know how much it cost me to make it so."

That's what I think my mother wanted to tell me. Not that she gave everything for me — but that God did, and still does, and always will. Those words tell me who I am and who God is. If you wrote a last, secret letter to your child or loved one, I wonder what you'd write in it. I think I know what I'd write in mine. I'd write the words of Hosea chapter 11.

Inseparable

I wonder if you've ever walked away from a funeral feeling really cross. Not so much with God, for taking the person away, but more with the clergy and even the family for not telling it like it was, for somehow fabricating a story about the deceased person that didn't have the courage to look into the reality of how the person really lived or the truth of how the person really died. It's almost like you want to do the funeral again, because somehow you can't believe it worked the first time.

That's how I felt when I walked away from my aunt's funeral, many years ago. She was diagnosed with cancer and died three weeks later at the age of seventy. At the funeral we sang happy songs and hymns and the pastor said how strong her faith was and what a great wife and mother she'd been. And I was screaming inside, "But she's dead! Can't you see it? Aren't you sad? Why won't anyone say it?"

But I wasn't just cross with the people who led the funeral. I was cross with my aunt, too. A couple of years earlier I'd injured myself playing rugby at college. My neck was damaged; I couldn't speak for a couple of weeks; and I was told I might never be able to speak properly again. I was moments away from being much worse. My aunt sent me a card with a Bible verse. It said, "All things work together for good for those who love God" (Romans 8:28). I could have screamed — except I couldn't because I had no voice and I couldn't even whisper. So I banged my fists against my hospital bed. This wasn't faith — this was just plain denial. This was a pious, sentimental Band-Aid over a mile-wide, gaping wound. Two years later what bothered me most at my aunt's funeral was not that I was hating it — but that my aunt would probably have been rather enjoying it.

Romans 8:28-39 is one of the most memorable, quotable, and mysterious passages in the whole Bible. In it Paul brings to a climax chapters 5 to 8, the central section of his letter to the Romans, and summarizes his whole theological outlook. And here we find my aunt's favorite words: "All things work together for good for those who love God." Has Paul joined the conspiracy? Has he stopped digging down to a faith that genuinely sustains us through painful injury and death and bereavement and fear, and instead thrown in his lot with the sentimental composers of greeting card platitudes and the straightforward deniers of harsh reality? Is faith just a groundless, stubborn, and counterintuitive refusal to come to terms with meaninglessness and mortality, or what is it really founded on? That's our question.

Paul gives us two answers. One redefines what we mean by good. The other redefines what we mean by God. Let's start with good.

Here's a common picture of God. We know we're not perfect, and life isn't always fair or easy, and we can't have everything we want. But that doesn't stop us from wishing that could all change. So God becomes the name for how all that changes. Because of Jesus, we get everything we could possibly want forever. And because of the Holy Spirit, we get a pretty hefty share of that wish list right now. That's the deal. God becomes a device, a piece of technology, that secures for us what we somehow feel entitled to have. If things go badly for us, we blame the technology — in the same way that we'd get cross with a spluttering car or a crashing computer. When we get sick, or our relationships fall apart, or our financial situation collapses, or our future prospects look thin, we think the system has failed. Either we haven't been keeping our side of the bargain, or God hasn't.

But Paul is saying, that was never the bargain. When he says, "All things work together for good," good doesn't mean a decent home, a healthy family, a rewarding job, a wholesome partner, and a long life. Paul has a very specific definition of "good." His definition is, "looking like Jesus." Here in this passage he gives us five verbs that describe the way in which the process of coming to look like Jesus takes place. God foreknew, predestined, called, justified, and glorified. Some of the church after the Reformation got hung up on the word "predestined": but here there's no ambiguity about what it means. Paul says, those whom God foreknew "he also predestined to be conformed to the image of his Son" (Romans 8:29). In other words, that was always the whole purpose of God among human beings: making us and remaking us to look like Jesus. Faith means cooperating with the process.

That's what "good" means. That's what we hope for. That's the bargain. We get to look like Jesus. Nothing about having a healthy family or a long and happy life. Jesus didn't have those things. Nothing about a rewarding job or a wholesome partner. Jesus didn't have those things. Nothing about a decent home or a loyal set of friends. Jesus didn't have those things. This is the deal: we are conformed to the image of Jesus. If God's doing a poor job at that, even when we're doing everything we can to cooperate — that's when we get cross with God. But bear in mind that Jesus was homeless, rejected, betrayed, tortured, and executed. We can't be surprised if we get a taste of these things, too. In fact, if we don't, we have to wonder if we're still part of the bargain — if we're still cooperating with the process.

Let's turn to Paul's second answer. I recall going to a seminar on a challenging topic. For a change I stopped listening to the speaker and started looking around at the rest of the audience. The most revealing moment was when the question-and-answer time began. There were about ten questions from the floor. What I noticed was that none of those who stood up asked a genuine question. Instead, each speaker said, more or less, "Thank you for your challenging lecture — but here's why the more difficult parts of what you're commending don't apply to me." Then the questioners added in a little about their life circumstances that made it clear why they were special cases. One had a disability. Another was retired. Another was in a second career. A fourth was a particular personality type on the Myers-Briggs Indicator. The next was a first-generation immigrant. Then there was someone who had an unusual learning style. And so it went on. And I came to believe that every single speaker was really saying, "I can't cope with what you're asking of me. Please tell me I have a get-out clause so I don't have to do it."

And then it struck me that this is exactly what we say to God. We sit in church and we say, "Yeah, yeah — I'm not saying all this stuff doesn't apply to everyone else, but it's different for me, because . . ." And then we go into our own carefully crafted get-out clause for why we find the claims of God don't work for us. We react like I did when I received that overpious card from my aunt — we say, "This is all very nice, but it's irrelevant and superficial compared to what I'm really going through."

What does Paul do? He exhaustively talks us through no fewer than seventeen kinds of exceptions for why we might think we are in an unusually difficult place. Here's all seventeen: hardship, distress, persecution, famine, nakedness, peril, sword, death, life, angels, rulers, things present, things to come, powers, height, depth, anything else in all creation (Romans 8:38-39).

Let's look at them in a bit more detail. He starts with hardship, distress, persecution. You could say these are the predicaments we find ourselves in through our own mistakes, the trouble that comes upon us through bad luck, and the misery we face because of the ill will of others. That may seem pretty comprehensive, but there are still fourteen more to come. Then Paul moves to famine and nakedness — in other words, lack of food and lack of clothing, two of our most basic needs. Then there are peril and sword — in other words, danger from adverse circumstances and danger from violent attack. Next come death and life, which between them cover pretty much every eventuality we could possibly fear. Then there are angels and rulers; that's to say those who are in charge of this earthly realm and those who hold sway over eternal realities. Then things present and things to come, which again incorporate everything our imagination can comprehend and everything it can't. Then finally there are powers, which seems to be a sweep-up term for everything that's preceded it, and, just in case something's possibly been left out, Paul finishes off with anything else in all creation.

Notice in this list that these are all things that Jesus himself was exposed to: hardship, distress, persecution, hunger, nakedness, peril, sword, death, life, angels, rulers, and all the rest. Paul's giving us a list of everything Jesus went through, and saying there's nothing we could go through that Jesus hasn't first gone through. But the list has even more authority because Paul has been through most if not all these things himself. He's not just appealing to Jesus, he's offering personal testimony. When the questioner in the audience says, "But I'm an exception," Paul replies, "Well, I'm an exception, too." By the end of Paul's list we're exhausted, but we're also stripped of all our exceptions and get-out clauses.

Except, perhaps, one. In this long list, there's still one thing missing. There's a lurking suspicion in the hearts and souls of very many people, and maybe you're one of them, that the problem of suffering, disappointment, sickness, and grief isn't about any of these things. It's that God has turned away from you. That God is punishing you, facing away from you, or just doesn't like you anymore. That God is cross with you or has lost patience with you. Paul knows all about that last, lingering fear. Paul knows that it's the most isolating fear of all, because it keys into our own profound feelings of self-hatred, and it ties into our helplessness in the face of the almighty power of God. But Paul shapes his whole argument to insist that this fear is finally, wholly, utterly groundless. God isn't against us. Any of us. God is *for* us. All of us. Why else would Jesus have gone through hell and high water for us? Jesus' death is proof that God is for us, and Jesus' resurrection is proof that nothing can separate us from God's love (Romans 8:31-35).

And so this long list of seventeen circumstances tells us two things. It tells us that nothing whatever, nothing we can possibly imagine in heaven or on earth, can separate us from God's love in Jesus. Here's my list, says Paul. Bring on yours. Nothing can force us and God apart. Jesus is the glue. But there's a second thing Paul's list tells us. If the point of life isn't to have a designer degree, home, job, family, spouse, leisure time, friendship circle, and the rest; if the point of life is to look like Jesus, then this is the kind of hell and high water we can expect to go through if we're going to end up looking like Jesus – or, to use Paul's language, if we're to be conformed to the image of God's Son.

If you're in distress, and you feel God's broken the bargain that was supposed to make you permanently content, you're wrong: there never was any such bargain. The bargain was, that you become like Jesus. If you're facing hardship, and you think it's because God's against you, you're wrong: God is for you. Always was and ever shall be. Nothing can separate you from the love of God. Nothing, nothing, nothing, nothing, nothing. Nothing. God is with you at every step, and Jesus has faced everything you're facing. You were with God in the very beginning of all things, you're with God now, and you always will be, and being with God in hardship is better than being separate from God in comfort ever could be.

I still think about my aunt's funeral, twenty-three years ago. I still feel her pastor got it all wrong. But I'm not cross with my aunt anymore. In fact, I admire her profoundly. She wasn't the favored child in her family, by any means. She went as a nurse to Kenya to give her life in service to others. She spent more than thirty years caring for a mentally disabled son. For much of that time she was caring at home for an infirm husband and an elderly mother too. Nothing in her assumed she had a right to an easy life of security and comfort. She was only interested in two things. She wanted to enjoy the freedom of knowing she'd never be separated from the love of God. And she wanted the Holy Spirit to make her look like Christ.

And she got all she wanted. And if, in my own hour of fear and trembling, she was able to say to me, "All things work together for good for those who love God," then, after all she'd been through, she had every right to. One day, if I've been through what she went through, with God at my side every step of the way, and if I've been made to look as much like Jesus as she was, then maybe I'll have the faith and the right to say those words too.

Everything's Relative

I want to tell you about three people whose lives I find instructive.

The first is Baxter. Baxter's a pilot. His life as an undergraduate was a daily process of trying to hold together his increasing confidence in his own skill and future in the air force and his chronically burdensome and embarrassing family relationships. He couldn't invite his father to his graduation because he couldn't trust him to behave; he hasn't seen his elder sister for years because her mental health has been so up and down; and he longs to be able to communicate with his younger sister but she seems to feel he's betrayed the family by moving away to go to college and graduate school. The one thing he adores is to strap himself into the cockpit of his plane, and head up into the freedom of the open skies and the far horizon. That feels like the only place in the world where he can relax and where his chaotic family can't poison his life.

The second person is Shannon. Shannon had a background in engineering. She was brilliant at getting machines to work and fixing things around the house. She was always pursuing a project or drawing up plans for something new to construct in her garage. She never quite turned all her technical expertise into a career. But then she decided to become a personal coach. She worked with a technique for helping people get past the blocks in their imagination and imagine their own success. After a couple of years she dropped out of coaching and went back to making things in her garage. When I asked her why, she said, "For a while there I got to thinking that you could fix people as easily as you could fix metal or wood. But it turns out people are harder to fix than things."

The third person is Clark. Clark went on a spring break mission trip. He was keen to go because he'd always felt powerless in the face of the poverty of much of the developing world and he was delighted to have the chance to do something practical about it. I asked him if he'd found the trip rewarding, and whether he felt he'd made a contribution to addressing poverty. He said, "Actually, the biggest part of the trip was the people I traveled with. I thought we were going to help poor people, but in the end we spent most of our time with each other, and what I found out about myself was from the people who saw me first thing in the morning and last thing at night. In some ways it's a disappointment, but in another way I found something important, even if it wasn't what I was looking for."

What Baxter, Shannon, and Clark have all been discovering is that when we want to score some quick victories in life, we try to keep things practical, and make sure people stay at arm's length. Once we let human beings – their fragility, foibles, and failures – get too involved, we quickly start to lose control of things. The trouble is, human beings are also where the joy lies. We can accumulate technological or practical or tangible successes, but what we really crave is fulfillment in our relationships. The things that matter most we can't get right on our own.

Let me give some examples. Take possessions. We can hide away from the clumsiness or the hurt of other people by putting what money we have into wall-to-wall TVs, state-of-the-art kitchen appliances, stylish and comfortable modes of transport, and breathtaking clothes. But where's the joy in having a car unless you've got someone to drive and see? Where's the fun in having a television unless you've got someone to talk to about what you've been watching? Where's the interest in having a nice kitchen unless you've got someone to share food with? Possessions aren't a protection or an escape from relationships. They're transitional objects to add dimensions *to* relationships.

Or take beauty. There's nothing like a magnificent sunset stretched out across a smooth and somnolent ocean. But don't you want to tell someone about it? It's wonderful to see a handsome face, but, in the end, people aren't for looking at – they're for talking to. Beauty isn't an absolute or abstract thing – it lies in the configuration of rawness and artifice, in the balance of nature and nurture, in the way people fit into their surroundings.

And perhaps most poignant of all is the question of suffering. We might think pain is about the body, about medication, about different forms of alleviation and avoidance. But so much of pain and grief is really about how we relate to other people. Sometimes it's *caused* by a relationship, by a betrayal or a bereavement or a broken heart. Sometimes it's the opposite, and a relationship is the only thing that gives us courage to keep going through a time of grief or suffering, or can even become the key dimension of our recovery. Whichever way, suffering is inconceivable without relationship. Suffering is perhaps our biggest form of isolation — but also our biggest proof of the centrality of relationship in our lives.

All these insights find their true significance in the doctrine of the Trinity. One could say that the doctrine of the Trinity is how the church celebrates the power, importance, indispensability, and everlasting quality of relationship. The Trinity celebrates that God is three persons in one substance. In other words, God isn't a thing, an achievement, an edifice, a piece of technology, an impressive sight, even a dazzling light or a blazing fire. God is a relationship. God is a relationship of three persons, so wonderfully shaped toward one another, so wondrously *with* one another, that we call them one, but so exquisitely diverse and distinct within that unity that we call them three. But that shape has a direction, a fixed purpose, an orienting goal. The life of the Trinity is so shaped, not simply to be in perfect relationship, but to be in relationship with us. Those are the two dynamics that lie at the center of the universe: God's perfect inner relationship, and God's very life shaped to be in relationship with us through Jesus in the power of the Holy Spirit. There isn't anything in God that isn't relationship.

There's a famous story of a public confrontation between a scholar and an elderly member of the audience to which he was speaking.

> A well-known scientist (some say it was Bertrand Russell) once gave a public lecture on astronomy. He described how the earth orbits around the sun and how the sun, in turn, orbits around the center of a vast collection of stars called our galaxy. At the end of the lecture, a little old lady at the back of the room got up and said: "What you have told us is rubbish. The world is really a flat plate supported on the back of a giant tortoise." The scientist gave a superior smile before replying, "What is the tortoise standing on?" "You're very clever, young man, very clever," said the old lady. "But it's turtles all the way down!"[1]

1. Stephen Hawking, *A Brief History of Time* (Toronto and New York: Bantam Books, 1988), 1.

That's what Christians discover in the doctrine of the Trinity. It's relationship all the way down. This is an incredibly difficult point to grasp. Most of us have huge resistances to allowing this discovery to affect our lives in any meaningful way. I want to dwell for a moment on why we get so nervous about it.

Think about the process of writing a will. Most of us delay, postpone, prevaricate, and deny in the face of such a responsibility. It makes us think about our own death, which is a reality few of us wish to dwell on. But it also makes us focus hard on two other realities, which are also uncomfortable, and hard to consider for very long. The first is the real extent, quality, and value of our personal possessions and assets. It's a cliché to say we can't take these with us, but it's only a cliché because it's a truism that needs repeating over and over again. Why do we put so much store by things that don't last forever? Why do we sacrifice so many relationships and so much trust in order to acquire more material security? Writing a will doesn't take long if all we have is what we need. Writing a will only takes a long time if we have things we don't need to have.

The second thing that makes us uncomfortable about writing a will is reflecting on the relationships a will requires. What about the brother I no longer talk to? What about the daughter who married the man I feel was unworthy of her? What about the former spouse I deep down feel I could have treated more graciously? Can leaving such people money, possessions, or even a meaningful trinket really make anything better after we've gone? If we're so keen to make things better, why don't we set about doing so now, face-to-face, while we really can?

What writing a will shows us is how little we truly trust relationships and how eagerly we spend our lives looking for hard currency to convert relationships into. The things our culture most values are what we might call transferable symbols that can only be acquired through relationships but don't somehow entirely depend on them. Money is the most obvious one, but there are others. A university degree is certainly one of the most significant. A good reputation is possibly the most telling one of all. A good reputation is all about relationships. But what we want is a tidy résumé. A résumé is a sign of the ways our culture expects us to turn all our working relationships into self-explanatory glittering accomplishments.

Before we too quickly bewail all such translation as cynical and manipulative, notice that this principle — of turning fragile relationships into reliable possessions — lies close to the heart of human civilization. That's what institutions are made of. The problem of writing a will is a microcosm of human civilization: How do you translate something of value into something that can survive death and distrust and decay? How do you turn delicate relationships into something you can keep? That's exactly what institutions do. That's what law codes do. That's what professions do. Laws, professions, and institutions codify the wisdom that has arisen from human interactions over decades and centuries, and turn it into the best practice that humans can aspire to. We have a word for following this approach to life. We call it being responsible. We call it being prudent.

But here's the crucial point. That's what *our* lives are like: constantly trying to turn relationships into something more tangible, more reliable, more predictable, more transferable. But that's not what *God's* life is like. *God's life is the complete opposite.* God's life is the 180-degree reversal of what we spend all our energies trying to bring about. *God's life is constantly turning the tangible, the predictable, the reliable into fragile, fallible, fickle relationships.* That's what we discover in Jesus. Jesus' coming, Jesus' ministry, Jesus' dying, Jesus' rising again are all showing us that there's nothing God wants besides us. And the doctrine of the Trinity reminds us that there is no residue in God beyond the relationship of Father, Son, and Holy Spirit. There is no solid rock, no lengthy beard, no gilded throne, no weighty scepter detachable from the interdependence of the three persons. It's relationship all the way down. All the way down.

God is turning reliable dust into fragile flesh. It's the wrong way round. It's God's way round. God is turning the economy of gold into the ecology of grace. It's the wrong way round. It's God's way round. God is turning the predictability of punishment into the adventure of forgiveness. It's the wrong way round. It's God's way round. God is turning death and taxes into healing and eternal life. It's the wrong way round. It's God's way round. God is turning the wood of cruel execution into the reconciled glory of restored companionship. It's the wrong way round. It's God's way round.

We want to turn relationships into something more substantial, more reliable. God turns the reliable and the substantial into relationships. Because God is a relationship. That's what God is — three persons in such perfect relationship that they are one substance. There isn't anything else. That's all there is.

John the Evangelist, by tradition the author of the Fourth Gospel and the three letters of John and the book of Revelation, lived out his days on the island of Patmos in the Aegean Sea. One day, one of his followers came and spoke to him. "Master," he said. "Tell me one thing. I've always wondered, why is it that you always write about love? Why don't you ever write about anything else?" Saint John paused for a very long time, waiting for his disciple to work out the answer for himself. Finally, he answered the question. "Because," he said, "in the end, there isn't anything else. There is only love."[2]

Only love, all the way down. Only companionship with us, all the way down. Only relationship, in the very heart of the Trinity. In the end, that's all there is. All the way down.

Searched and Known

"There's no escaping my love." I wonder if you've ever said those words to anybody. I know someone who routinely signs her e-mail messages to friends and colleagues with those very words. "There's no escaping my love." In fact, she used to shout those exact same words down the street to her children when she dropped them off at school, accompanied by much gorilla-style long-distance arm-encircling. "There's . . . no . . . escaping . . . my . . . looooooove."

Think about what it might mean to be a child, hearing those words. Would it not be suffocating and oppressive — not to mention embarrassing and unsettling — to be on the receiving end of more love than you had any idea how to deal with? Or would it rather be glorious

2. I owe this story to John Inge.

and releasing, freeing and empowering, to know that however much you might feel a fool, a failure, a freak, or a fraud, this woman with the forgiving eyes and the warm embrace would always adore you? Or could it be somewhere in-between? What I want to describe here is that somewhere in-between. "There's no escaping my love," says the beckoning voice with the everlasting arms . . . and we say, "Errr . . . can I get back to you on that?"

Psalm 139 puts us in exactly that somewhere in-between, poised between suffocating enclosure and empowering embrace. Except in this case the subject isn't a bighearted mother casting aside her social inhibitions. The subject in question is God.

I wonder if you've ever had a dream, maybe a recurring dream, where you're running away from a mysterious pursuer, and becoming breathless and exhausted as you find fewer and fewer places to hide, until suddenly, at the point when you're about to be caught, you find yourself awake, sweaty and confused, trying to recall what was chasing you and why you were so desperate to get away. Psalm 139 is as intense and sweaty as that dream. It turns out that what was chasing you – what was searching you out – was God. And why you were so desperate to run away . . . well, that's what the psalm leaves you wondering about.

"I know you." I wonder if anyone has ever said those words to you – maybe in the hurly-burly of a networking social event, maybe in the faraway parking lot of an anonymous vacation beauty spot, maybe in the raised voice of an argument with a long-standing but mistrustful family member, maybe in the intimacy of loving touch. "I know you." Feel the layer upon layer of meaning and resonance and texture in those brief words. They may be simple recognition, turning a stranger into a previous acquaintance, carrying the pleasure of remembrance or the fear of rejection and forgetfulness. "I know *you*." They may be words of reproach and bitterness, as someone names a history of deception and broken promises and manipulation and betrayal, in such a way that says, "And I'm never going to make that mistake again." "I *know* you." Or they may be words of gentleness and joy, of feeling understood and appreciated and comprehended and loved, for all one's clumsiness and blunders and follies – words that are spoken with tender eyes, only inches from yours, with a compassionate smile, and with palms enfolded in one another. "I know you."

That's what Psalm 139 says to each one of us, in all its multi-textured complexity. "I know you."

I know you in four dimensions. First, depth.

> O LORD, you have searched me and known me.
> You know when I sit down and when I rise up;
>   you discern my thoughts from far away. (vv. 1-2)

This is such a domestic picture. God knows me so well that he antici-pates when I'm going to sit down, when I'm going to wake up, what I'm thinking about and what I'm going to be thinking about, which route I'm going to take to where I'm headed, what I'm about to say. We all want people to think we're beautiful, and clever, and fun, and wonder-ful. But isn't it even more flattering to be studied so minutely, to be in-tricately examined and scrutinized as profoundly as this. "You really know me," we say, and we glow because we are enormously touched — but we also shiver because we're a little scared at the same time. The psalm says,

> You hem me in, behind and before,
>   and lay your hand upon me. (v. 5)

It's affirming and intimidating at the same time. "There's no escaping my love."

Then there's the dimension of height.

> Where can I go from your spirit?
>   Or where can I flee from your presence? . . .
> If I take the wings of the morning
>   and settle at the farthest limits of the sea,
> even there your hand shall lead me. (vv. 7, 9-10)

One of our most instinctive reactions when we're scared of what people know about us is simply to run away — to put ourselves physically in a place where we don't have to endure the shame or exposure of being known. There's an urban myth about a person who sent an identical anonymous message one Friday to a random selection of six senators that simply said, "They know everything: flee" – and by the end of the weekend, so the story goes, all six had abruptly left town. The psalm proclaims that we can't hide, and we can't become invisible to God, however far we run. "There's no escaping my love."

The third dimension takes this discovery even further. It's cosmic.

> If I ascend to heaven, you are there;
>> if I make my bed in Sheol, you are there. (v. 8)

God's presence isn't limited to this life, this earth, this existence. If we die, if we go into perpetual darkness, if we go into dazzling light, if we are buried in the earth – wherever we are or in whatever form we come to be, there God is, beside us, with us, among us, before us. Probably every one of us has, at some time or other, maybe frequently, wondered what it would be like to end our own life, and have held back, maybe from fear, maybe from conscience of hurting those who love us. These words suggest something that seldom occurs to us. Not that our death would change and ruin and destroy everything – but that it wouldn't change anything, at least not in God's sight, because God would still be there, as present as ever, probably more so. "There's no escaping my love."

And there's yet a fourth dimension, not about space but about time. These are perhaps the most precious and mysterious words of all.

> For it was you who formed my inward parts;
>> you knit me together in my mother's womb.
> I praise you, for I am fearfully and wonderfully made. (vv. 13-14)

God knew me before there was a "me" to know. God knew the days of my life long ago, as if they were words and sentences in a book. God made me as delicately as a brain surgeon makes stitches. Again, we have this poignant mixture of fear and wonder: I am "fearfully and wonderfully made," because it's astonishing that God cares about these tiny particulars of my existence, but it's also evident that God knows me oceans better than I know myself. Listen again to the fear and wonder in these words: "There's no escaping my love." We were with God, all along. And God will be with us, to the end of all things and beyond.

"I know you." When God says those words to us, they mean all four dimensions – they mean depth, they mean height, they mean beyond this space, and they mean beyond this time.

Who knows you? Who really knows who you are? Have you ever let another human being see into your soul? In 1969 singer-songwriter Peter Sarstedt released a song entitled "Where Do You Go To (My Lovely)?"[3] It's addressed to a young woman named Marie-Claire who lives a jet-setting lifestyle in Paris with diamonds and pearls in her hair and, in her apartment, a painting she stole from Picasso. But the singer can see through these superficialities, and he's skeptical about where her soul truly lies. He sings,

> Where do you go to my lovely
> When you're alone in your bed
> Tell me the thoughts that surround you
> I want to look inside your head, yes I do.

You can never quite tell how he really feels about this alluring but infuriating young woman. Eventually, as if he's giving her a last chance, he tells of how they grew up together in abject poverty.

> I remember the back streets of Naples
> Two children begging in rags
> Both touched with a burning ambition
> To shake off their lowly-born tags, so they try.

Finally, he pleads with Marie-Claire to look into his face and remember just who she is. He knows she still bears the scars of her upbringing deep inside, and he's sure that he knows her better than she

3. Peter Sarstedt, "Where Do You Go To (My Lovely)?" World Pacific, 1969.

wants to know herself. But here's the same poignancy: Do we really want anyone to know us that well? Do we really trust that if someone truly knew us, he or she wouldn't expose us and reject us and humiliate us and shame us? That's what makes this song to Marie-Claire so memorable. We never quite know, all the way through, if the words are ones of enduring, long-suffering love (of the "no escaping" variety) or whether they are the embittered venom of a slighted admirer, now resolved to destroy the maiden who'd always evaded his advances. There are a lot of Marie-Claires in the world, who have tried to reinvent themselves and have plenty of good reasons to keep secrets. Maybe you are one of them. It can be very hard to believe that if someone truly knows you, he or she will truly understand and love you. Even if you've known that person all your life.

The woman I mentioned earlier, who insists there's no escaping her love, doesn't limit herself to cascading words of affection down the street to her children. She makes extraordinary friendships. Some while ago she got to know a man who'd lived a really rough life. He'd been shot in the face, and part of his cheek and ear were disfigured. And he'd spent a long time in prison. My friend first loved this man; and, through loving, she came, over a period of years, to know him. Some days they ran errands together; other times they just talked. But gradually she began to realize something was wrong. This is how she told me the story: "He kept getting sick, and what was happening never occurred to me until I was sitting in the infectious disease clinic with him, and he was telling me how he felt. And I said, 'Darling . . . I think you have HIV. I think that's why you're sick all the time, and why I have to wear the gowns.' And he said, 'No!' And I said, 'Honey, it's me. I know your doctor, and he's an AIDS doctor. I think you should ask.' And he said, 'No . . . ! You won't love me!' And I said, 'Oh, darling, I already do. You can't stop me. *There's no escaping my love.*'"[4]

Most of our attempts to love and know like God aren't quite as successful as that. In one of the strangest passages in the whole Bible, this

---

4. This story is told in more detail in Samuel Wells and Marcia A. Owen, *Living without Enemies: Being Present in the Midst of Violence* (Downers Grove, Ill.: IVP, 2011), 88-89.

most exquisite of psalms drastically changes gear near the end to express purple anger on God's behalf, calling on God to slay the wicked, and celebrating the speaker's "perfect hatred" for those who hate God (Psalm 139:19-22). From marveling at how profoundly God knows, the speaker suddenly displays how little God is truly known in return. Before we ridicule and distance ourselves from such an absurd parody of God's mercy and compassion, we should pause for a moment and wonder if this isn't exactly how we think when the blood rushes to our head and we boil with anger with our own self-righteousness — which we invariably persuade ourselves is the righteousness of God. In a curious way this furious digression only underlines how complex is the relationship between knowing and loving. Because here the speaker claims ardently to love God, but evidently doesn't really know God at all. Love is often founded on such ignorance.

But then the speaker halts this intricate exploration of the complexities of knowing by comprehensively submitting to God's loving knowledge. The psalm started with a description ("You have searched me and known me"); it now ends with a demand: "Search me . . . and know my heart" (Psalm 139:23). What does such an abrupt conclusion mean?

The speaker has discovered the difference between *our* knowing and *God's* knowing. With us, knowing and loving are separate, and there's always the fear that if others really knew us, they'd have a power over us that they could use to hurt us, or that they'd see through us and cease to love us. But God's knowing is different. *God's knowing and loving are indistinguishable.* There's never a moment when God knows but doesn't love, or loves but doesn't know. That is the gospel we can hardly begin to imagine. God wholly knows *because* God wholly loves; and God wholly loves *even though* God wholly knows.

Look back upon your life. Have you made knowing and loving enemies of one another? Write this psalm on your heart. Tell your friends and family to read it to you on your deathbed. Because when your life ends, it will be time for those estranged companions, knowledge and love, to be reunited in you, just as they are in God. And when you're raised to life eternal, you'll for the first time be known and loved not just by God, but by everyone else as well. That will be heaven.

Put a Lid on It

I wonder whether you've ever had a moment when someone else has seen who you really are, and looked you straight in the eye, and said nothing . . . but somehow, for ever after, you've known you couldn't pretend with that person, because even if he or she had gone on to forget that moment, *you* never could, and would always recall it whenever you would later see the person. I had a moment like that a few weeks after I was ordained and first began in parish ministry.

As in every church since the days when Joseph played wide receiver for Israel, the new associate pastor led the youth group. That new associate pastor was me. And so it was that with my coleader I hosted the church youth in my apartment living room one August evening. As we played some nonsensical but purportedly faith-building or at least team-bonding game, I handed round my newest food discovery: sour cream and onion Pringles. You have to understand that this was 1991, and this was just about the most addictive food invented up to that point in human development. It turned out everyone liked them as much as I did, and I was alarmed to see fistfuls of curvaceous wedges being rapidly funneled down adolescent consumption chutes. Five minutes later my coleader spotted the cylinder of Pringles with the lid firmly back on, lodged between my protective backside and the bottom of the sofa. I've never forgotten the look she gave me. It said, "Are you *really* keeping all those for yourself? I never realized you were so greedy, so selfish . . . and so *mean*."

I want to leave aside for a moment my pathetic attempt to put a lid on the Pringles, because I'll come back to that, and focus on the moment when the consumption of the Pringles started to take on wildfire proportions. Because that's precisely the moment where we enter into the story of Jesus' encounter with a Syrophoenician woman in Mark's Gospel:

> From there he set out and went away to the region of Tyre. He entered a house and did not want anyone to know he was there. Yet he could not escape notice, but a woman whose little daughter had an unclean spirit immediately heard about him, and she

came and bowed down at his feet. Now the woman was a Gentile, of Syrophoenician origin. She begged him to cast the demon out of her daughter. He said to her, "Let the children be fed first, for it is not fair to take the children's food and throw it to the dogs." But she answered him, "Sir, even the dogs under the table eat the children's crumbs." Then he said to her, "For saying that, you may go – the demon has left your daughter." So she went home, found the child lying on the bed, and the demon gone. (Mark 7:24-30)

The healing of the Syrophoenician woman's daughter is a key moment in Mark's Gospel. It sums up the sequence of miraculous events that have come before this point in the Gospel. There have been stories of an unclean spirit (1:23-26), of a woman drawing improperly close to Jesus (5:25-29), of a parent distressed over a daughter (5:22-24). It's as if all the previous miracles are coming to a head in this story of the Syrophoenician woman and her demon-possessed child.

And why is that so important? Well, this story is also equidistant between the two decisive miracles in Mark's Gospel – the feeding of the five thousand in chapter 6 and the feeding of the four thousand in chapter 8. Let's look more closely at those two stories. The feeding of the *five* thousand took place in *Jewish* territory and resulted in *twelve* baskets left over. These numbers five and twelve are significant. Five is shorthand for Israel because of the five books of the Law that begin the Bible. Twelve is the number of the tribes of Israel. Meanwhile the feeding of the *four* thousand took place in *Gentile* territory and resulted in *seven* baskets left over. The numbers four and seven are also significant. Four refers to the four corners of the earth, and seven refers to the seven days of the whole creation, before the calling of Israel as a people set apart.

And now for the missing link. The Phoenicians were a widely dispersed people, because their trade was all by sea. This woman is a Syrophoenician because she is from one branch of this Gentile people, this global people, the branch who'd settled to the north of Israel in the land broadly known as Syria. Listen to what Jesus says to this Syrophoenician woman, this global woman: "Let the children be fed first" – or, more literally, "Let the children be *satisfied* first" (7:27). Why is the word "satisfied" so important? Because it's precisely the same word that appears in the feeding of the five thousand where it says "and all ate and were satisfied" (6:42), and again in the feeding of the four thousand where it says, almost identically, "they ate and were satisfied" (8:8).

So what's happening in this intense dialogue between Jesus and the Syrophoenician woman is not just the climax of all the ways in which Jesus heals but more exactly an enactment of the transformation from Jesus as the messiah for the Jewish people to Jesus as the savior of the whole world. The debate between Jesus and the woman starts as a conversation about healing — but Jesus quickly turns it into a debate about food. In just the same way in the two feeding stories, Jesus crystallizes the question about the extent and depth of his mission into a drama about food.

Jesus comes first to the Jews; they are hungry, and then they are satisfied. Jesus has an argument with a Gentile woman: he says, let the Jews be satisfied first — then we'll worry about the Gentiles. She says, you've got more than you need for the Jews — you've got enough to feed the whole world with the leftovers, the crumbs. And I'm hungry! Hungry for the food that only you can give! Then Jesus goes to the Gentiles; they're hungry, and then they're satisfied too. What the feeding stories tell us *visually* with their image of the baskets of leftovers, this conversation tells us *verbally* with its words about feeding the Gentiles with the crumbs that are left over from the Jews. The first feeding tells us that after Jesus has fed the Jews, there's plenty left over for the Gentiles. The second feeding tells us that, after satisfying the Gentiles, there's *still* plenty left over.

But over and over again the story of the Syrophoenician woman tells us that that's all very well — there may be plenty left over, but that's not what it *feels* like. First, we start with Jesus getting a long way away from the action. Tyre is way up in Yankee territory, where it's all Gentiles. There are not a lot of Jews around. Mark says that Jesus "did not want anyone to know he was there" (7:24). He's a long way from Israel and he's keeping a low profile. So no one should be bothering him, right? Wrong.

Here's this woman, breaking every cleanliness code in the book, bursting in through the closed doors and spending time alone with a male stranger. As a Phoenician, she's breaking national boundaries; as a Gentile, she's breaking religious boundaries; as a woman, she's breaking gender boundaries. She's breaking courtesy and propriety boundaries, as a person who won't respect a messiah when he needs a bit of space. And the degree of transgression she's asking from Jesus matches her own. He's already crossed a territorial line by being in lands north of the land of Israel. She's asking him to take on the boundary of the demonic by encountering her daughter. And she raises the whole issue of food laws — the most common stalling point in Jewish-Gentile relations — by all her talk of giving food to the dogs.

In Mark 7:1-19, just prior to the story about the Syrophoenician woman, Jesus breaks through these dietary laws by declaring all foods clean. Now he makes an even *more* radical step by declaring all *eaters* of food clean. That means salvation can apply to the Gentiles; they too can become members of the inrushing kingdom; they too can eat and be satisfied at the Lord's table — which is exactly what is depicted happening a few verses later when the four thousand are fed.

By presenting this miracle as the synthesis and climax of many previous miracles, by piling up the symbolism of numbers and settings, by noting the wave upon wave of gendered, national, religious, dietary, decorous, demonic, and territorial pressures on Jesus, the story is portraying Jesus — and through Jesus, Israel — as being overwhelmed by the inrushing need and longing of the Gentiles for God. There is so much God, so much grace, so much kingdom, so much forgiveness, so much eternal life, all crystallized by the astonishing abundance of the two feedings and the many baskets left over. But while the gospel is one of overflowing glory, here we get the other side of the story too, the sense of drowning in overwhelming *anxiety*. The woman in this story represents the simple truth that the gospel means overwhelming grace. Jesus' reaction reflects Israel's fear that overwhelming grace means overwhelming anxiety.

Here's the challenge of this story to us today. On the one hand we see the woman with her simple, persistent demand that Jesus take the logic of the gospel to its obvious conclusion. She may be high maintenance, she may be a disciple with more elbow activity than we'd think polite or well-mannered or respectful. But she's obviously right. And here on the other hand is Jesus, representing the ancient loyalties of Israel, to be set apart and so reflect the holiness of God understood in the Torah, the Jewish law.

Let me ask you this. Why do we always assume we are on Jesus' side of this story? Why do we expend all our energy on willing Jesus to be more generous, on suppressing our dismay that he's so rude to the woman, and on wondering how Israel could be so small-minded as to keep salvation to itself? That way the story merely underwrites our managerial reading of the gospel, that, granted, it's clearly intended for everybody, but that's going to take a huge amount of administration and infrastructure, and it's inevitably all going to fall to us, so please bear with us, we're getting there, but privately we're overwhelmed with anxiety and the gospel is really too much for us. Why don't we instead identify with the woman? Knocking, nudging, demanding, teasing, even flirting our way to get Jesus' attention and *let us into the kingdom*, for God's sake. (Literally.) That's the question this story puts to us. Is it because everything in us is trying so hard to avoid seeing ourselves as beggars?

This story is offering us the gospel. But it's up to us how we hear it. If we assume salvation belongs to us, our gospel is going to be one of entitlement and responsibility, where Jesus seems to be dashing off some kind of unfulfillable public policy memo. But if we allow ourselves to be like this pleading woman, our gospel is one of astonished grace that God has bent his ear even to us and showered upon us healing and forgiveness and eternal life. Both of these gospels describe degrees of overwhelming – but only one of them is a gospel of joy.

Look at the way this story starts and finishes. It starts with Jesus trying to keep his presence in the region a secret. In no time his day off and the kingdom of God are broken open by a woman whose thorough understanding of the implications of the gospel makes her both impatient and dangerous. Immediately after Jesus heals the woman's daughter, he makes the ironic gesture of releasing a man's tongue and then telling him to say nothing to anyone about it (Mark 7:31-34). The more Jesus ordered the healed man and the onlookers not to tell anyone, "the more zealously they proclaimed it" (7:36). The lesson is clear. The gospel is not a cylinder of Pringles. You *can't* put a lid on it when its infectious,

addictive character makes things spin out of control. Whoever you are
– Jew, Gentile, synagogue leader, or mother of a demon-possessed child
– the gospel is going to overwhelm you.

What was going on in my sitting room back in 1991 was not just me
being greedy and hoarding the tasty Pringles to myself. What was happening was that I was realizing, like many young pastors before me and
since, that this youth group were starting to take over my life, that their
needs and discoveries and questions and tender faith were beginning to
disturb my deep-rooted introversion and my newly minted financial
independence. Ministry was beginning to overwhelm me. So I literally
and metaphorically put the top back on the Pringles. What a fool I was.
You can't put a lid on the gospel. You can't manage it. You can't keep it
under control. The moment you try to do so you look as mean and ridiculous as I did that day in my apartment. It just can't be done.

It may be that right now you're feeling overwhelmed. It may be
that you're longing for a bit of peace and quiet because your domestic
or professional life is overwhelmed – overwhelmed with the pressures
of trying to be generous and kind without becoming totally exhausted
and humiliated and bankrupt. Well, I've got news you don't want to
hear. Maybe you're reading this story from the wrong point of view.
The gospel is all about being overwhelmed – but not by responsibility
and anxiety and strategic administrative policies and domestic chores.
The gospel is all about being overwhelmed by the discovery that there's
room in the kingdom even for one like you. That's what the Syrophoenician woman discovers in this story. If church or Christianity
has become for you just one burden among others dragging you down
into bewildered exhaustion, maybe it's time you started reading the
story from her point of view. You can't put a lid on the gospel. You
can't keep it under control. The gospel is all about being overwhelmed.
But are you being overwhelmed by burdens – or by grace?

Who Are You?

I wonder what you feel like when you see a photograph of yourself. I
know a number of people who claim they always look bad in photo-

graphs. Think about the logic of such a conviction. You see yourself in a photograph. You think, "That person doesn't look as beautiful, charming, witty, relaxed, and cool as I like to think I look. Either the equipment is faulty, or the photographer is hopeless, or I have a gene that makes me drop all my fine qualities the moment someone points a camera lens at me – or, and this is the most likely, I have the kind of warm and effusive personality that's just impossible to capture in a single two-dimensional image." We could simply say, "That's what the photograph shows, so I guess that's what I look like, and maybe I should deal with it." But no. We say, "I always look terrible in photographs." In other words, "I know who I am. No one else does. Least of all that cruel, distorting, coldhearted camera."

"I know who I am." Do you? Fair enough – you know you're more wonderful, more exquisite in looks, intelligence, character, taste, talent, and style than anyone could describe or capture. But do you really know who you are? One of the features of our culture, with its obsession with youth, its social media networks, and its transitory love of the latest fashion, is that it becomes tempting, almost unavoidable, to try to present ourselves to one another at our best. Isn't that what a Facebook page is? A chance to say, "Hey y'all out there, I'm in the middle of a wild party right now but I love ya and here's a few photos of me that don't do me justice but at least remind you that I'm lotsa fun!" We're constantly making it easy for people to understand how brilliant but unthreatening we are. One thing people have started putting on résumés is a little line under their full name that says "Goal." What follows is a succinct but generic summary of everything they have to bring to the world – something like "High achiever who selflessly wants to use my outstanding gifts with inevitably less wise and gifted people, and to apply my mastery of all technology (including that not yet invented) to bring about lasting change in the world."

When we're immersed in such a culture of digitally enhanced appearances and fleeting connections, it's very hard to answer the question, "Who are you?" Instead, we're constantly answering the question, "Who can I *persuade* people I am?" What we call successful people are those who've convinced a large number of the public that they're brilliant but unthreatening. And that's why successful people often find this question, "Who am I?" particularly hard to answer: because they've peddled their publicity so many times, they've started to believe it themselves. Success is a drug that makes you think your identity and character are products you can market to unwary consumers. You think you're fooling them, but in the end the one you're really fooling is yourself.

By contrast, when you've had months or years out of work, when you've had the courage to admit the one thing in life you truly want and yet it's never happened for you, when you've experienced a terrible illness or injury that's left you in need of long-term care, or when you or your family have had to bear a private burden together that, if exposed, would bring down a cloud of public shame; if this is your story, then the likelihood is, you do know who you are, even if who you are is a daily struggle with distress, disappointment, or despair. That's one of the few things an experience of genuine deprivation can give you: a deeper understanding of who you truly are.

John's Gospel begins with a great sweeping prologue locating Jesus at the heart of God's purposes and at the heart of the universe: "In the beginning was the Word, and the Word was with God, and the Word was God" (John 1:1). And then a few verses later we find ourselves abruptly face-to-face with a man giving testimony, a man also called John, a man who sets up stall some way from the epicenter of Israel, some way from Jerusalem, from the temple, from the people who decided what was godly, indeed on the other side of the Jordan, outside the traditional boundaries of the Promised Land. John doesn't have a website, he doesn't have a Facebook page; it's hard to know who he is and what he stands for. Think about the Occupy protesters, and their many imitators — they really wind people up, some of them challenge hygiene norms, and they won't translate their protest into concrete demands, so no one knows who they really are. That's where they get their power. In many respects they're like John.

The high and mighty send their lackeys to say to John, "Who are you?" He has an answer for them. "I am not." It's a funny kind of answer. He repeats it several times (John 1:20-21). There's something almost aggressive about it. But that quickly makes sense when you realize that the people John is talking to are messengers from the very same

44

crowd of leaders who will put both John and Jesus to death two or three years after this conversation. This isn't an idle game of Twenty Questions, where only John knows the answer and everyone else has to guess, and he takes delight in shaking his head and saying "Uh-uh." This is a cross-examination with John's head on the block. His life depends on his answer to this question.

Eventually John puts his interrogators out of their misery and gives them a straight answer.

> "I am the voice of one crying out in the wilderness,
> 'Make straight the way of the Lord.'" (John 1:23)

These words are a quotation from the prophet Isaiah. They're a clear statement from John that he's well in line with the way God has worked over centuries and has prepared Israel for this moment. But they also say a lot about John. They say what he is — a voice; where he is — in the wilderness; what he's doing — crying out; and what is really going on — the Lord is coming soon. John is asked the question, over and over again, "Who are you?" And his answer is, "I can't answer that question except in relation to Jesus." Think about those words for a moment. "I can't answer that question except in relation to Jesus." Is that your answer?

The French film *A Very Long Engagement* tells the story of Mathilde, a young woman from northwest France who is crippled by polio.[5] She falls in love with a young man named Manech. Manech goes off to fight in the trenches of the First World War, but before he does so, the couple seal their love and promise their hearts to one another. Manech takes a knife and carves into the trunk of a large tree the capital letters *MMM*, which stand for "Manech loves Mathilde" — the middle *M* representing the French verb for love, spelled *aime* but pronounced "M." Manech repeatedly carves these three capital letters on trees and paints them on walls wherever he goes — it becomes his signa-

5. *A Very Long Engagement*, directed by Jean-Pierre Jeunet (Warner Brothers, 2004). Based on the novel by Sebastien Japrisot. Originally released as *Un long dimanche de fiançailles*.

ture tune, his logo, the one thing he knows about himself and wants to tell the whole world.

But things don't go well in the trenches for Manech. He's accused of injuring himself to avoid combat and is court-martialed. As punishment, in the middle of the Battle of the Somme, he is pushed up and out of a trench and into no-man's-land. That's the last anyone hears of him.

His beloved Mathilde refuses to believe this is the end of the story. After the war she hires a private investigator and searches high and low for news of him. She finds a letter from another soldier in the trench. The letter describes Manech's final walk in no-man's-land and how he was last seen carving into a tree the letters *MMM*. She realizes that at the brink of death the one thing he knew about himself was his union with her. But she won't stop there. She continues her intrepid investigation, en route finding that Manech had received a pardon from the president of France, but that the pardon had been suppressed by the commanding officer. Eventually Mathilde's all-consuming search bears fruit, and she discovers to her unbridled joy that Manech survived the ordeal, is still alive, and is being cared for in a rehabilitation community. In the final scene of the film, Mathilde is reunited with her beloved fiancé Manech. But Manech is a changed man. He doesn't know who Mathilde is. He doesn't remember anything about their love or about the trenches. He doesn't know who he is.

This is where the film ends, but just imagine how the story might continue. Loving this man, and having spent so long searching for him when everyone thought she was crazy and obsessed and chasing an impossible dream, and having finally found him, surely Mathilde is not going to stop there. Surely she's going to stay by his side until he learns to think and feel again, until life begins to come back into focus. Even if he can never remember their youth together in France, before too long all his memories and impressions will be infused with Mathilde, just as they were before, only with different details. It's not hard to imagine that one day again, perhaps without knowing he's done it before, and that he did it at the defining moment of his life, Manech might carve the same three letters into a tree trunk, *MMM*. The truth is, he doesn't know who he is without Mathilde. He never did. And now, the other side of hell and oblivion, he never will.

That's what John is telling us in saying "no" to all his interrogators' questions. He's saying, "I don't know who I am. I only know who I am in relation to Jesus. I am a voice. I'm one crying in the wilderness. I'm one making a way for Jesus. I don't have any purpose in life, any goals in life, any satisfaction in life, any bearings in life, any wisdom in life, any security in life, any identity in life, aside from Jesus. Jesus is the way I know who I am."

Think back to the story of Mathilde and Manech, and their very long engagement. Think of yourself as Manech, and Jesus as Mathilde. Imagine the story in three scenes: scene one before the war, scene two in the heat of the battle, and scene three after the war.

Some of us identify with the story before the war. Manech could follow a number of paths in life, but he chooses to associate himself with Mathilde. In just the same way for many of us Jesus is a choice, a figure with whom we choose to identify, and our faith is something from which we could theoretically disentangle ourselves, just as it's possible to loosen oneself from an inauspicious engagement.

But others of us might see ourselves more in scene two, at that moment when Manech has been rejected by his own superior officers and thrown into the wilderness of no-man's-land, and is facing his near-certain death. Here he knows no truth other than Mathilde. Will that be us, moments before our near-certain death? Will we know no other truth than that Jesus loves us? Will all we know be that Jesus carved his love for us onto the trunk of a tree and has been carving it ever since?

And yet again others of us may feel that the most profound portrayal of our faith comes in the final scene of the film, where Mathilde, who has already given so much and loved so deep and searched so far, begins to whisper words and make gestures of faithful, abiding love to a man who no longer knows who he is or who she is. Here are we, like Manech, not knowing who we are, where we are, what's going on, hidden away in our little self-absorbed existence; and here is Jesus, kneeling beside us, whispering, playing, teasing, drawing us into this new world that we half-remember, half-yearn for, partly resist and partly embrace. But without Jesus we would have no idea of it, and scarcely ever do we realize that it's only possible because of this same Jesus who's telling us about it. And one day we may carve our love onto the trunk of a tree. But we might be blissfully unaware that Jesus has been in the tree-carving business not just for us, but all along.

Without Jesus, we don't know who we are. Sure, we can discover our home, our tastes, our dreams, our sexuality, our colors, our rhythms, our learning styles, our psychological metrics, our star sign, our DNA, our genes, our ancestors' dwelling place, our voice, our family tree. These can all be helpful in their own way. But none of them discloses the most important thing about us. Like John, what really matters about us is to what and to whom we are a witness. What is a witness? A twentieth-century French cardinal had the answer to that question. He said, "To be a witness consists not in engaging in propaganda, nor even in stirring people up, but in being a living mystery. It means to live in such a way that one's life would not make sense if God did not exist."[6]

That's the answer. John was a mystery to his interrogators. But he knew who he was. He was a living mystery whose life made no sense if Jesus was not coming. Maybe you feel your life makes no sense right now. Maybe you don't know who you are. Maybe your life is a mystery even to yourself. But Jesus has carved your name beside his into the trunk of a tree. Jesus is calling you to be a witness. Jesus is kneeling beside you, whispering your memory and imagination into a life for which he has searched you out and which he has made possible for you to enter. Jesus is the living mystery in whom alone you can discover who you are.

6. Emmanuel Suhard, *Growth or Decline* (South Bend, Ind.: Fides Press, 1948); quoted in Stanley Hauerwas, *Sanctify Them in the Truth: Holiness Exemplified* (Nashville: Abingdon, 1998), 38.

CHAPTER 2

Learning to Live Again

We think we choose how to think and how to live. In fact, we im-
bibe much or most of what we take for granted from our wider
culture. The discussions in this chapter and the next consider how
Christians may configure their relationship to forms of life and
thought that pervade secular culture. I take five themes and seek to ex-
amine them scripturally and theologically. The first discussion sets
the tone for the chapter. It presents itself as a cultural and exegetical
survey of the differences between contract and covenant. But it is intended to indicate a whole ethic of how church relates to world. It seeks
a nuanced way of living in the world that is incarnational — that is, one
that recognizes that God's revelation in Jesus was as fully God but also
as fully human. Christians must learn to live in what Augustine called
the city of God, but they must also learn to navigate the heavenly city.
Early theologians tried to ensure that our understanding of Jesus' nature didn't so separate his divinity from his humanity as to make him
an entirely split personality. Our contemporary understanding of the
church's vocation faces a similar challenge.

The subsequent parts explore this ethos in regard to significant dimensions of contemporary society. I begin with health care, exploring
the theology underlying (and sometimes buried beneath) modern
medicine. I then explore sport, recognizing the grip it has over the contemporary collective imagination, and the ways it parallels religion in
today's culture. Then I turn to science, particularly in the wake of the

"new atheist" brand of scientific fundamentalism. And finally I consider the arts.

There Are Two Ways We Can Do This

Let's imagine that you're in an apartment and there's water dripping through the ceiling. You don't want to get your neighbor upstairs in trouble, but you also don't want the apartment and your furniture to be damaged. You get on well with the landlord, but you think it's unreasonable to wait seven days to get the problem seen to. You keep wondering, "What's the Christian way to behave right now? Should I be a doormat and say, 'No, really, that precious rug I brought back from my year abroad is all the better for being moist and damp'? Or should I protest my rights and talk about justice and attorneys and compensation?" A conversation goes through your head that says, "I want to be generous, and understanding, and patient, and forgiving. But I don't want to be stupid and taken for a ride. I know that people can be worse off than me, and under a lot of pressure, and in financial trouble, and have nowhere to turn. But I also know that people can be lazy, and mean, and thoughtless, and selfish."

Situations like these are microcosms of a huge question. The huge question is, what does it mean to be God's companions but at the same time to live in the world? How can we be captivated by God's holiness without being naïve, but mindful of human clumsiness without being cynical? Must we live a double life, inhabiting two worlds simultaneously? I don't believe so. Instead, we live in one world; but we must learn to speak two languages.

Here's the first language. It's rooted in philosophers from three hundred years ago like Thomas Hobbes and John Locke. This language imagines a time when human beings had no way of trusting one another, no way of making binding agreements, and no way of holding one another to promises or navigating disagreements. This condition is sometimes described as the "state of nature." It's not a happy condition to be in. Everyone is at war with everyone else, and no one lives very long. These philosophers suppose an original agreement by which everyone once upon a time gave up some of his or her individual rights to a sovereign in return for peace and security. This is called the "social contract." The state exists to protect the people's rights, and to arbitrate disputes.[1]

This kind of thinking is at the heart of America's founding documents and is the fabric of Western culture. It's so foundational to our lives that we scarcely notice it. The dominant word is "contract." A contract is a voluntary agreement between two free agents that creates an obligation that can be enforced. If a contract is broken, compensation can be expected. When you're sitting in your damp apartment with water dripping through the ceiling, and you don't know what to do, and you call a wise friend, what does your wise friend say? Most likely, "Have you got a contract? What does it say about maintenance in the contract?"

If you have a contract, in normal circumstances you shouldn't have to feel guilty about holding the other party to their side of the bargain. With a contract, you know where you are. Most contracts are built out of previous contracts, with language and stipulations derived from experience over generations. They're a residue of accumulated wisdom. While contracts can be pretty dull to read, they also evoke a kind of relief. It's reassuring to realize that someone has thought in advance about all the things that could go wrong and worked out a fair way of naming responsibilities and anticipating solutions. You really can begin to imagine almost all the complex parts of your life in terms of contracts. In the 1994 congressional election campaign, when the Republican Party issued its "Contract with America," the phrase had a certain rightness about it. You thought, "That makes sense. Yes. We can rely on that." That feeling of security is everything a contract can give you.

That brings us to another, older language that goes back before the language of contract. And that's the language we find in Genesis 9.

---

1. Thomas Hobbes, *Leviathan* (Oxford: Oxford University Press, 1998), chapter 14, "Of the First and Second Natural Laws, and of Contracts," pp. 86-89; John Locke, *The Second Treatise of Government* (Oxford: Basil Blackwell; New York: Macmillan, 1947), 3-120.

This is the language of covenant. Genesis 9 describes the covenant God makes with Noah and with every living creature after the flood (9:8-17). The covenant says that never again will God cut off all flesh by the waters of a flood (9:11). This is the foundation of the whole of the Old Testament. God will have to resolve the shortcomings of creation by some route other than destruction. This is the covenant of life.

A few chapters later God makes a covenant with Abraham that says through Abraham's line, through the people who came to be known as Israel, and whom we know as the Jews, all nations will find a blessing. Abraham and Sarah's descendants will be as numerous as the stars in the sky and the sands in the desert, and as a guarantee God will give them Canaan as their possession (Genesis 12:1-3). This is the covenant of the land. Then in Exodus God makes a covenant of holiness with Moses that sets the bounds within which Israel must live and keep the land (Exodus 19:1-20:17). This is the covenant of the law. Finally God makes a covenant with David to bless him and his descendants with kingly authority (2 Samuel 7:4-17). This is the covenant of the lineage.

Life, land, law, lineage. All the parameters of the Old Testament are set by these covenants. The whole dynamic of the Old Testament story is about whether God will be faithful to these covenants even if Israel breaks them. How will God restore Israel when the covenant is in tatters? That's the question on which the whole Bible rests.

In the end, Jesus is God's answer to this question. Jesus is the representative human being, the new Noah, the new Abraham, the new Moses, the new David, the embodiment of Israel, with whom God makes a covenant that won't ever be broken. And Jesus is at the same time the God who won't ever break the covenant. Jesus is the Lamb of God who in his body suffers the pain of all the broken covenants. But at the same time Jesus is the shepherd who goes and fetches the lost sheep to bring them into the fold of the new, unbreakable covenant.

Let's look at these two languages. Let's consider the difference between a contract and a covenant. Contracts cover limited matters and are a way of keeping them under control. By contrast, covenants are about powers that we can never truly hope to control. And that's why, when we look at the most precious things in our lives, we find they're run by covenants, not by contracts. Who will be holding your hand when you die? That's not something you can put in a contract. That's all about a covenant. Who do you turn to when you're at a crossroads in your life and you've searched your soul and you don't know what to do for the best? Someone you know and trust in a way no contract can ever guarantee. What gives you a sense of community and belonging and of being understood and at home? A group of people and a place with whom you share a covenant. No contract can give you that.

One of the differences between a contract and a covenant is that signatories to a contract can always appeal to a third party. There's a law court lurking in the shadows of every dispute. But parties to a covenant have no court of appeal. There's no compensation for the breaking of a covenant, because the covenant wasn't a means to some more useful end. A covenant, be it between friends, or family members, or churches, or neighbors, is an end in itself. If it's over, there's no consolation prize to put in its place to make it better. But if it lasts, it's maybe the most tangible sign of God's abundant provision we can experience.

The idea of governing all our lives by contracts is superficially attractive. But on closer inspection it turns out to be the road to hell. By turning every relationship into a contract, we end up regarding everyone as a stranger, and we come to live as if trust and community are bonus items that we generally factor out — while God's provision becomes something we exclude altogether. Eventually we find we've factored trust and community out so many times that we wake up and discover that they've ceased to exist, and God's provision becomes a hypothetical we never have time to dwell on. That's pretty much the process that our culture finds itself in the middle of. The fear of litigation is taking a lot of the care and most of the discretion out of the caring professions. One reason why medicine is so expensive and so many interventions take place is because the trust between patient and doctor and the watchful "Let's wait and see" are fast being gobbled up by the constant threat of legal proceedings.

Sometimes people in business ask me what they should aim for in their dealings. After all, business is all about contracts. It's about driving hard bargains and maximizing profit margins. I usually say, the sign of doing business well is that you can have cordial relations not just with your colleagues but also with your suppliers and your customers. That indicates you haven't exploited the one or taken advantage of the other. In other words, good business is a process of gradually turning contracts into covenants. In fact, that's a pretty good aspiration for all our lives: turning contracts into covenants.

You may be expecting me to argue that contracts are worldly and covenants are heavenly, and we should be wary of the one and aim always for the other. But I've been a pastor for twenty years and hung around churches all my life, and I've seen that kind of thinking go wrong too many times. Here's the mistake Christians often make. We start by assuming a covenant and we don't take the time and care to get the contract right. We hire friends as employees or put congregation members on the church staff, and it quickly turns out that they're a hopeless fit for the job and their work habits fall well below the reasonable, and our desire to keep the covenant inhibits us from facing the truth about the breaking of the contract. What we should have done was be more modest and set the contract out explicitly and hope and pray (but never assume) that a healthy covenant would in time blossom. I always say to new colleagues, "We don't have to be friends. That may come in time, and in fact it most often does, but we mustn't let our need or desire to be friends get in the way of the more important work we have to do together for something bigger than us and our personal needs." That's my rather blunt way of saying, let's get the contract right and not rush into a covenant.

Look at your life for a moment and the painful relationships that get you down. Think of an in-law or a boss or a colleague or a person you're still vainly trying to pretend is a friend. I wouldn't mind guessing that this confusion between contract and covenant names a big part of your misery; you're going through the motions of relating to one another as if you're in a covenant, but the reality is, you feel the other person isn't even keeping the terms of a contract. I bet it's driving you crazy. And all the talk of being in a loving family or a Christian organization just becomes a smoke screen that makes a mockery of the covenant and leaves you finding it almost impossible to have a long-overdue conversation to straighten out the contract. The result is public confusion and private fury.

On a macro scale this can be a problem for whole denominations.

Think about the response to the clergy sex abuse scandals. The judicatories want to act in a covenantal way of love and forgiveness, but they find it hard to see that they and their representatives have broken basic contractual obligations to safeguard the vulnerable. The general public gets very angry if it sees Christians talking piously about covenants while not even keeping their contracts. Here's the critical point: we should aspire for every relationship to become a covenant, but we should never let any relationship fall below the level of a contract.

So here's the good news for Christians trying to speak both languages, the language of contract and of covenant. *Take contracts seriously*. Caring for contracts and their details is a form of love toward those we don't know very well. It's a recognition that life is full of unexpected pitfalls, and contracts are a way of holding one another to honesty and honor in the face of temptation and distraction. *Never assume we can run our whole lives by contracts*. If we do, we'll find ourselves unprepared for the deepest and most beautiful things God has to give us. Instead, *try to turn contracts slowly but surely into covenants*. Contracts can give us security and trust, but only covenants can bring joy and delight.

And most of all, *never treat our relationship with God as a contract*. We never made a deal. God owes us nothing. We aren't God's equal. There's no court of arbitration we can go to if we get it into our head that God's not keeping the divine side of the bargain. There is no contract. What we have with God is a covenant. A covenant of grace that we did nothing to earn or deserve.

In the end, all contracts will fade away, and our covenant with God will be all we have. Forever.

Entertaining Angels Unaware

Medicine today is a victim of its own success. If you think of novels set in the nineteenth century, the world of *Little Women* or *Gone with the Wind*, there's always a scene where a physician in a black overcoat emerges from the bedroom of a much-loved but sickly sibling or parent and somberly announces, "I'm afraid there's nothing we can do." In nineteenth-century fiction that's all doctors ever say: "I'm afraid there's nothing we can do." These days, physicians dress in white coats and are more likely to say, "There's a new drug that's just come on the market, and I think it could be just the thing to have you back on your feet in a few days." Catastrophic diseases like tuberculosis have now been virtually wiped out in the developed world; better diet and safer living and working conditions mean that most of us can expect to live a lot longer than people once did; and medicine has been transformed from the discipline of managing tragedy to the offer of perpetual remedy. The clinician's drug and the surgeon's knife have done so many wholesome things and saved so many lives, my own included. Only one thing has moved faster than medical skill and innovation, and that's the public expectation that medicine can solve pretty much everything.

People look to physicians today the same way that, in the distant past, they looked to priests: as those who carry the keys to the kingdom. When, in the Christian West, confidence in the resurrection of the body was almost universal, a long and healthy life first time around was not the only or even the most important thing to be wished for. The real life was the one to come, and this life was just the introduction — so if it was uncomfortable or even harsh, that wasn't an insuperable problem. But medicine rose to prominence at about the same time that confidence in the bodily resurrection of the dead began to falter. Over the last 150 years people in industrialized countries have increasingly come to place their hope on this life more than on the next; those that seem to have the key to the door of longer, healthier life have become the new priests of our culture. Because of this, medicine is in danger of being transformed from a practice conducted by those whose faith in the life to come enabled them to cope with the tragedies of this life, into a new religion that seeks to extend this present life for as long as possible.

That brings us to the first key word in medicine: "care." The fact that medicine can do so many new things raises a host of questions about what it should or should not do. Most of these surround the beginning and end of life. Should the fetus die if the mother's health is at risk? Should the fetus die even sometimes when the mother's health isn't at risk? Should the patient be brought to an early death if he or she is overwhelmed by pain? And so on. These are the stuff of the ethics textbook and the single-issue campaign manual. But together they miss the most significant issue in all of medical ethics — the commitment by those in society who are not sick to care for those who are, particularly for those who are not likely to be economically productive again in any measurable way. This is not a commitment that hardnosed economics can comprehend. It goes against the principle of the survival of the fittest. And yet it's the most basic assumption of medicine, and is at the core of the vocations of the huge majority of health professionals. Medicine is fundamentally about caring for people, even if one can't cure them — perhaps *especially* if one can't cure them. In my experience, very few health professionals ever forget this, but the same is not true of the general public, many of whom have come to believe that medicine is precisely about curing. To be fair, the quantity of investment that goes into research and development toward more extensive forms of treatment for more previously untouchable ailments does give the impression that curing has become a much bigger part of the culture of medicine. But the truth is that most common diseases are incurable with current countermeasures, and most of what physicians do is to try to help people manage a bit better with the burden of the chronic but incurable illnesses they bear.

Don't get me wrong — I want my physician to give me a cure as much as anyone else. When a loved one is facing pain and distress, of course we yearn for a cure. But when curing becomes the heart of medicine, medicine loses its heart. Health professionals become service providers, and hospitals become hives of hyperactivity, because anything that could possibly be done must be done — or else the attorneys will bang on the door. More and more drastic kinds of interventions start to be described as cures, and patients can forget that a cure is worthless without the care that accompanies it. A system obsessed by curing will always be critically short of money and resources, whereas a system that continues to assert the primacy of care will be able to rejoice in the gifts that money can't buy — gifts we will all need in the end, when we reach the moment when curing can do no more and we face dying alone.

That brings us to the second key word in medicine: "patient." Medicine remains a moral practice rather than an economic transaction so long as the physician remembers the duty to care and the patient remembers to be exactly that – *patient*. Anyone who has endured a serious illness, or anyone who has cared for a loved one through such a time, knows that finding the patience is as trying as fighting the pain. When I was a teenager my mother knew for three years that the cancer she had long carried was going to kill her, but I found the strain of not knowing how long it was going to be almost unbearable. After she died I had nightmares in which she would come back to life and I would say to her, "Really, it's easier if you die. I just can't bear not knowing anymore." Patience is fundamentally about learning to live in God's time rather than our own. Like caring, it rests on Christian assumptions. Caring rests on the conviction that however tough life is this time around, God has something better in store beyond our own deaths, and so we can treasure each other's lives as gifts that invite us into new life. Patience rests on the conviction that we live our lives in the palm of God's hand and that God's palm is always the best place for us to be. When medicine doesn't rest on this kind of faith, it's almost inevitable that it becomes a religion all its own.

A hint of the third key word in medicine is to be found in the book of Hebrews: "Show hospitality to strangers, for by doing that some have entertained angels without knowing it" (Hebrews 13:2). A hospital is many things: a large employer, a scene of triumph and tragedy, a business always struggling to balance its books, a place of research and training, a theater of devoted care and anxiety and professionalism and pain and hope. But fundamentally, more than anything else, a hospital is a place of hospitality. If you go to France you will see, in town centers, medieval buildings with inscriptions inlaid by the front door, saying "Hôtel-Dieu" – the hostel of God. These are the places where the sick and dying were cared for, especially during the plague. And they were called God's hotels. Hospitals are God's hotels. Hospitals are the places God earmarks to stay when in town. And those who work in hospitals, if they do so in the spirit of Christian mission and charity, welcome strangers because they believe that in so doing they are entertaining angels. That doesn't mean they look for wings and halos on all their patients. The word "angel" has the more general meaning of "messenger." So those who seek to serve God and their neighbor through being physicians and nurses and physical therapists and a host of other health professionals look at each new patient as a messenger — a person through whom God is bringing wisdom, grace, humanity, kindness, friendship, humility, or many less immediately attractive gifts.

You may know the story of the monastery where the monks were tetchy and cross and at each other's throats until one night there was a knock at the monastery door. The monk who answered saw a shadowy figure who leaned forward and whispered, "One of you is the Christ." The whole life of the monastery began to be transformed, as the monks came to treat each other in a very different way, conscious that in every conversation or gesture, they could be encountering Jesus.[2] That's the practice of Christian hospitality — the belief that whenever people come to us in need or distress, the chances are they could be Jesus, so we'd better make sure we treat them as if they were, not out of fear of judgment but out of the wonder of being in the presence of God.

Health systems in our day face three challenges: our obsession with technology, our consumer culture, and our unresolved tension between public health and private insurance. In regard to these three great challenges, I propose three ancient Christian practices: care, patience, and hospitality. About the obsession with technology, I wonder how Christians can help hospitals and society in general to remember that medicine is fundamentally about caring and only secondarily about curing. About consumer culture, I wonder how Christians can exhibit patience in such a way that shows that real health is fundamentally rooted in right relationships and only secondarily in dynamic drugs. And about public health, I wonder how Christians can help make hospitals places of genuine hospitality, where the stranger is regarded not as a problem or a danger or simply a "case" but as a gift. I have suggested that belief in the resurrection is the key to medicine and that without faith in the resurrection the practice of medicine risks falling into a host of insoluble dilemmas. But such an observation requires a response. It's up to Christians to embody what the resurrection

2. Story adapted from M. Scott Peck, *The Different Drum: Community Making and Peace* (New York: Simon and Schuster, 1987), 13-15.

means in medicine today — and I believe that embodiment lies in care, in patience, and in hospitality.

Feeling God's Pleasure

Few things in America attract more media attention and heartfelt devotion than sports. Yet there's one thing we don't do very much: talk about the role of athletics in society.

Universities funnel an enormous amount of resources into athletic programs, which in turn generate millions of dollars. College athletes today face unprecedented pressures. Cable television has every interest in nonstop scheduling and no interest in students getting to lectures or getting any sleep. Likewise, professional sports in the United States are a multibillion-dollar industry. Adulation of sports stars blurs the line between athletics and entertainment.

Maybe it's time to ask ourselves what this avalanche of emotional, physical, and financial investment is really all about. What are the features of athletics that put it at the heart of society and cause it to evoke so much admiration, so much disdain, and so much controversy? And what do sports have to do with Christianity? I'm going to reflect on three themes.

The first is simply put: *practice* makes perfect. You want to know how to sink a ten-foot putt to win the U.S. Open? You go out at six o'clock in the morning every day for years and sink ten-foot putts from every conceivable angle. You want to know how to snatch victory with three seconds left on the clock by getting a slam dunk after having started under your own basket? You get out there with your teammates and work out fifteen ways of doing so and how to communicate to each other which one you're going to try. Sort out your 99 percent perspiration, and your 1 percent inspiration comes easy. Practice, practice, and practice some more. Keeping our eyes on the prize keeps us honest, keeps us disciplined, keeps us loyal. Wanting not just to win but to win well and to win again and again teaches us sportsmanship, teaches us hard work, teaches us how to set priorities. Making ourselves better athletes more often than not makes us better people.

Athletics today is one of the best places to learn about obedience. Think about a medieval monastery: the monks had to learn teamwork, keep regular hours, attune their bodies, listen to one another's souls. Monasteries in the Middle Ages were the engine room of education, economic growth, and character development. Today, that role has largely been taken by sports teams. If you're looking today for commitment, obedience, dedication, and people who will give everything for one another, you look at the Olympic Games, you look at the NCAA, you look at Real Madrid. The individuals who have thrived there are likely to be leaders elsewhere.

A friend of mine used to be a senior executive in a famous engineering company. He conducted a survey of what salaries people were earning ten years after joining the company. It turned out that the people with the highest salaries were not the cleverest, or those with the best academic achievement, or those who'd been the highest earners when they'd joined the company; they were the people who were capable of persuading others and communicating a vision. These are the qualities you need to lead a sports team. These are the qualities you need to get the best out of any group of people. These are things athletics teaches you.

Look at these words from Saint Paul in his letter to the church in Rome: "For as in one body we have many members, and not all the members have the same function, so we, who are many, are one body in Christ, and individually we are members one of another" (Romans 12:4-5). He could be talking about a baseball team, a hockey team, a football team. When the 4 x 100 meter leadoff woman runs out of her lane and gets disqualified in the track relay, the woman on the anchor leg is brokenhearted, but she realizes it's a team sport and they can only cross the line as a team. We practice not just to make our individual bodies better but also to make our team more one body. We can't get there unless we all get there. Life is a team game. Athletes know this. If only the church did too.

The second blessing of athletics is *play*. The great Liverpool soccer coach Bill Shankly famously said, "Some people think [soccer] is a matter of life and death. I assure you, it's much more serious than that." Sports talk is notoriously prone to exaggeration, and no doubt he was half in jest. But these widely quoted and oft-repeated remarks indicate a transition from joy to obsession and from obsession to pathology. The whole point of athletics is precisely *not* to be about life and death, but instead to be a glimpse of timeless, intense play. The second-century theologian Irenaeus said, "The glory of God is a human being fully alive."[3] Athletics is about exploring what it means to be fully alive.

In the film *Chariots of Fire*, the Scottish sprinter Eric Liddell explains how his running is not only play but also prayer. "I believe God made me for a purpose, but he also made me fast. And when I run I *feel his pleasure*."[4] Feeling God's pleasure. That's got to be about as good as it gets. That's being fully alive and experiencing eternal life at the same time. At the 2008 Olympic Games, the Jamaican sprinter Usain Bolt was criticized for showboating as he crossed the line in the 100-meter final. But he was in unknown territory. He was running faster than anyone had ever run. I'd like to think he was showing us what it's like to feel God's pleasure.

Several coaches and commentators are associated with the phrase "Winning isn't everything; it's the only thing." Again, this seems to miss the whole point of play. To play is to become so absorbed in a circumscribed and in some ways ritualized activity that you lose all track of time and space. As much as the physical exercise or the camaraderie, surely it's this sense of play that makes athletics so refreshing for the mind and body. Once winning becomes everything, the play stops being an end in itself and is relegated to being a means to an end. That immediately opens the door to a whole host of ungracious, dishonorable, and sometimes illegal practices that technically count as winning but don't genuinely count as sport.

Winning with grace is an attribute you expect athletes to learn. But athletics isn't just about learning to win. It's also about learning to

3. Irenaeus of Lyons, *Against the Heresies*, in *The Apostolic Fathers: With Justin Martyr and Irenaeus*, vol. 1 of *The Ante-Nicene Fathers*, ed. Alexander Roberts and James Donaldson (Grand Rapids: Eerdmans, 1979), 4.20.7, p. 490.

4. *Chariots of Fire* (1981), directed by Hugh Hudson, original screenplay by Colin Welland, produced by Allied Stars Ltd. and Enigma Productions, distributed by 20th Century Fox.

lose — with dignity, generosity, and grace. Every loss is a kind of preparation for death. After all, in the game of life we all lose in the end. Athletics shouldn't preserve the illusion that it's possible not to lose. It should help to train us in how to live and what things are worth living for even though we all lose in the end. Competitors are often quicker to understand this than fans are. (It's often the fans that drive the obsession with winning, as a displacement from a personal sense of loss that they know sometimes all too well.)

And that's where competition comes in. There's a brand of Christianity that suggests that all competition is wrong, and should always be displaced by cooperation. But that's not Saint Paul's view. Also in his letter to the Romans, he says, "Outdo one another in showing honor" (Romans 12:10). There *is* such a thing as healthy competition, provided the prize sought and the methods used are appropriate. Competition is usually against others, but is always fundamentally within oneself, to be the best that one can possibly be, win or lose. In that sense competition is a way of showing gratitude for the faith and the gifts one has been given by not letting them go to waste but making the most of them. Notice also the very human lesson in Paul's words: if there's something you know is right but you struggle to do, rather than just earnestly trying harder, consider making a game of it and involving others in a playful competition.

The third vital feature of athletics in addition to practice and play is *peace*. In the Middle Ages, Italy wasn't one country. It was a host of city-states, and these states had tin-pot wars against each other with relentless regularity. I sometimes think sports teams are like Italian city-states, maintaining a host of intense rivalries. But there's a vital difference. The rivalries are intense, but they're not about killing people. In fact, in a crucial way, they're a *substitute* for killing each other. A lot of the activity of our sporting contests is like war — putting on face paint, camping out as if mounting a siege, pumping iron, getting sick in the stomach, shouting war songs, and manufacturing truckloads of testosterone — but at the end nobody dies.

On Christmas Day, amid the carnage of World War One, the British soldiers heard the German infantry singing "Silent Night." The British and German soldiers ended up playing soccer together in no-man's-land between the opposing trenches.[5] Why couldn't they have made that soccer match a substitute for the whole war? A similar principle applied with the original Greek Olympic Games, where chronic hostilities between the city-states were suspended in order for athletes to compete with one another in wrestling, chariot racing, and the like.

One of the problems with peace is that we find it difficult to imagine a peace that isn't desperately boring. War may do terrible damage, but for many participants it gives meaning to their lives. Intercollegiate athletics is a picture of the kind of competitive but nonviolent interaction that peace involves and perhaps even requires. If you think of the virtues of battle — the building of trust between comrades, the attempt to give your very best for the cause, the balance of patience and constant awareness, the development of skills for use at crucial moments, the power that comes through undying loyalty, the galvanizing of whole nations around a greater cause — competitive athletics grooms each of these qualities, without anyone getting killed; and these qualities become the foundation of peace.

Here's the heart of why athletics are about peace. Saint Paul says, "Do not be overcome by evil, but overcome evil with good" (Romans 12:21). Every athlete, every sports team, sooner or later comes up against a player or a team that's bigger, stronger, faster, or more talented than they are. That athlete or that team must then work out a way to win regardless. That's where sport really gets interesting. Life is a series of challenges where the other guy or the other set of people seem to have all the advantages. Violence arises when you can't think of any better way to get level, get even, or get ahead. Athletics at its best is a training in how to overcome apparent disadvantage without violence.

The 1975 Wimbledon final provided an amazing example of this principle. Everyone knew that the defending champion Jimmy Connors, the ultimate counterpuncher, was going to be the champion for years to come. He seemed unbeatable. Along comes Arthur Ashe, thirty-two years old (which, in case you didn't know, is ancient in tennis terms), not as fast, not as strong, not as intense a player as

---

5. Stanley Weintraub, *Silent Night: The Story of the World War I Christmas Truce* (New York: Free Press, 2001).

Connors. But Ashe just takes the pace off the ball with his dolly back-hand slice . . . and in no time Connors ties himself up in knots like a cat with a ball of wool. Ashe demonstrated the kind of intelligence that's required to wage peace: not making himself bigger and stronger, but learning to play *beyond the imagination of the opponent*. And that's the kind of intelligence athletics teaches.

So what athletics is really about isn't a huge stadium, big money TV deals, or celebrity egos. Athletics is really about practice, and the qualities needed to blend and lead a team. Athletics is really about play, and the competition that's ultimately with your own limits. And athletics is really about peace, and the overcoming of evil with good. Athletics belongs in society, because sports can model the goods that we all seek: disciplined practice at the limits of human endeavor; profound, imaginative concentration and the absorption of play; and the discovery of the paths that lead to peace.

In Christian language, athletics is a way of understanding the Holy Spirit. It is the Holy Spirit who makes us holy through the constant *practices* of discipleship; it's the Holy Spirit in whom we dwell when we feel God's pleasure in our *play*; and it's a sign of the fruit of the Holy Spirit that we see when we realize we are living in *peace*. The problem only comes when we mistake athletics for Jesus, and mistakenly think athletics is eternal, is more important than life and death, or is the meaning of our existence. Jesus is all those things. Athletics is not.

Athletics is not Jesus, but it can be one of the most profound experiences of the Holy Spirit we can ever know. Remember Eric Liddell's words. "God made me for a purpose, but he also made me fast. And when I run I feel his pleasure." When we have practiced hard, when we have become a team, when we have used our collective imagination to overcome evil with good, when it all comes together, we can discover that remarkable experience of feeling God's pleasure. God has made you for a purpose, but he may also have made you fast. Run, leap, hurl, soar — and *feel* God's pleasure.

Refashioning the Clay

Not long after my sister began life as an undergraduate, she had a high-noon meeting with her roommate and the dorm housekeeper. My sister had been on a couple of dates, and had seen just about enough. "Men!" she expostulated. Her roommate shared my sister's exasperation and bewilderment. "We should shoot them all, and have done with it," she concluded. The housekeeper interjected, in a kindly but experienced tone, "Don't waste your energy, my dearies. They're not worth the bullets."

The first few years of the twenty-first century witnessed the publication of a series of books, from a variety of authors, attacking religion with a virulence not seen for a long time. This movement has been called "the New Atheism." It believes religion should no longer be tolerated but should be exposed, challenged, and refuted at every opportunity, with a conviction founded on scientific certainty. I have tended to take the advice of my sister's housekeeper, and reckoned that the work of Christopher Hitchens, Sam Harris, Daniel Dennett, and others was not worth the bullets. The New Atheists have said many new things and many true things, but the new things they've said are not true and the true things they've said are not new.[6]

I'm taking exception to this stance for two reasons. One is that many Christians have a lingering anxiety, maybe even dread, that perhaps science really has disproved it all. The second reason is that I want to use New Atheism as an opportunity to dwell on the relationship between science and Christianity.

The prophet Jeremiah describes God as a potter, handling and cherishing the clay, and making something beautiful out of clay that has been deformed or damaged (Jeremiah 18:1-4). The Christian life begins when we realize that we are that clay. But I also want to see how Jeremiah's picture of God as a potter might inspire us to handle precious things the same way God cherishes us. The relationship between

6. To paraphrase Samuel Johnson, who reportedly said, "Voltaire said many new things and many true things; but the new things he said were not true, and the true things he said were not new."

science and Christianity is like clay: it's moist and full of potential, and if cherished, should become something beautiful. But currently this clay is spoiled in our hands. The relationship between science and Christianity seems less about understanding and more about bullets. I want to suggest a refashioning of the relationship of science and Christianity, and to suggest a way that they can be a blessing to one another.

To understand the backlash of some prominent intellectuals against religion, one has to scroll back a few decades. The New Atheists came to adulthood in a world where it was assumed that an atheism inspired by the discoveries of science would soon fill the earth as surely as the waters cover the sea. In 1988 the moviegoing public was captivated by *Fatal Attraction*, which portrays a professional woman having a wild weekend affair with a man while the man's wife is out of town, and then obsessively stalking him for months afterward. Her activities become increasingly alarming, until finally she breaks into the man's house in murderous mood. The man fights her off and forces her into the bathroom, where she becomes submerged beneath the surface of the bathwater for several minutes. Her body goes limp, blood rises from the corner of her mouth, and the man and his wife finally relax. But the stalker defies apparent death and, in a scene rated number 59 on Bravo network's *100 Scariest Movie Moments*, she rises up from the bathwater to mount one final, deranged, but ultimately unsuccessful attack.

This is how the New Atheism sees religion. Given up for dead forty years ago, religion is rising anew from the bathtub. Reports of its death have been greatly exaggerated, and it's not only alive but unhinged and eager to fight. The dismay of making such a baffling discovery in large part accounts for the almost hysterical tone adopted by some of the New Atheist arguments.

The first thing to say in response to these assaults is that Christianity has only itself to blame for being criticized in such a way. Most people who reject faith as vehemently as this do so not on scientific grounds but on moral ones. While the portrayal of Christianity offered by the New Atheists is, to most Christians, an absurd caricature, there are undoubtedly some who sincerely hold the lurid views Dawkins and his friends take to be the norm. We Christians have often propounded an impoverished faith, and have even more frequently failed to live up to the faith we profess, so we are bound to invite criticism from those who scrutinize our lives and convictions. At the same time, just because we are often poor witnesses to our beliefs, that doesn't mean our beliefs are untrue. The novelist Evelyn Waugh was reportedly asked how he could behave the way he did and claim to be a Christian, to which he replied, "If I were not a Christian, I would scarcely be human."[7]

The relationship between Christianity and science can't be left to extremists, who believe that only one or the other can make legitimate claims. Instead it must begin with respect and awe. Natural science has plausibly been called "the most successful enterprise human beings have ever engaged upon."[8] The more that science discovers about life, about the universe, about the tiniest detail and the mightiest power, the more one can only be amazed and enthralled. Yet if one has awe toward the known, one must have at least equal awe toward the unknown. That awe is not always in high profile. In 1928 the German Nobel physicist Max Born announced, "Physics, as we know it, will be over in six months."[9] It turned out not to be so. The only trustworthy science is a humble science, which acknowledges the tentativeness of the known and the vast extent of the unknown. But the same is true of theology. There is so much that remains unknown, and claiming to know more than we do, especially if it's done with a hectoring tone and without a listening ear, substitutes arrogance and ignorance for true faith, and attracts the antagonism it deserves.

And that's why it's such a blessing for science and theology to be in dialogue with one another. Some believe truth resides only in natural science and there should be no place for literature or philosophy, let alone religion, because they have no testable data and refuse to play by the rules. Some few believe that theology is the queen of the sciences, and that the findings of science should be filtered through the truths of faith, because theological questions of *why* always precede scientific

7. I am grateful to John Inge for sharing this story with me.

8. Peter Medawar, quoted in Alister McGrath and Joanna Collicutt McGrath, *The Dawkins Delusion* (Downers Grove, Ill.: IVP, 2007), 38.

9. Stephen Hawking, *A Brief History of Time* (Toronto: Bantam Books, 1988), 156.

questions of *how*. But the challenge and privilege of trying to value both religion and theology are that we can enjoy and benefit from the different methodologies of the respective disciplines, valuing each for what only it can do, while relishing the interaction and the challenge of the moments when the disciplines overlap and spark fascinating parallels and tensions.

For example, for most of the last 150 years there's been a lively debate about the question, "Where do we come from?" One branch of science goes a very long way back and dwells on the nanoseconds surrounding the big bang; another branch goes back to the beginning of life on earth and to the processes of evolution. These are gripping investigations. It's useless for theologians to claim they have an inside track on the truth or falsity of scientists' findings in such areas. Instead, theologians interrogate the Scriptures to ask a related, but different, set of questions. One is, "Was it always in the mind and heart of God to be in relationship with creation, and for that relationship to be focused by entering creation as a coparticipant at some stage in the story?" That's not a question science can answer, but it's hard to deny it's an exhilarating question to set alongside the others. Just imagine the attentiveness and absorption of God in beholding the evolution of creation, and awaiting the right time to enter it in order to be a coparticipant with that part of it that could show some conscience and awareness in return. That's not a manipulative picture. That's a picture of astounding, patient, devoted, indescribable love.

Here's a parallel question. It's fascinating to ask, "Where do we come from?" – but isn't it at least as interesting, and perhaps more urgent, to ask, "Where are we *going*?" Theologians at this point hold no naïve optimism that as a species or as a universe we're intrinsically heading for candyland. We're sinners, no better or worse than our forebears were or our descendants will be. But Christian theology is committed to the notion of a sudden, final intervention of God in history that brings time to an end and inaugurates an era of glory and fulfillment. Most scientists keep a respectful silence on the question of where we're all going. But some of the New Atheists fuse the theory of evolution with a notion of progress that suggests humans are heading for a happy place all on our own. That's why the New

Atheists are so cross with religion, because it's inhibiting our species' free ride to happiness. It's hard to fathom how you could live through the era of the gulags and the gas chambers and still believe in such a notion of progress. But that just shows how important the question of where we're going is. Scientists may disagree with the answers some theologians give, but the point is, you can't avoid the question, and any answer to the question is going to depend on information science alone can't provide.

Once you put these two questions together, where are we coming from, and where are we going, you're into territory where science and theology can have a really interesting conversation. *Now* the question is, "What, if anything, is the *logic* at the heart of the universe?" The big bang and evolution are huge contributions to science and philosophy. But here's the danger. Once you turn them uncritically into theology, as the New Atheists tend to do, you get a single-word answer: *survival*. Survival of each creature, because death is the end, and survival of each species, because extinction is forever. The whole dynamic of history mutates into survival, and adaptation that enables survival is called progress. Conflict is the dynamic at the heart of every encounter, and survival is the reward for those who win the battle.

But Christianity has a very different answer. Christians believe that the logic — the *logos*, or word — at the heart of the universe is not about survival. It's about death and resurrection. The ultimate future doesn't belong to those who have fought and prevailed; it belongs to those who have laid down their lives for others. This timeless logic is exemplified not in the species that survives, but in the single human being who accepted brutal execution and yet was raised to new life. The real big bang that dominates the Christian imagination is not the detonation that inaugurated the universe, but the rolling away of the stone that signaled the death of death. The real evolutionary pattern that baffles and amazes the Christian imagination is the history of humanity's extraordinarily elaborate hide-and-seek, and somersaulting attempts, to escape the logic of God's relentless, humble, sacrificial, and limitless love, and the constant adaptation God makes to be present to us and in relationship with us anyway.

Constant adaptation. That's a fascinating theme in evolutionary biology. That's a fascinating theme in ecology. That's a fascinating theme in climate studies. That's a fascinating theme in civil engineering. Constant adaptation. That's also a fascinating theme in the prophet Jeremiah. Jeremiah portrays God as a figure making constant adaptations. The vessel, observes Jeremiah, was spoiled in the potter's hands, *and he reworked it into another vessel* (Jeremiah 18:4). This is the story of Israel: the vessel was broken, the covenant was spoiled, and God made something beautiful by fashioning it into a pot shaped around the Jew named Jesus. This is the story of the church, over and over; our common life is spoiled and broken, and God refashions it into something old but new. This is your story. Your life was spoiled, your pot was cracked, your hopes were broken, your plans were ruined; and God the potter made something that could never have been out of something that should never have been. Constant adaptation. That's not a disputed scientific theory. That's what Christians call the Holy Spirit.

And this is why Christians honor and cherish and pursue studies in natural science. Not just because science can solve things and find things and prove things and make things. Science can do all these things. But in them science is simply *used* as a means to an end. If Christians are fully to embrace science, they must learn to *enjoy* science as an end in itself. In science Christians can find a pattern, and a logic, with analogies and parallels to the very purpose of God. They can see depth, and complexity, and diversity, and simplicity, which together reflect the activity and character of God. They can see energy, and creativity, and adaptation, which portray the dynamism of God. The study of science, understood this way, is nothing less than a form of prayer. It's an attempt to enter the presence and be enthralled by the mystery of the form and logic and wonder of all that is.

Scientists, be humble. Remember that science is an art, and that what you study is clay, being constantly fashioned and refashioned. Christians, be humbler still, and remember that science is a form of wonder, and that scientists, if you let them, will teach you to wonder, to love, and to pray.

Turning All into Alleluia

The painting *The Death of Chatterton* by the Pre-Raphaelite painter Henry Wallis is an archetypal image of what it means to be an artist. Thomas Chatterton, a poet and native of my hometown, Bristol, England, died in London in 1770 at the age of seventeen, penniless, desperate, and alone. His art was seldom understood and scarcely ever appreciated. In the painting, he is lying in disarray on his bed, one arm flung off the edge. His clothes are Bohemian and raffish. His talent is enormous, and in his tiny garret apartment he has clearly had spurts of breathtaking and rapid creativity. Yet the scraps of torn paper on the floor next to his bed demonstrate his tortured struggle. We vividly see the contrast between the intensity of his life's purpose and the terrible waste brought about by his poverty and lack of critical acclaim. The painting is telling us, to be an artist is to be possessed, impassioned, alone, tragic, and tortured; but nonetheless glorious and beautiful.

Why then would anyone want to be an artist? The answer is that art is not simply tortured and lonely and tragic. Art is the threshold you cross as soon as you move from the indicative of what things are to the subjunctive of what things could be, from grabbing something in one hand to use it, to cherishing something in two hands truly to enjoy it; from regarding an abundance of meanings as exasperating and distracting, to seeing plurality of possibility and interpretation as joyful and life-giving.

Art is not so much the production of distinguished artifacts or even the experience of profound creativity. Art is what happens within a triangle of forms, media, and ideas. For example, the form might be a landscape, the medium might be a watercolor, while the idea might be the healing goodness of living things. Within the triangle of forms, media, and ideas lies a myriad of possibilities, and art refers not just to acts of creation but also to moments of appreciation and interpretation and revised understanding. Artists are those who live their lives within that triangle of forms, media, and ideas, refining their skills, understanding their tradition, enjoying the interplay of genres, and finding new ways to configure and present them. A true artist is not so much one who dies a tragic, tortured, histrionic death, as one who embodies the disciplines of his or her craft so as to make it a way of life, and whose art evokes imaginative constructions, fertile conversations, and engaged responses in the lives of its audience. These are all the reasons that art in its many forms enriches all our lives.

But what does the Christian faith have to bring to this world of art? How do Christians come to discern a call to be a visual, literary, or performance artist, and continue to see that calling within their Christian vocation as a whole?

Five centuries ago the theologian John Calvin described the ministry of Christ as a threefold office. Calvin looked at the three roles for which persons were anointed in Old Testament times. The roles were prophet, priest, and king. Calvin described how Jesus exercised all three offices, as prophet (especially in his life), as priest (especially in his death), and as king (especially in his resurrection).[10] I'd like to explore what it might mean for an artist to exercise these three roles — or, more collectively, for the arts in general to carry this threefold purpose in our society.

Many artists today can readily identify with the role of the prophet. What a prophet does is to hold a mirror up to society or an individual, and ask, "Are you proud of what you see?" A prophet recalls the founding commitments of a person or a body of people, and asks, "Have those commitments been honored?" A prophet casts a dream of what it might mean for a person or society to fulfill their true potential, and says, "Look, here is the painful gap between ideal and reality." Artists are drawn to all these questions.

A prophet says, "Let's see what this looks like upside-down. I wonder how life would be if all the light shone from the back. Let's imagine we hear this baritone several times, but each time it becomes more threatening, or more mysterious." Prophets challenge, reconfigure, expose, highlight, ridicule, and shock. That's what artists do. Sometimes when an artist's ideas stick outside the triangle and leave the form and media behind, or when the medium is so distressing it ob-

10. John Calvin, *Institutes of the Christian Religion*, trans. Ford Lewis Battles and ed. John T. McNeill, 2 vols., Library of Christian Classics 20 (Philadelphia: Westminster, 1960), 2.15.1-6, pp. 494-503.

scures the form and ideas almost altogether, art becomes notorious for upset and scandal. The offended people who crowd in to condemn the artist, or art in general, at such a moment, have often forgotten, or never appreciated, that artists are prophets. Prophets often shock people too. Jesus shocked people, with his prophetic actions of cleansing the temple and healing on the Sabbath. Not all offensive actions are prophetic; but some prophetic actions are offensive, and just because an artifact offends some people, that doesn't inherently mean it's not art. It just means it's testing the boundaries of idea or medium.

Composer Benjamin Britten was a pacifist, and in his *War Requiem*, he weaves the bitter and ironic poetry of Wilfred Owen with the traditional words of the Latin Mass for the Dead. Britten's composition is a prophetic work of art. It shocks some, transforms many, and moves almost everyone. It asks two questions: "How can we live with the Christian faith, after all this horror?" And, "How can we live without it?" That's what prophets do.

The second role of the artist is to be a priest. The poet George Herbert says,

A man that looks on glass,
On it may stay his eye;
Or if he pleaseth, through it pass,
And then the heaven espy.[11]

But just imagine if that glass is stained glass — just imagine if that glass is the music of Bach or the painting of Giotto or the poetry of Shakespeare. For the artist, every work of art is an icon, through which the observer can look and see ultimate truth, profound wisdom, the heart of God. The artist strives to approximate that epitome of all things, and hopes that the audience will, at least in its imagination, transcend whatever limitations there are in the work or performance or presentation and see beyond even what the artist can see, see beyond the horizon, beyond the stars. In a general way, this is what Christians mean

11. George Herbert, "The Elixir," in *The Works of George Herbert* (Oxford: Clarendon, 1941), 184.

by the notion of a sacrament. In a sacrament, a priest takes the ordinary stuff of life – bread or water – and makes it speak of heaven. A sacrament lies at the intersection of actions and words, where the presence of God is felt or tasted or touched in the faithfulness of what comes about and the way it imitates the pattern and character of God. An artist takes the ordinary stuff of earth – wood, or metal, or canvas – and makes it speak or sing of the divine. It's a priestly role.

When you listen to the trailers for a classical radio station, you'd be forgiven for thinking that classical composers throughout the centuries have really been in the therapy business, and that Mozart, Beethoven, and the rest devoted their lives to making background accompaniments to bubble baths and foot massages. But this simply reflects the way our society has transformed priests into therapists and therapists into priests. The point is that Mozart and Beethoven roll back the gates of heaven and bring us face-to-face with God. And that's a priestly role. When you stop believing in God, you still know you want what Mozart and Beethoven give you, but you don't want to call it God, so you call it soothing or searing; but that's just because you don't trust the word "holy." Artists are high priests of creation; they gather around them all the fruits of creation, just as a priest does around an altar, and order those gifts in such a way as to show the divine in the human and earthly. That's what priests do.

And then there's the artist as king. By king, I don't mean being in charge. I mean showing what humanity can do when it fulfills its potential. The architecture of a cathedral is kingly art – full of majesty and splendor. Kingly art is art that thrills, and delights, and excites, and enthralls – art that stretches our imaginations to their limit in exaltation and awe and delirious rejoicing. I want to tell you about one of my most treasured encounters with kingly art.

Twenty years ago when I first started out as a priest in the Church of England, I lived in a town that was both large enough and small enough to have its own road sweeper. When the truck had gone down every street spraying and blowing and sweeping, the road sweeper followed with his cart full of brushes and buckets and hoses. I would pass the gruff and heavyset road sweeper many days of the week as I walked around the town doing home visits, and we would exchange respectful monosyllables of mutual acknowledgment. One day I got a call to say an elderly woman in the parish had died. I headed to her home, where I was told her son would greet me. Her son, who did indeed greet me, turned out to be the road sweeper. He sat me down and wept as he mourned his mother, and we planned the funeral together. "What keeps you going?" I dared to ask, as I viewed his bare apartment, now even emptier without the presence of his elderly mother. "These," he said, sweeping his hand across a swathe of videotapes, covering the wall from floor to ceiling.

I thought it might be "Great Boxing Matches of the 1980s," or maybe "Classic Truck and Trailer Escapades of All Time." But I was wrong. "Op-ra," he said, with a tear in his eye. I thought, "You mean *Oprah*," and I pondered how a talk show hostess from Mississippi could cross the Atlantic with such ease and stir the heart and soul of a road sweeper. Maybe, I speculated, he and his mother had watched Oprah's shows together. "Op-ra," he said again, with his throaty voice. "This is my glory." And I looked closely, and opera it was. Verdi, Puccini, Mozart, Rossini, Bellini, Strauss, Wagner, Stravinsky — *The Magic Flute*, the Ring Cycle, *La Traviata* — every opera you've ever heard of was on those shelves. "This is my glory," he said, with tears falling down his cheeks. Here was a man who spent his life in the gutters, and had just lost maybe the only person that had ever loved him. And he was showing me where to find beauty. I heard a voice in me saying, "Dust we are; but we are dust that dreams."[12] That's the kingly power of art.

Psalm 150 is a resounding celebration of the kingly dimension of art.

> Praise the LORD!
> Praise God in his sanctuary;
>   praise him in his mighty firmament!
> Praise him for his mighty deeds;

12. Adapted from A. E. Housman's translation of Horace's *Ode* 4.7: "But oh, whate'er the sky-led seasons mar,/Moon upon moon rebuilds it with her beams:/Come *we* where Tullus and where Ancus are/And good Aeneas, we are dust and dreams." Quoted in J. D. McClatchy, *Horace: The Odes; New Translations by Contemporary Poets* (Princeton: Princeton University Press, 2002), 3.

praise him according to his surpassing greatness!
Praise him with trumpet sound;
  praise him with lute and harp!
Praise him with tambourine and dance;
  praise him with strings and pipe!
Praise him with clanging cymbals;
  praise him with loud clashing cymbals!
Let everything that breathes praise the LORD!
Praise the LORD!

This is a call to pull out all the organ stops, and, as conductors like to say in rehearsal, play it "Once more, with feeling." The psalm also has a subtle prophetic message, because there's nothing elitist about this psalm. On the contrary, it is determinedly inclusive. It's a psalm about what art is like in heaven — what the psalm calls God's "mighty firmament." In heaven, the music is joined by men, who in ancient Israelite culture traditionally played trumpet, lute, harp, and cymbals; and also by women, who traditionally joined with dance and tambourine. In the final line, everything that has breath — every single creature on earth — joins the heavenly chorus. Here is a prophetic statement that art may be the realm of genius, but it also has its democratic moments. Perhaps even more than the kingly and prophetic dimensions, Psalm 150 is profoundly priestly, because it's fundamentally a call to worship. The whole psalm is about the wonder of God, and the infectious character of celebrating God's glory. The word "praise" occurs thirteen times in six verses. Every instrument, every person, and in the end every living thing on earth discovers its ultimate purpose in glorifying and enjoying God forever. This is the crescendo that brings the hymnbook of Israel and the church to a rousing conclusion.

That's the discovery that lies at the heart of a Christian notion of art. Art is finally about glory. Artists fundamentally construct acts of worship. They may be so prophetic that their bitterness and irony are more about lament than praise — but lament is still a form of worship. They may be so ordered and bumptious that it seems to be more about cleverness or vainglory than genuine exultation — but vainglory is merely a distorted form of worship. The artist strains for what cannot be said, cannot be expressed, cannot be contained in conventional forms. It cannot be contained, because it's from God; and God cannot be contained, or fathomed, or comprehended. That's why art is exhausting, compelling, and ultimately fundamental to human existence. Art is where we imitate the nature of God, in the excess of energy that created the universe, the exquisite miniature that constituted the incarnation, the harrowing agony that underwent the cross, the restorative joy that burst out in the resurrection, and the dance of delight that caught fire at Pentecost. Because *God* is the great artist, and each human life is an event of recognition, interpretation, and improvisation on the wondrous imagination of God.

Are you an artist? According to Psalm 150, you are. Is there a yearning in you to express the depths, the ache, the fury, the glory? Are you a prophet, seeking truth and a closer social embodiment of it? Are you a priest, rolling back the veil between heaven and earth? Are you a king, rousing all creation to its potential and praise? Are you allowing the Holy Spirit to make you a work of art that turns all creation into alleluia?

CHAPTER 3

Learning to Think Again

My scholarly training is in Christian ethics, and I have written a number of books in the field, both introductory texts for students and more advanced texts for practitioners and scholars. I therefore feel a particular sense of responsibility in addressing issues that arise in public life — and issues that should arise in public life more than perhaps they do.

This chapter is self-consciously entitled "Learning to Think Again" because it covers subjects that have given the church's public voice a bad name. My contention is that this means these subjects need especially careful treatment — but not avoidance. I start with a consideration of abortion, because abortion is perhaps the issue on which the church's prophetic, pastoral, and political voices have become most tangled. If we can talk about abortion, then we can probably talk about most things. In the rest of the chapter I explore some of the territory within that area of "most things." Torture is, like abortion, not an area for the church to point the finger but one where the church might better look into its own heart and life. Taxes are perhaps the most pressing ethical issue, particularly among those issues whose theological significance is underexplored. There follow two sections about food, which is close to the heartbeat of any ethic and at the center of the church's liturgical practice. And the chapter concludes with justice, which, like the treatment of contract and covenant that opened the previous chapter, offers reflections on questions that pervade the other issues.

Choosing Life . . . and Living with Choices

"Choose life." This is God's plea to Israel on the eve of her entry into the Promised Land. "I have set before you life and death. . . . Choose life" (Deuteronomy 30:19). These are among the most powerful words in the Bible. They've also become the most divisive words in America. "Choose life." Half of America hears the word "life," and immediately identifies the plight of the unborn child. The other half of America hears the word "choose," and zeroes in on the rights of the pregnant woman.

I'm talking about abortion. We are a nation of 300 million people. We have just over 4 million live births a year. And we have nearly 1 million abortions.[1] However diverse the list of ethical issues of our time, abortion is always right at the top of it. On the whole, the main-line church has come to a clear position on the question. That position is, "Let's not talk about it."

There are some good reasons for not talking about it. Everyone knows there are plenty of Christians who talk about nothing else, and it sometimes seems their passion around this issue has obscured their sense of love, joy, peace, kindness, gentleness, and self-control. So it's a natural reaction to say, "We want the world to see our compassion and understanding, not our fanaticism and judgmentalism." Meanwhile, most of us have been close enough to this question, if not for ourselves, then for our family or friends, that we're not going to be too hasty to push the buttons labeled right and wrong. If every abortion in America is as complex and tortured as the ones we've been close to, then there's a huge amount of distress, silence, and anguish going on behind our nation's closed doors.

A typical pro-choice advocate would say, "In an ideal world there would be safe and reliable means of contraception; men and women

1. According to the Centers for Disease Control and Prevention (CDC) and the U.S. Census, in 2008 there were 4.2 million live births and over 820,000 abortions. The abortion rate has dropped slightly almost every year for the last decade in the United States. See http://www.cdc.gov/reproductivehealth/data_stats/index.htm and http://www.census.gov/compendia/statab/cats/births_deaths_marriages_divorces .html.

would share responsibility for procreative choices and children's well-being; and there would be no sexual violence or abuse. Thus saving the mother's life would be the only pretext for abortion. But this isn't an ideal world. The damage of our flawed lives is repeatedly inflicted on the most vulnerable. Abortion is a tragic way of protecting those most vulnerable people. Ardent pro-lifers, in their relentless attention to the unborn child, often fail to see the unjust social relations within which unwelcome pregnancies arise, and so tacitly underwrite the terms of a fallen world." It's a strong argument, and a similar one to that used to justify war. After all, war is state-sanctioned killing to bring about a more just world. So, in this perspective, is abortion.

But wait a moment. If pro-lifers are failing to see unjust social relations, surely pro-choicers are failing to hear something. A fetus of only a few weeks may not be a fully fledged human being, but, barring an unfortunate miscarriage, its future is only going one way. I was that fetus once. So were you. I'm rather glad I was allowed to come to term. I expect you feel the same about yourself. To take the strong pro-choice line is to close your ears to the cries of the never-born, the wailing of lives begotten but never lived.

And that's the real reason, I believe, why so many Christians have decided not to talk about abortion. Not because it's controversial; not because they fear seeming judgmental; not because their own lives have taught them that the line between right and wrong is more fragile than they once believed; but because to talk about abortion means to open our eyes to the unjust social relations in our nation and to open our ears to Rachel weeping for her children. And we can't bear it.

But we *have* to talk about abortion. Because seeing injustice and hearing the cries of the innocent are at the heart of discipleship and at the heart of God.

Several years ago I sat down with two people whom I'll call Brian and Clare. Clare was fifteen weeks pregnant. They'd recently been told that the child she was expecting would be so severely disabled that it might survive only a few agonizing days after birth; maybe only minutes. I asked them the two questions I always ask. "What's the best thing that can happen?" Clare said, "That I might find peace." "What's the worst thing that can happen?" She said, "That I might have this child, and it might live, terribly troubled and hugely disfigured, and that my friends might come round once or twice, and then I'd be left all alone."

So I said to Brian and Clare, "What you want is peace, and what you fear is being alone. But may I suggest that what you *need* is the church?" "Oh," said Clare. "My dad is dead set against abortion. He thinks people who have abortions go to hell. My mom is all for women's rights. She thinks it should be my choice." I replied, as gently as I could, "Can I suggest to you that we're not really talking about campaigning for abortion or campaigning for women's rights? I'm not sure it's really about legislation and I don't think it's really about going to hell. Because all these people with their certainties, for all their self-importance, have left you all alone. Alone now, with your decision: and alone in six months' time, when you might need all the help you can get. You don't feel able to ask for real help, and you sense, probably rightly, that real help isn't there. It's perfectly understandable that you're drawn to a technological solution. But the real problem is one that a termination won't solve. You need people who won't leave you on your own. You need a hope that knows there are things worse than physical suffering. You need people around you who will make your life beautiful even if it's not happy. What you need is the church."

When the conversation ended I stared into space for some time. I knew I'd broken most of the accepted conventions of pastoral counseling, but that's not what bothered me. What bothered me was whether this couple could possibly find the congregation they needed. I saw before me two churches. On the one hand was the church represented by Clare's father. I saw it captivated by two notions: personal assurance and righteous judgment. And on the other hand was the church of Clare's mother. I saw it captivated by two corresponding notions: individual freedom and progress through legislation. Two churches: one that's made the Bible its constitution; the other that's made the Constitution its bible.

As I stared out at these two churches, they looked so alike to me. They were both obsessed with the nation-state, and they were both preoccupied with the individual. And they'd both made the church invisible. On the one hand they'd assumed America was their church, and they'd gone to battle to win America, with the weapons of campaigns and lobbying and government and legislation. On the other hand they saw Christianity as largely a vehicle for personal fulfillment and individual choice. So the church became little more than a pawn in a personal or political game. But meanwhile both churches had failed Brian and Clare, because they'd both left them alone. Alone in the defining crisis of their lives. Clare's mother's church had proudly secured their right to choose, but had then left them alone with an impossible and agonizing choice. And Clare's father's church had sternly demanded they uphold life — but when the time came for supporting that life, it was nowhere to be seen. These two young parents were all alone. What they needed was the church.

That's why the church can't agree to say, "Let's not talk about it." Because that becomes yet another way of leaving people all alone to make a choice, and all alone to face the life that results from that choice.

What kind of church might we need to become if we were going to be a people who could talk about abortion? I'm going to make three suggestions, each of them inspired by Jesus' language in Matthew 5:21-37. In this passage, Jesus takes a law from the Torah and says, "You have heard it said . . . but I say to you," and then reinterprets that law in light of the gospel.

Number one: You have heard that it was said, "Live a flawless, irreproachable life, and don't make terrible mistakes." But Jesus says to you, "Life isn't about never making mistakes. It's about what you do when you've made them. Life isn't about not having regrets. It's about what you turn your regrets into. Christianity isn't about effortless perfection. It's about costly forgiveness. If you're floating along pretending you're living a flawless existence, you're living a lie and you're living in fear, because one day the truth is going to bring you crashing to the ground. Come down from that lofty place right now, and get in the dust where the mistakes are happening and the regrets are being felt, and meet the true redemption and the painful reconciliation that the gospel's all about."

Why do we have abortions? One big reason is that we're ashamed. We're desperate to maintain the outward appearance that everything is impeccable and respectable, long after the train of truth has left the

83

station. And let's not pretend that we as the church don't collude with that. Is ours a community where the unexpected, unwelcome, and inexplicable pregnancy is greeted with gentleness, understanding, and a little mischievous joy? Or do we replicate precisely the judgment and self-righteous condemnation that lead to secrets and lies and furtive solutions to avoid public shame? Have you ever made a terrible mistake? If it resulted in public humiliation, no doubt you have compassion on others like you. If no one ever found out, does that not make you have even more compassion for others less lucky than you?

Number two: You have heard that it was said, "Make enough money, get enough qualifications, invest wisely, so you can always be independent." But Jesus says to you, "That's not the gospel. That's an insurance policy in case the gospel turns out not to be true. The gospel is, 'bear one another's burdens.' The gospel is that we find a strength in one another we could never discover left to ourselves. Independence is a myth exposed by the threat of sickness and failure and the certainty of death. The reality of life is about dependence, about working out whom and what to be dependent upon. The heart of life is friendship and companionship, with one another and with God; those are the foundations that survive long after the qualifications, investments, and money become useless."

Why do we have abortions? Because we feel abandoned. We don't feel we have the emotional support or the money or security to meet all our commitments or give a child a chance in life without destroying our own. And let's not pretend that we as the church don't collude with that. Do we challenge, not just with our words but with our lives, the unjust social relations within which many unsought pregnancies arise? Do we genuinely welcome the unexpected and untimely stranger with open arms? Do people see us and say, "If you have friends, you don't need financial independence"? Really?

Number three: You have heard that it was said, "Have a perfect body, a trophy spouse, and may all your offspring be poster children." But Jesus says to you, "The body that matters is my body, not yours. I know how broken you are inside, even if you keep up a tidy appearance outside. We're all disabled, it's just that in some of us it's harder for a stranger to see it. One day you'll be given a new body to share with me

84

forever, but for now you'll find joy as much in learning to inhabit your limitations as in transcending them." Discipleship lies not in proudly saying, "My body is not broken," but in finding people to whom you can truly say, "My body is broken . . . for you."

Why do we have abortions? One reason is we fear that a disabled life is less than a full life. We don't trust that God will shine through the holes in our minds and bodies. We're so concerned to abolish suffering that we would rather end life than watch a life in distress. But when we look at Jesus on the cross, we see that the body of Christ *is* a disabled body. If we're going to call ourselves the body of Christ, we have to realize that the church is a disabled body too.

Here are the false laws of perfect bodies, material independence, and flawless lives. These are among the idols that lead us away from becoming the forgiving, companionable, disabled body of Christ. Is it surprising, in the face of this smoke screen of shame, that when we discover our unwanted pregnancies we find our refuge, not in the church, but in the clinic? Can we deny that there is more forgiveness, more companionship, and more acceptance of brokenness in the clinic than in the church? Lord, have mercy upon us.

Now we realize, once and for all, why we say, "Let's not talk about abortion." How can we demand legislation, how can we call for personal responsibility, how can we expect a sacrificial choice, unless we embody the slow redemption of costly mistakes, unless we exhibit the mutual interdependence of generous friends, unless we display the transparent grace of broken-open lives? Until, that is, we become what we were saved to be — the church? We don't want to talk about abortion because we might have to become the church.

That's the choice that matters most. That's the life Jesus calls us to. Brothers and sisters, choose life. Choose God's life. Choose to become Christ's church.

Our Tortured State

I wonder if you've ever been truly afraid. I wonder if your stomach has twisted in knots and your throat run dry, your backside begun to quake and your forearms become too heavy to use — because you realized something violent and painful and horrifying was about to happen and there was nothing you could do to stop it, because you realized there was no one you could call to for help. It's one thing to realize something dreadful is going to happen. But it's another thing entirely to realize there's someone who's actually trying to make it happen, someone who is trying to cause you genuine, physical harm.

The seventeenth-century philosopher Thomas Hobbes perceived that without civilization this state of perpetual fear is the natural condition of all of us, all the time. He said this is exactly why citizens organize themselves around common security, universal respect, and mutual well-being — because such commitments give them freedom from fear, and only in such freedom can they live dignified and productive lives.[2]

I wonder whether 9/11 was a day when you were truly afraid. For many Americans, 9/11 declared that we are not safe within our borders, that our national identity alone makes us all targets, and that attacks may come anywhere, anytime, on almost any scale. In other words, 9/11 took many Americans back to the core of our civilization — back to the horror of Hobbes's state of nature, back to a primal fear of everyone toward everyone else.

That's why the idea of a war on terror seemed so necessary, and so appealing. The narrative that had been widely assumed, at least since the end of the Cold War, but arguably since the founding of the nation, that history was a gradually unfolding story of progress toward greater security and flourishing — that narrative suddenly seemed a delusion. Of course, there's no way to abolish or defeat fear, and declaring war on terror risks appearing ridiculous, because you can't defeat an abstract noun. But if America was going to recover its confidence and sense of well-being, it seemed it simply had to eradicate the sense of being perpetually exposed to limitless Hobbesean fear. And the only way to do that was to do something about the people seeking to manufacture that fear: to wage war on terror.

2. Thomas Hobbes, *Leviathan* (Oxford: Oxford University Press, 1998), chapter 14, "Of the First and Second Natural Laws, and of Contracts," pp. 86-89.

That quest, which has included the invasion of Afghanistan and Iraq, the detention of many thousands of suspected insurgents elsewhere, and the implementation of countless counterterrorism measures at home, has brought Americans face-to-face with profound questions about their own identity. The central question is this: What is it that we're proud of about America, and seek to protect at all costs?

For many the answer to this question is law. America has a Constitution and a Bill of Rights. These protect the citizen and prevent the majority dominating a minority, assuring well-being and security for all. The history of adherence to such principles makes America a great nation. But what happens when America meets an enemy that doesn't play by the rules, and exploits American freedoms to undermine American democracy? Such a scenario provokes a second answer to the question of what makes America great. This answer lies in sovereignty. America is great because, when it chooses, for an immediate emergency, to set aside the rule of law, it has the power to subdue any adversary by the might of its military and economic resources.

The trouble is, we're not at all sure which of the two answers we want to give. Most of the time we stand behind the rule of law. We say, "America has rules, it has signed international treaties, it has passed legislation, it believes in human rights. We don't torture." There are some things, like waterboarding, forced hypothermia, sleep deprivation, mock burials, and ritual physical humiliation, that you just don't do to people if you want to call yourself a civilized nation — let alone a world leader. But then, from time to time, we find ourselves saying, "We're not talking about an enemy that plays by the rules. Only a strong and ruthless America can protect itself and the free world from the evil, unscrupulous forces that seek to undermine it, and so America not only *does* torture — it *must*, and the grief of this is part of the troubling burden America and her protectors have to bear."

This results in a face-off in our public discourse. One side says, if the way you fight a war means you have to give up your nation's core values, then winning that war does you more harm than good, because it turns you into a monster. The other side says, only by putting your whole credibility at risk do you prove that you're willing to go to any lengths to defend your country.

87

At this point a more subtle criticism of torture appears. It argues not just that torture's wrong, but that it doesn't work. The standard defense of torture is that if you caught a terrorist who knew the location of a time bomb due to explode on Manhattan, and the terrorist wouldn't talk, you'd want to torture him or her to save the lives of millions of people. But the truth is that almost none of the scores of thousands of recent instances of U.S.-sponsored torture have arisen in cases of that kind, that what people say under such duress is notoriously unreliable, and that gaining a reputation for torture produces myriads of new enemies while jeopardizing the well-being of American forces and civilians when they themselves are captured.[3]

These are formidable arguments, and they thoroughly dismantle the sovereignty argument. Yet U.S.-sponsored torture persists, in contravention of the rule of law. That has to show us that torture isn't really about a cost-benefit analysis, and in fact never was.

To map out how we as the church might participate in this conversation at the heart of our nation's life, I want to look at three passages in the New Testament that shape a Christian response to torture.

The first passage is Jesus' trial before Pilate and the Sanhedrin (the Jewish court). "The men who were holding Jesus began to mock him and beat him; they also blindfolded him and kept asking him, 'Prophesy! Who is it that struck you?'" (Luke 22:63-64). Jesus was tortured. And this brief account tells us a lot about torture. It's not really about eliciting information. It's not simply about rogue soldiers behaving liked bored bullies. What it's about more than anything else is the attempt by those in control to *degrade the body in such a way that they dominate the mind and spirit as well.* It's their attempt to show that the god of the prisoner, in this case the God of Jesus Christ, is a sham — or else why doesn't he save the prisoner now? It's a kind of alchemy, which tries to rub together physical dominance and quasi-liturgical procedure and produce spiritual and mental ascendancy, by removing

---

3. See the essays "Getting Away with Torture" by Philip Roth (3-12, esp. 7); "Confessions of a Torturer" by Tony Lagouranis (27-35, esp. 33); and "Torture Is the Ticking Time Bomb: Why the Necessity Defense Fails" by George Hunsinger (51-72), in *Torture Is a Moral Issue* (Grand Rapids: Eerdmans, 2008).

every source of respect, authority, or security and leaving the victim utterly in the hands of the torturer.

Let's not pretend America started torturing prisoners only after its identity was attacked on 9/11 and the War on Terror began. It's long been an open secret that a great number of those who perpetrated widespread torture in South and Central America over the last fifty years were trained on American soil. The point to recognize is that to uphold the cause of your country in troubled overseas terrain requires you to believe in your country with an almost religious zeal; and that when you discover your physical strength isn't enough to win the battle, you find you almost *have* to impose your mental and spiritual superiority lest your religious fervor for your country be exposed as an empty fantasy. So torturing the terrorist isn't about locating the ticking bomb — it's about discrediting and degrading and ritually dismantling the cause the terrorist is fighting for.

During the Reformation, Catholics and Protestants burnt each other at the stake. The torture was designed to make the victim recant at the very moment of death. This history should make Christians more reluctant to take the moral high ground on torture. But it also shows us that torture has always been a ritualized method of degrading the body to win the soul. It's an almost inherently religious activity.

But it's not an activity that properly belongs in Christianity. Why? For our answer we need to look at a second New Testament passage: "When they came to the place that is called The Skull, they crucified Jesus there with the criminals. . . . And the people stood by, watching; but the leaders scoffed at him, saying, 'He saved others; let him save himself if he is the Messiah of God, his chosen one!'" (Luke 23:33, 35). Jesus reverses the logic that creates torture. The conventional logic goes like this. "I have your body, but I don't have your soul and mind. So I will enact a liturgy of sacrificing you, to within a hairsbreadth of killing you, to force you to hand your soul and mind over to me, and to make you worship what I worship." Jesus' logic is the reverse. It goes like this: "I want your mind and soul, and your body as well, but I will seek it by giving you my body."

Torture says, "Give me your body." Jesus says, "This is my body, given for you." Torture says, "I will win your soul by dominating your body." Jesus says, "I will heal your soul by giving you my body." Torture says, "I will show you what power is, and force you to bow down to me." Jesus says, "I will show you what love is, and inspire you to follow me." Jesus suffered torture, that his followers might never torture again. That's the Christian gospel in the face of torture.

This brings us to our final New Testament passage. The torture of Jesus indeed meant that his followers never contemplated inflicting torture themselves. But it didn't mean they avoided becoming victims of torture. Far from it. Listen to the words of Paul: "Five times I have received . . . the forty lashes minus one. Three times I was beaten with rods. Once I received a stoning" (2 Corinthians 11:24-25). The logic of torture was alive and well in the ancient world. Paul was an infuriating opponent, a human ball-bearing that seemed indestructible in body, mind, and spirit. No degradation of his body could turn his heart and mind from the worship and mission of his savior Jesus Christ. But why did people keep attacking him? Because to the political and religious authorities he was a threat to their whole raison d'être. In the face of their dominance over him he showed his willingness, like Christ, to hand over his body, and their inability, even through torture, to trouble his mind and soul.

The question I want to address derives from this witness of Saint Paul. Imagine that this country was invaded by a ruthless power. Imagine the enemy had occupied almost all the country and was now bent on stamping out pockets of resistance. Imagine the resistance they found most objectionable was not so much the force of arms, which they knew they could defeat, but the hearts and minds of some troublesome members of the population who insisted on remaining loyal to the God of Jesus Christ and wouldn't worship the gods of the invaders. Imagine, like many invaders before them, in every age including our own, that they sought to change the souls and minds of these troublesome people by degrading and dominating their bodies and enacting sacrificial rituals upon them to within a hairsbreadth of their death.

This is my question. Would we be among those they considered worth torturing? Would we be enough of a trouble, enough of a nuisance, enough of a threat, for them to create elaborate mechanisms of pain and domination? If we were simply a collection of individuals, the answer would surely be no. As individuals we could easily be picked off and manipulated. But what if we were part of a greater body than just our own body; what if we were part of a body that had a heart and soul the invader envied and even feared; what if baptism and Eucharist, and the holy disciplines of Lent, and the history of shared struggle, and the wisdom of suffering, and a shared commitment of money, and the solidarity that comes through forgiveness, and the willingness to make sacrifices for one another had formed us into a body more significant than our own individual bodies, a body that could truly be called the body of Christ? Maybe then they'd have to torture us.

Yes, we'd be afraid. Yes, we'd wonder if our body could withstand becoming part of the disappeared. Yes, we'd face pain, and degradation, and humiliation. But maybe then we'd truly see how radical Jesus truly is. Maybe then we'd truly see what following Jesus means. Maybe then we'd truly discover the political significance of the cross, as the Christian answer to torture. Maybe then we'd find it in ourselves to say, "These are our bodies, given for you." Maybe then, and only then, we'd truly be able to call ourselves the church.

Ordinary Rendition

I want to discuss taxation. That's a bit like saying I want to discuss going a week without indoor plumbing. But if there's a bad smell in the house, at least everyone thinks it's time to call the plumber. There's been a bad smell coming out of Washington these last few years, but no one seems at all agreed on what to do about it.

What's the fight really about? Sure, there's been an economic crash. We all know the economy is teetering on the brink of a double-dip recession. But there's nothing much to fight about in that. We've all been affected by it, some of us savagely and devastatingly; but it's not inherently controversial. There's a problem about the debt, but again, there isn't anyone out there who actually thinks having a massive debt is such a great idea. Everyone wants to reduce it: the question is, how much more sacrifice is needed to reduce it, and who gets to pay?

That's the heart of the issue: Who gets to pay? As Milton Friedman put it, "Congress can raise taxes because it can persuade a sizable fraction of the populace that somebody else will pay."[4] Liberals are those who believe they have a great debt they need to pay off to the weak and heavy-laden, but intend to pay that debt not with their own money but with someone else's. If you realize *you're* that someone else, you feel mad. Meanwhile conservatives are those who regard taxation, and government in general, as being forced to pay for the violation of their own liberty. If you feel, like George Washington, that "to have revenue there must be taxes; and that no taxes can be devised which are not more or less inconvenient and unpleasant,"[5] then you're going to wonder whether conservatives have done the math.

If there's a subject that can make people go from placid to furious in five seconds, it's taxation. If there's an exercise that makes people lie and deceive and cheat and write imaginative fiction more than any other, it's filling in a tax return. If there's an issue that lies at the heart of the hatred and filthy smell in Washington right now, that issue is tax. Everyone knows there's an economic and financial crisis. That's not controversial. What's controversial is what we do about it. Do we tax more and spend more? Winston Churchill said, "for a nation to try to tax itself into prosperity is like a man standing in a bucket and trying to lift himself up by the handle."[6] Or do we spend less and tax as little as possible? But hang on — didn't we just spend eye-watering amounts of money on two foreign wars in the last decade? Wouldn't avoiding useless foreign wars have solved the debt crisis rather painlessly? Will Rogers supposedly once quipped, "The difference between

4. Widely quoted; see, e.g., Mike Gearhardt and Will Gates, *The Financial Tsunami* (Bloomington, Ind.: AuthorHouse, 2010), 57.

5. George Washington's Farewell Address, 1796; see the Avalon Project at Yale Law School, http://avalon.law.yale.edu/18th_century/washing.asp.

6. Although this version of Churchill's words is widely quoted, the original source of the quotation seems to be a speech Churchill delivered at the Free Trade Hall in Manchester, England, in 1904: "Can foreign nations grow rich at our expense by selling us goods under cost price? Can a people tax themselves into prosperity? Can a man stand in a bucket and lift himself up by the handle?"; see Richard M. Langworth, ed., *Churchill by Himself* (New York: PublicAffairs, 2008), 387.

death and taxes is death doesn't get worse every time Congress meets."[7] That's about the only thing everyone seems to agree on.

Arguments about taxation are written into the DNA of America. Everyone knows that the revolt against the arrogant and perfidious British, a protest epitomized by the Boston Tea Party, wasn't about tea — it was about tax. But it turned out that "taxation *with* representation wasn't so hot either."[8] Deep in the founding mythology of our country lies a sense that America was not to be like other nations, where people were curtailed by overbearing governments, religious discrimination, and burdensome taxation. America was to be a place where individuals were set free from such constraints to pursue their own dreams and their own happiness, and prosperity was to lie in the surplus of creativity and fruitfulness arising from the untrammeled energy of the people. In such a vision taxation can only seem like a monstrous constraint on liberty.

Jesus has something to say on the subject of taxes. The Pharisees and the Herodians come to see him during his last week in Jerusalem, and they flatter him, and they ask whether it's lawful to pay taxes to Caesar or not (Matthew 22:15-22). It's a tough question, because the choices are idolatry or suicide. When Jesus asks to see the coin used for the tax, he's drawing attention to the head that's found on the coin. It's the head of Tiberius Caesar, the Roman emperor. Tiberius freely referred to himself as the Son of God. When the Pharisees ask, "Is it lawful to pay taxes to the emperor?" they're saying, "Okay, Jesus. You know the Jewish law. You know the first two commandments: 'You shall have no other gods before me,' and 'You shall not make for yourself an idol.' Tiberius has called himself a god, and put his head on his imperial coinage. So which is it: Pay tax, and collude with the idolatry of putting the head of this Roman god on a coin? Or don't pay, and declare a war that could lead to the suppression and extinction of our peo-

7. The line is often credited to Will Rogers, although it is also attributed to newspaper writer Robert Quillen, who wrote a similar line in 1931; see http://www.barrypopik.com/index.php/new_york_city/entry/the_difference_between_death_and_taxes_is_that_death_doesnt_get_worse_every/.

8. Humorist Gerald Barzan is usually credited with this line.

ple. So it's idolatry if we pay, suicide if we don't. Which is it, Jesus?" A tough question.

Jesus replies, "Well, well, well, here are my friends the Pharisees, come to ask me a question. But just look who's with them — a bunch of Herodians. We all know what the Herodians stand for. They're a cynical bunch of quislings, who've completely sold out to Roman rule and more or less lost their Jewish identity in the process. So, my dear Pharisees, if this is who you're hanging out with, I can see you've already made your choice. You're carrying the coin in your pocket, which suggests you're content with the benefits of Roman rule. You're not supporting the revolutionaries who are refusing to pay this tax. But you've brought along your friends so that if I say anything out of line you can be sure it'll get straight back to Pontius Pilate and I'll be eliminated by tomorrow morning. I know what you're up to."

But then we get Jesus' famous answer. "Give therefore to the emperor the things that are the emperor's, and to God the things that are God's" — or more famously, "Render therefore unto Caesar the things which are Caesar's; and unto God the things that are God's" (KJV). We've seen that Roman coins bear the image of Caesar; they clearly belong to Caesar, and even to use them is to recognize that you're living under Caesar's authority. But human beings bear the image of God. So Jesus seems to be saying, "By all means give your money to Caesar — but make sure you give yourself to God."

Don't miss the way this turns American notions of taxation on their head. Remember, for much of the history of this country people have said, "My body and soul belong to America, but my money, now . . . my money belongs to me." Jesus comes pretty close to saying the opposite. He seems to be saying, "Your money is given to you by America, and might as well go back to America. But your body and soul don't belong to America. They belong to God."

Maybe he's saying even more than that. Listen to the irony in his words. "Give to God the things that are God's."

What precisely is there that isn't God's? God is the creator of heaven and earth. God is the sustainer of all that is. If you accept these things, the very idea that something belongs to us and not to God is absurd. Caesar may think everything belongs to him. But he's a fool. Everything belongs to God. Remember Joseph's words to the brothers who sold him into slavery: "You meant it for evil; God meant it for good" (Genesis 50:20, paraphrased). In other words, you may think you're in charge, but more fool you. God's in charge. You can't use Jesus' words to suggest that some things belong to the state and some things belong to God.

So what *can* you use Jesus' words to mean? If taxation is the most hotly contested issue in our country right now, what does Jesus have to tell us about it, and how can we make filling in our tax return an act of discipleship, rather than one of resentment, confusion, and fury? I suggest four things.

Number one, taxation is not in principle a monstrous extortion. Imagine that you were living in Somalia or Afghanistan or the Congo, or any other failed state today. When there's chaos, nothing can flourish. Without a minimum of order, it's hard to foster the fruits of the Spirit or the habits of trust and love, let alone health and education. Paying taxes is a concrete gesture of commitment to the state as a joint enterprise in which you and everyone else give up a degree of liberty for an umbrella of security, a degree of freedom for the establishment of the rule of law, a degree of independence for the expectation of justice, a degree of income for the common good. These things aren't a birthright; they're bought at a price. But without them we're at the mercy of the warlords.

Number two, taxation is an entry ticket to a civilized politics. And the first thing you have to let go of in politics is the assumption that you can always get your way. It's ridiculous to expect that Congress will ever vote a fiscal measure that any single citizen will entirely agree with. Civilization depends on each of us saying to one another, "I don't ever expect fully to agree with you, but I'll always seek a compromise with you, because I believe we are always stronger combining our energies to tackle projects together than opposing our energies to fight and destroy one another." You can't say, "I'm only going to pay two-thirds of my taxes because I only agree with two-thirds of the government's policies." That's like the government saying, "We're only going to defend two-thirds of America from foreign attack because only two-thirds of America voted for us." By all means protest, and shout, and argue, and persuade representatives that they're wrong. But if you're losing the game, you can't just pick up the ball and take it home. Our forebears worked so hard to establish a democracy. We can't just wreck it and withdraw from it when we haven't persuaded a majority to agree with us. If Jesus said one can pay taxes to Tiberius Caesar — megalomaniac, tyrant, self-proclaimed god — then I think we can have a sense of perspective and bring ourselves to pay taxes to Washington, however much we might run things differently if and when people finally came to their senses and put us in charge.

Number three, think about the notion of currency. There are a lot of words for money in the Gospels — the denarius is mentioned in this story. But there are also the parable of the talents, the story of the widow's mite, the thirty pieces of silver given to Judas Iscariot, and the shekel of the temple tax. These episodes all involve different currencies. Jesus asks to see the denarius to make the point that it's Caesar's money. Jews had to change their money in order to pay Caesar's tax. Think about that notion of currency. Maybe if Christians have a problem today, it's because we've forgotten that we have our own currency. Like the Jews in Roman-occupied Palestine in the first century, we have to change some of that currency to participate in society and recognize we're part of a politics that doesn't just involve people like us. But I wonder if we've forgotten that we actually have a currency of our own. It's a currency in which the big denomination notes are called forgiveness and resurrection, mercy and grace, walking the way of the cross and washing one another's feet. We have our own vocabulary and our own ways and our own currency, and when called to do so we translate them into dollars and use our country's language and our country's customs and our country's coin. But maybe the real problem we Christians have in America is that we've been using the denarius so long and so happily that we've forgotten we also have a currency of our own, and only that currency buys the things of eternal value.

Number four, let's give up thinking that our freedom lies in an overhaul of the fiscal system. Give to Caesar what is Caesar's. Have done with it. Don't think for one moment that in Caesar's strength lies your true security, and don't think for one moment that what Caesar is taking away from you is your heart and soul. If you're obsessed with how much tax Caesar is taking away from you, you're giving Caesar too much power over you. You're worshiping the wrong God. Government probably spends your money about as wisely as you do — some good, some foolish, some bad, some wasted. Government isn't any more perfect than you or I.

There's only one freedom that really counts, and it doesn't come from zero taxation or from lavish government spending. You can't get to it through enviously denouncing how scandalously little some people pay in tax or judgmentally exposing how some recipients of welfare have no impulse or will to help themselves. You can only get to it through recognizing that God's currency is grace, that left to ourselves we're hopelessly and catastrophically in debt, and that no one is willing or able to pay off that debt on our behalf. But Christ has forgiven our defaults. Christ has paid our dues. Christ has offered us membership in his kingdom. Christ has bestowed upon us the glorious liberty of the children of God. That's where our security rests. That's where our freedom lies. That's why in the end we can give Caesar as much or as little as we or he may like — so long as we give everything to God.

Facing Down Hunger

"Hunger" is a terrifying word. It's physically terrifying to imagine the process of wasting away with hunger. Let me describe it in five short sentences. Starvation begins with a few days' gnawing pain before your stomach shrinks. Then there's a longer period where the pain is replaced by widespread physical irritation as your body feeds off its own fat and then its muscle. There follow a shrinking away to skin and bone and terrible tiredness. That tiredness leads to a loss of interest in everything, even food. Finally, there's a deadly vulnerability to minor infection that in the end will probably kill you.[9] Just the thought of this process makes our shoulders shiver and our stomachs wince.

9. This description of the process of starvation is condensed from Robert Song, "Sharing Communion: Hunger, Food, and Genetically Modified Foods," in *The Blackwell Companion to Christian Ethics*, ed. Stanley Hauerwas and Samuel Wells, 2nd ed. (Malden, Mass., and Oxford: Wiley-Blackwell, 2011), 440-41. Song uses Paul Vallely's description in David Blundy and Paul Vallely, *With Geldof in Africa* (London: Times Books/Band Aid, 1985), 70.

It's an emotionally troubling thing to imagine being in the presence of real hunger. We've all heard stories of thirsty sailors cast adrift on flimsy life rafts facing desperate choices about how to stay alive. And it's not hard to project from those nightmares a more general terror of being in proximity to someone who's half-crazed, who might want what you have, who might stop at nothing to get it.

As well as being physically and emotionally terrifying, it's psychologically humiliating to live as we do in a culture soaked in the myth of progress, and yet to know that 5 million children die of hunger in the world each year. It's sobering to admit that in the United States, where we can be tempted to speak of hunger as another nation's problem, one household in six struggles to put food on the table.[10]

So hunger is physically terrifying, emotionally troubling, and psychologically sobering.

Why is there so much hunger? Is it because the world has too many people and not enough food? Quite simply, no. The world produces enough food to feed everyone one-and-a-half times over. The causes of hunger vary, but they usually include one of the three Ws.[11]

W number one is war. War disrupts food production, diverts investment from agriculture to armaments, makes food supplies a focus of conflict, displaces populations, and creates refugees.

W number two is waste. Waste refers to the corruption that absorbs around a quarter of the wealth of some of the world's poorest countries. But waste also recognizes that nearly half of the food ready for harvest in the United States each year never gets eaten, and that huge transfers of food from wealthier nations to poor countries in times of famine or crisis sometimes undermine local agriculture and destroy the local economy. And waste names the reality that many

---

10. World Hunger Education Service (http://www.worldhunger.org/articles/Learn/us_hunger_facts.htm); World Food Programme, "Hunger Stats" (http://www.wfp.org/hunger/stats); Bread for the World, "U.S. Hunger" (http://www.bread.org/hunger/us/).

11. Sources: Marc J. Cohen and Don Reeves, "Causes of Hunger," International Food Policy Research Institute, 2020 Brief 19, May 1995; and the World Hunger Education Service (http://www.worldhunger.org/articles/Learn/world%20hunger%20facts%202002.htm).

people in stronger economies, who don't necessarily feel hungry, are still eating foods that leave them undernourished.

W number three is world trade. Much of the most fertile land in developing countries is used to grow products for rich world markets that yield no benefit for local consumers. Global ownership of grain and seed production remains in a very small number of hands, and the pattern of trade agreements and food subsidies prevents the flourishing of local food production in much of the developing world.

Notice that none of these Ws is weather. Famine isn't primarily about drought. If you're living in vulnerable circumstances in a developing country that is in the grip of war, waste, and the imbalances of world trade, you have very little margin for error when it comes to keeping hunger at a safe distance. You can die of hunger without regard to the weather. Thousands do every day.

Put in this context, the first book of Kings is not so strange and foreign as it may appear. The land of Israel is a dry land, where famine is always a possibility. But it's also a land flowing with milk and honey, where the destructive damage of war, the misuse of power, and the economic realities on the ground shape people's destinies more than simply the weather. It's not so different from many developing nations today.

I want to look at the physical, emotional, and psychological way the prophet Elijah faces the reality of hunger in his encounter with the widow of Zarephath (1 Kings 17:8-24). The Lord commands Elijah to go to Zarephath, where he will find a widow, who will feed him. When he arrives, the widow and her son are in a desperate state: all she has left is a handful of meal in a jar and a little oil in a jug. Elijah instructs her to make a little cake for him to eat, and then to make something to eat for herself and her son; then he tells her that according to the word of the Lord, her jar of meal will never be empty and her jug of oil will never run dry. The woman obeys, and the word of the Lord regarding the jug and the jar comes true. But then the widow's son falls ill, to the point of death; whereupon Elijah heals the boy and restores him to life.

Two moments leap out of this story as strange and jarring and provocative. One comes near the beginning and the other comes near the end.

Elijah obeys God's instruction to go to Sidon, the territory north of Israel. Then he meets a widow on the edge of the town of Zarephath. This should ring a bell, because a meeting between a man and a woman on the edge of town is a tell-tale sign in the Bible that God is going to do something important (for example, when Jacob meets Rachel or when Isaac meets Rebekah in the Old Testament, or when Jesus meets the Samaritan woman in the New Testament). And then Elijah says something really surprising. "Bring me a morsel of bread" (1 Kings 17:11). Isn't that strange? Isn't it an insult to ask a hungry widow for food? After all, she's just about to cook her last-ever meal.

So why does he do it? Because it respects her dignity and it calls out her faith. Elijah respects her dignity because he begins by assuming the widow is the agent of her own salvation in relation to hunger. He doesn't try to buy her off with a handout. When we see TV pictures of starving people, we easily think, "Why doesn't someone just give them lots of food?" But that's not a solution. They'll just be hungry again the next day. Any long-term solution has to come from the people themselves, and eventually it has to be based on how they can generate their own income by doing things for others. Even in a desperate situation, Elijah's request recognizes this. He proposes a plan that will benefit both the widow and himself.

Saying "Bring me a morsel of bread" is also a call to faith. Faith means living in the world God promises until the promise comes true. That makes people of faith look strange to everyone else, because everyone else isn't living in the world God promises. Elijah is asking the widow to live in a very different world from the one in front of her. The woman knows that feeding Elijah will require everything she has — her last handful of meal and drop of oil. Here she faces the moment of truth.

If you have so little left that there's not even enough for yourself, will you cling to it all the tighter — or make it feed another and thus entrust it to God? You might think that generosity is worth a try in these desperate circumstances. After all, she's going to die either way. But how many of us would take a risk on generosity, even as a last resort? How many of us ever do?

Step back from the story a moment. What if that meal and oil represent the last few days or years of your life? Would you take a risk giving those last few days or years to others, and thus to God, or would you rather cling to them for all you're worth, making them stretch as long as you can, despite knowing deep down that they'll run out soon enough? Would you take a risk on generosity, even as a last resort?

Well, the widow does give him the morsel of bread. God chooses to ask something more of her at just the time when she's worn out. God does just the same to us. It's when we've got nothing left that God asks us for something more. That's when God finds out who we really are and we find out who God really is. In the defining moment of her life, when she's at her lowest and most self-absorbed, the widow faces the challenge of recognizing God in the stranger who is asking something of her.

And great is the widow's reward. "The jar of meal was not emptied, neither did the jug of oil fail," until the rains came and the famine was over (1 Kings 17:16). When the widow saw her destiny in the stranger, God gave her abundance even amid hunger.

There's another curious moment in this story. The widow's son fell ill, and "his illness was so severe that there was no breath left in him" (17:17). The widow erupts with anger toward Elijah, expressing all her grief and despair. "What have you against me?" she says. Elijah's response is similar to the first conversation. He asks something more of her, a second time. Elijah says, "Give me your son" (17:18-19). Again, does she part with her dead or dying son, trusting this strange foreign man, or does she cling to her son in her ocean of agony? How many of us would rather be left alone, clinging to our grief and anger and despair, rather than allowing someone to come close to us and be in it with us? But, in spite of herself, the widow gives Elijah her son. And Elijah cries out his own lament and grief to God. He takes the widow's despair and makes it his own, saying, "O LORD my God, have you brought calamity even upon the widow with whom I am staying, by killing her son?" (17:20).

Here's the most remarkable part of the story. Elijah "stretched himself upon the child three times" (17:21). A few minutes from the end of West Virginia's defeat in the 2010 NCAA men's basketball Final Four, their star player, Da'Sean Butler, fell to the floor, screaming in pain. His coach, Bob Huggins, leaned over him and placed his own face no more than an inch or two from the player's agonized mouth and despairing eyes for what seemed like forever but must have been only thirty seconds. The intimacy of these two men was startling and the poignancy of the scene was mesmerizing. That's what Elijah does over this widow's son. He goes flat out for him three times. Remember, a dead body was thought to be unclean. Elijah is not made unclean by death. Death is made clean by the faith of Elijah. He lays his life down for the boy — and the boy is raised from death, and Elijah brings him back to his mother and says, "See, your son is alive" (17:22-23).

Here are the two surprising things about this story. Number one: God doesn't simply solve our problems for us. He gives us abundance when we give away our last morsel. Number two: God doesn't hide his face from our grief. He goes flat out for us, and faces down our death with his intimate touch.

What we see in Elijah is what we later come to see fully in Jesus. God meets our desperation face-to-face. God asks something more of us when we feel we have nothing to give. God enters into our suffering and faces it down with us. God goes flat out for us and restores us to life. What we have in this story of Elijah is a prefigurement of the whole of Jesus' story.

And that brings us back to hunger. How should Christians in the West think about world hunger? Like anything else, we should study the issue, and learn about war, waste, and world trade. But we should also study the gospel, and see how God works. Then we come face-to-face with the issue the way God does.

More precisely, we can learn from the two surprising parts of this story. First, Elijah meets a woman who's desperate, and he asks more of her. This is a lesson for our head. We can't divide the world into the poor, who have the need, and the rich, who have the answers. Hunger isn't simply about lack of food. Addressing world hunger means setting to work on all the factors that contribute to a person facing starvation, and always working so that the person is empowered to find his or her own solution, often in partnership with many other such people around the world. You can't solve other people's problems. The best you can do is to help them solve their own. On a personal level, when you yourself are desperate, don't be surprised if that's the moment when God asks a little bit more of you. It feels unjust and unfeeling and unfair, but it's the way God respects your humanity and begins to set you on your feet again.

Here's the second surprising thing. Elijah stretches out and lies facedown on the boy three times. Elijah's approach to the widow's suffering is physical and intimate and all-consuming. This is a lesson for your heart. Having a heart doesn't mean shedding sentimental tears at the end of the movie. Having a heart means sharing the widow's cry of grief and anger and despair and laying down your life because you believe God hears your prayers when you put yourself in another's place, and pleading with God to visit the poor in their affliction. If you want to address global hunger, you can't just get the head right and understand the causes and work out the right strategies. You've got to get the heart and soul right and physically and intimately put your body wherever God needs it to be to pray and strive for change.

Write on your hearts these two ways to face down hunger. Come face-to-face with the realities of need and suffering in their complexity and their humanity. And go flat out with your body and soul to give your whole life in an enacted prayer for change. That's Elijah's challenge to you. Come face-to-face. And go flat out. And together, in the power of the Holy Spirit, you'll face down the most terrifying horrors in the world.

Food Is Politics

We are what we eat. These five words explain why there is nothing more fundamental to human life than food.

I want to suggest four things about food. First, food is politics. In other words, food is at the heart of our common life. Second, it was always so. Third, only when we have seen that it was always so can we understand why Jesus transformed human existence from the inside out by transforming food. Fourth, when we have seen how Jesus transformed food, we can see what it might mean to envisage and embody a Christian politics based on food.

When I say "politics," I don't mean specifically primaries, caucuses, and elections. I mean the whole ordering of the things people hold in common. I mean the way we human beings come to terms with the fact that we don't get to choose whom we share the planet with. I mean what really makes societies tick.

Food is politics.[12] The food industry is the largest manufacturing industry in this country. Anyone who disputes the description of agriculture and animal farming as an industry hasn't been outside lately. The reality is, the old distinction between food on the one hand, which was about the country and the soil, and industry on the other, which was about the city and the factory, has broken down. We all go to the supermarket and shop for groceries. But did you know that the average item of food in a grocery store has traveled 1,500 miles?[13] This means that putting food on our dinner plates is a global project. Let me give two examples, one of meat, the other of bread.

The first example concerns soybeans. Our national economy has an enormous appetite for meat and isn't too fussy if the animals that yield the meat are intensively reared in unpleasant and sometimes hideous conditions. What are those animals going to eat? Increasingly, the answer is soybeans. Where are these soybeans going to be grown? On the whole, Brazil. How will Brazilian farmers get enough land to grow this new crop? By ripping out the rain forest, and jeopardizing the ecology of the whole planet in the process. Is the tropical soil suitable for soybean farming? As it happens, no, it isn't, and after a few years the land is exhausted and more forest needs ripping out, leaving a desert behind. And who funds all this so-called development? It turns out that 60 percent of it is underwritten by three agricultural corporations based in this country. This is the politics of food.

The second example concerns bread. Once a seed is sown, it is aided by fertilizers, pesticides, and herbicides. Only strenuous procedures prevent these fossil-fuel derivatives from poisoning the water supply. After a combine harvests the grain and a truck transfers it to a silo, it's sprayed with fungicide and stored for months or years. Even-

12. I have drawn this phrase, along with several of the biblical examples in this essay, from Michael Northcott, *A Moral Climate: The Ethics of Global Warming* (Maryknoll, N.Y.: Orbis, 2007).

13. Sarah DeWeerdt, "Is Local Food Better?" *World Watch Magazine* 22, no. 3 (May/June 2009), available at http://www.worldwatch.org/node/6064.

tually it reaches a large flour mill to be refined and treated, and then goes to a bread factory where a conveyor belt mixes flour, yeast, and water. Then it's mechanically sliced, slotted in a plastic bag, and trucked to a supermarket, where consumers, having been persuaded by advertising that bread is the truly natural option, drive to purchase it in cars, but in fact buy so little of it prior to the "best before" date that much of it is discarded and trucks come and take it away. Thus bread production is one long fossil-fuel consumption exercise from beginning to end.[14] This is the economy of food.

Food is politics. And that's before we recall that 40 percent of our country's population struggles with obesity, while as many as 10 million women are struggling with an eating disorder, along with an increasing number of men.[15] Food is domestic politics just as much as it is global politics.

And of course, it's always been so. This is my second point. The world of the Gospels was as highly charged politically as any congressional committee or local anti-immigration caucus. The outer reaches of Tiberius's Roman Empire had one central purpose in the imperial economy: to be a breadbasket and source of other agricultural surpluses. If you lived in an Italian villa and your taste was fish paste, olive oil, or wine, then Galilee was your key supply base.[16] Perhaps the most significant Old Testament practice in this regard was the Sabbath. The soil of Israel was perpetually at risk from erosion or becoming too salty. The constant imperial demands for food and the extensive taxation system both feature in the Gospels. Consider in the story of Legion and the Gadarene swine why pigs were being reared in a Jewish country, where no one ate pork, except to satisfy Roman needs (Mark 5:10-20). Consider in the story of Zacchaeus why tax collectors were regarded as traitors (Luke 19:1-10). In these conditions a bad harvest could force a smallholder off the land, and the temptation to ignore the Sabbath day and the Sabbath of the fallow year was immense.

14. The previous two paragraphs are dependent on Northcott, *A Moral Climate*, 242-43, 244-48.
15. National Eating Disorders Association (http://www.nationaleatingdisorders.org/information-resources/general-information.php#facts-statistics).
16. Northcott, *A Moral Climate*, 248-49.

The politics of food dominates the Gospels just as much as it dominates today's global economy. This is my third point. When Jesus set about transforming human reality, he went to the core of the culture: the production and consumption of food.

The Gospels are an account of the storyteller who becomes the story, the healer who becomes the one in whose body the world is healed, the messenger who becomes the message. Jesus' new politics addresses the politics of food in two principal ways – through speech and through embodiment.

Most of Jesus' talking about food comes in his parables. It's often supposed that Jesus was a simple agrarian figure telling homespun yet subversive stories of small-town folk, a kind of cross between Huckleberry Finn and John Denver. But when our eyes are opened to the politics of food, the parables take on a new dimension. When we read the story of the landowner who built bigger and bigger barns (Luke 12:16-21), we start to ask, "Whose land had now come into his possession and why? Was he in the Romans' pocket or simply exploiting his fellow Jews?" In other words, it's no longer just a parable about greed but now also a story about the politics of food. Think again about the parable of the sower (Matthew 13:1-23; Luke 8:4-15; Mark 4:2-20). The stony ground and the thistles aren't just figures of speech. They're agronomic reasons why peasant farmers remained in grinding poverty. And when the good soil produced a hundredfold, this isn't just some kind of Middle Eastern penchant for exaggeration. This is saying, at last this struggling peasant farmer could pay his taxes, pay off his debts, and finally buy his own land and be free of bonded oppression for good. This becomes Jesus' image of salvation, of the kingdom of God – the ability to have more than enough food in a culture of extortion and exploitation.

But Jesus embodies his new kingdom politics of food in the way he eats. Remember that we are what we eat. Jesus *is* how Jesus *eats*. Luke's Gospel recounts seven definitive meals Jesus ate on his journey to the cross.[17] The first is a banquet with Levi the tax collector, who has just

---

17. For another discussion of these meals, and the way they turn alienation into companionship, see Samuel Wells, *God's Companions* (Malden, Mass., and Oxford: Blackwell, 2006), 27.

left everything to follow Jesus (Luke 5:27-29). Then a sinful woman washes Jesus' feet with her tears at the house of Simon the Pharisee (7:36-50). Already Jesus' way of eating food has incorporated social and personal sin. Then at the feeding of the five thousand, Jesus becomes a new Moses offering God's manna to Israel in the wilderness (9:10-17). Next, at a Pharisee's house Jesus transforms the notion of outer purity when he does not perform the ritual act of washing his hands before the meal (11:37-52), and then when he goes to eat with a leader of the Pharisees Jesus transforms the notion of Sabbath by healing a man with dropsy (14:1-4). The Pharisees wrote the book on the right way to eat, and by challenging the way the Pharisees ate, Jesus was starting a revolution. Then Jesus goes back to a tax collector's house, by the name of Zacchaeus, and at the meal Zacchaeus decides to embark on a radical program of welfare and restoration (19:1-10). That's six meals.

Remember that the number seven is the perfect number in this tradition. The seventh meal is the Last Supper (22:13-23). At the Last Supper the storyteller becomes the story. The Passover deliverance is embodied in Jesus' coming death and resurrection. The transformation depicted in the parables is absorbed into Jesus' body. The teaching becomes a practice to be repeated by the disciples ever after. The meal becomes a parable. Meanwhile, another dimension of food is added. In addition to food as parable, and food as the embodiment of what Jesus is, we see food as sacrifice. The Old Testament tradition of sacrifice, going back to Noah, linked the sacrifice of an animal with atonement for sin and thanksgiving for abundant life (Genesis 9:4-5; Exodus 12:5-7, 12-13; 29:10-28). The sin part was dealt with through the animal's death, while the abundance part was embodied in the feasting that followed. At the Last Supper Jesus becomes the Lamb of God, whose blood atones for sin and whose body gives the world abundant life. The body of Christ becomes food, in order that through the way we produce and consume food — through the way we order our economy and the people with whom we eat food — we may become the body of Christ.

Finally, there is an eighth meal. The eighth day is the first day again. Creation was on the first day. New creation is on the eighth day. The eighth day is resurrection day. The eighth meal is on the eighth day, and it takes place on the road to Emmaus (Luke 24:13-35). On the road to Emmaus, Jesus appears to two people whose faces are down-cast, looking sad. Jesus teaches. Jesus says, "Didn't you realize? Don't you *get* it?" Jesus receives the ridicule and misunderstanding of his fol-lowers, who say, "Are you the only one in Jerusalem who has no idea what's been going on?" Feel the irony of those words, said to the only one in Jerusalem who actually does know what's going on. And then Je-sus tells a story. It's a parable of the way God saves Israel. It's a story of healing. It's a story of sacrifice. It's all the things those seven meals have been in Luke's Gospel — moments of the reassembling of God's people from exile, moments of storytelling, moments of discovering the real purpose of food in God's new order. And then what happens? They eat a meal, of course. At the meal Jesus takes, blesses, breaks, and gives. And they think, "Hey — this is the whole gospel story — Jesus teaches, reveals, transforms, and finally sits down to summarize the whole story in one meal," and then as soon as they've realized what's going on, Jesus is gone, and they're left to embody the gospel for them-selves. Every element of those previous seven meals is drawn together in this transforming eighth meal. Jesus has shown us the transforming politics of his kingdom, and it's all about food.

This brings me to my final point. We've seen how food is politics. We've seen how it was always so. We've seen how Jesus transforms us through transforming food. Now, finally, it's time to see how we might embody a Christian politics based on food. I have three suggestions.

Number one, we should realize that there's nothing more political than what we eat. We can lament the demise of the rain forest; we can lobby our senators to address climate change; we can cry over the bro-ken marriage between humanity and the planet. But we don't have to eat the food that emerges from this system. We don't have to eat beef from intensively reared cattle whose fodder makes the rain forest dis-appear. Let's not get into a fantasy about uncontaminated food. But let's realize that the world's economy is based on choices about agricul-ture. The world is what we eat.

Number two, we should ask ourselves, "Who am I eating *with?*" Food is both need and pleasure. It's all of humanity in microcosm. Food is best eaten in the company of those in need and those who give us pleasure. Companions are friends we eat with. Those in need become friends, rather than simply objects of benefaction, when we eat with them. As for those we love, the balance of need and pleasure in food perfectly reflects the balance of need and pleasure in love. And when those in need and those we love come together in such a way that they get all tangled up around the meal table, we call it the kingdom of God.

Number three, whenever we eat, we should be aware of what we're doing. The Eucharist is a meal that depicts a new society in which we each bring different things to the table and receive back the same. But if worship is food, could it be that food is worship? Can we perceive the risen Christ not just in our Sunday bread, but also in our daily bread? Could it be that *every* act of eating is a moment that discloses our own humanity transformed by God's divinity? Could we imagine how good eating might become a sacrament of reconciliation between human beings and our planet?

Think one last time about that meal on the road to Emmaus. The disciples saw Jesus' scars as he broke the bread. They remembered his story and realized it was their story. They discerned his body as it became their body. They left the table with hearts on fire. They who before had stood alone were united with the believers. They looked forward to every future meal as a moment of encounter with the risen Christ. They had become what they had eaten, the body of Christ. Seven transformations that shape the Christian politics of food. Not just at the Eucharist — at every meal. Let our prayer be that every supper be an Emmaus supper, and that our politics be the politics of transformed food.

The Justice of God

The strangest thing about freedom in America is not how invisible it is to a foreigner or how cherished it is by those who live here but how frequently it's portrayed as being under threat. Unlike almost every other country in the world, America went through the twentieth century without being invaded or living under totalitarian government, and left the century with the same constitution with which it entered it. And yet nowhere else is public discourse so saturated with the rhetoric of freedom being in daily peril. When one political party looks to be elected, the right of abortion on demand is on the point of being snatched away. When another party looks to be elected, the right to bear arms is in dire jeopardy. When America is attacked by an unknown force, the president assumes the attack comes from parties who "hate our freedoms."[18]

One feature of American life that fascinates me is the degree to which the law in general — and the Constitution in particular, and what might be called the amphitheater of the Supreme Court — has become the focal point of our culture. We've come to believe that the best place to discover right and wrong, to identify good and bad, and to resolve ambiguity is the law court. I would guess that of all the dramas broadcast on network television over a regular month, more than half include some kind of pivotal courtroom scene. The wonderful dimension of this is the remarkable statement of hope that our diverse culture really can function harmoniously and that rules can emerge to govern this flourishing effectively. The risk is that the attention given to getting the rules right can distract from the fact that a healthy society is always primarily about relationships and only secondarily about rules.

The question is, whether it's ever possible for a society to reach a point that could be called justice. For all the drama and excitement of electing a new president to occupy the White House every four years, it sometimes seems the most significant job a president gets to do is to appoint new members of the Supreme Court. And no one for a moment thinks the president will be impartial. Everyone assumes the president will want to stack the court with like-minded judges. It makes you wonder whether anyone really believes in justice, or if we've all settled for the manipulation of the legal system to get the results we want. But that shouldn't make us cynical. After all, a flawed legal system is a whole lot better than no legal system at all. As Martin Luther King Jr. said, "It may be true that the law cannot make a man

18. President George W. Bush used this phrase in an address to a joint session of Congress on September 20, 2001, after the 9/11 attacks; see http://www.american rhetoric.com/speeches/gwbush911jointsessionspeech.htm.

love me, but it can keep him from lynching me, and I think that's pretty important."[19]

And that brings us to the story of Naboth's vineyard, from 1 Kings 21. This is a salutary story of what happens when there's no justice and the powerful get to crush those who stand in their way. Ahab is king of the northern territory of the land of Israel. Beside his palace lies a vineyard, and Ahab wants to purchase it. But Naboth adheres to the ancient property laws of Israel, by which land cannot be transferred from one household to another. So he refuses. Ahab sulks on his bed. But his wife Jezebel says, "What kind of a king are you?" She sends instructions to the nobles in Jezreel, instructing them to have Naboth lynched. The nobles obey Jezebel's instructions to the letter, and in no time the vineyard belongs to Ahab.

On the face of it, the story of Naboth's vineyard is a precise illustration of Martin Luther King's point. If there's no law, or at least no law enforcement, there's nothing to keep someone from lynching a person, and that does seem pretty important. In a society where the king and queen have unbridled power, justice is an early casualty. Of course, the kingdom of Israel was not, in fact, a lawless society. There *was* a law, and that law was the covenant made between God and Moses at Mount Sinai, a covenant designed to help Israel keep the freedom God had given her by bringing her out of the land of Egypt. And because Israel was always in danger of ignoring or forgetting the covenant, God sent prophets to remind the people of their story and restore their faithfulness. One of those prophets was Elijah. Elijah pays a visit to Ahab as he's sitting in the vineyard that so recently belonged to Naboth. And Elijah speaks God's justice to Ahab as only an Old Testament prophet can: "In the place where dogs licked up the blood of Naboth, dogs will also lick up your blood" (1 Kings 21:19).

So the bad guy doesn't get away with it. But this is a rather depressing portrayal of justice. It's depressing for several reasons. Number one, justice appears to have no preventative power. It can't stop people doing terrible things to one another — it can only punish them for doing so. Number two, it seems that any system of law enforcement is

19. Speech delivered at Dartmouth College, May 23, 1962.

only as effective as the force that lies behind it. And that makes justice little more than a grand word for the exercise of power. Number three, justice doesn't do the one thing that Naboth's family really want and need it to do — and that is, restore the life of Naboth himself. Justice can identify the transgression, justice can pass sentence, justice can ensure punishment, justice can stop the wrongdoing; yet justice can't heal, can't restore, can't reconcile, can't genuinely make anything better.

But there's a lot more going on in this story than a gruesome tale of ruthless oppression and its just deserts. Let's look for a moment at what this story is really about. It's really an Israelite horror show.

In the first place, look at the way Ahab rehearses all the sins of the Old Testament. Like David with Bathsheba, Ahab takes what is not his and arranges the death of the one who stands in his path. Like Cain with Abel, Ahab attacks his brother out of jealousy and impatience. Like Adam with Eve, Ahab takes the fruit of the vineyard when it is evidently God's will for him not to do so. The story of Naboth's vineyard is all of Israel's sins in one go.

Then, look at how this story represents Israel choosing slavery over freedom. The vineyard is a frequent metaphor for Israel. But Ahab wants Naboth's vineyard as a "vegetable garden" — a term used only one other time in the Old Testament, where it refers to Egypt (Deuteronomy 11:10). So Ahab's desire to turn Naboth's vineyard into a vegetable garden is a symbol of Ahab's intent to take Israel back to the conditions of slavery in Egypt. When Ahab kills Naboth and takes possession of the vineyard, what we're supposed to recognize is an ironic echo of exactly what Israel did under Joshua in driving out the Canaanites and taking possession of the Promised Land.

On top of that, notice how in this story injustice is portrayed in the disordering of relationships. First, the relationship with the land. Naboth understands his own land to be like the Promised Land, a gift in trust from God that can't be sold or traded away. Ahab, by contrast, sees land as a transferable commodity. Second, the relationship with the king. Israel saw the monarchy as a gift of trust to help the people embody the will of God. Ahab saw the throne as a mechanism for him to acquire anything he wanted by force. Third, the relationship with

God. Elijah has already been shown to follow God's orders to the letter. When in this story the nobles of Jezreel follow the behest of the Gentile Queen Jezebel to the letter, we're being shown that she has become their God. Israel has completely lost the plot.

So this is what the story of Naboth's vineyard is comprehensively showing us. Justice unravels when we lose sight of who we are in relation to God, and, once justice has had a great fall, it's a tall order to put it back together again. I wonder if you yourself have been close enough to an experience of justice or injustice to feel the profound pain of this story. Maybe you've been the victim of cruelty or crime and no legal attempt to make amends can ever truly address the repercussions and the damage. Maybe you yourself have done something seriously wrong and don't know how you can ever restore the relationships and the trust. Maybe you have been close to someone who's been some part of this spiral of justice and injustice, and you've seen how lives can be wrecked as if visited by a tornado, and how seldom the criminal justice system really makes things better.

There really is only one thing that can make things better. There really is only one thing that can make any difference in a situation where you can't bring Naboth back. There really is only one thing that can prevent an act of merciless force and the crushing of an innocent life from turning into a spiral of retribution, a vendetta of vindictiveness, and a cascade of vigilante revenge. And that single thing is forgiveness.

Today there are plenty of dispossessed Naboths and plenty of unjust Ahabs on which to focus our reflections. When we see Naboth die we tend to push forgiveness back until later. We're outraged by the lynching. We're full of horror about the way Ahab treats land and law and liberty. We're worried about seeming naïve or soft or being powerless to stop Ahab and Jezebel from doing it all over again to someone else. In short, we push forgiveness aside because we think it will get in the way of justice. So we charge in with our own version of justice. We get so consumed with that version of justice that we never get round to the forgiveness part. And in the process we forget the gospel just as much as Ahab forgot the covenant.

Put the Naboth story alongside the story of Jesus being anointed by a sinful woman (Luke 7:36-50). Jesus is in the house of Simon the Pharisee. A woman enters whom everyone knows to be a sinner. She bathes Jesus' feet with her tears and dries them with her hair. Simon is furious. Jesus turns the tables on Simon. He points out the multiple ways in which Simon has been rude to him. Jesus says there's only one thing to be done with wrongdoing, whether it's a sin of commission, like the woman's, or a sin of omission, like Simon's. And that's forgiveness.

Forgiveness shouldn't be the last thing Christians have to say in the face of injustice. It should be the first thing. Forgiveness says, "You can hurt me, but you can't take away my allegiance to Christ. You can be cruel to me, but you can't make me become like you. You can crush me, but you can't put yourself outside the mercy of God."

Why do we forgive? Because we don't want to turn into creatures of bitterness locked up in the past, and we don't want to be given over to a hatred that lets those who've hurt us continue to dominate our lives. Why do we forgive? Because, unlike Simon, we know we're sinners too and we can't withhold from others the forgiveness we so desperately need for ourselves. That's why in the Lord's Prayer we say, "Forgive us . . . as we forgive those . . ." Why do we forgive? Because Jesus in his cross and resurrection has released the most powerful energy in the universe and we want to be part of it and be filled with it. Why do we forgive? Because we know that every form of justice, all the systems for setting things straight, has failed. Why do we forgive? *Because Jesus is dying for us to forgive.* Jesus is dying for us to stop our shame and secrecy and beg for forgiveness. Jesus is dying for us to end our enmity and hard-heartedness and offer the hand of mercy. Jesus is dying for us to forgive. Why do we forgive? *Because forgiveness is the justice of God.*

Forgiveness is the justice of God. That's why a society that has forgotten how to forgive can never be truly just. Because the best that justice can do is to set the stage for forgiveness. Justice can't make things right. Even forgiveness can't make things right on its own — it takes repentance, it takes reconciliation, it takes making amends, it takes healing. But all these start with forgiveness. Forgiveness isn't the end of the process. It's the beginning. Forgiveness is the Christian word for justice.

The lesson of Naboth's vineyard is that in the end there's only one kind of injustice. All Ahab's sins come down to one. The fundamental injustice is that Ahab fails to honor God. Ahab forgets who God is and what God is really like. Failing to honor God is, in the end, the real injustice from which all other kinds come. And here's the Christian version of that injustice. We forget that God's character is fundamentally about forgiveness. Because when Christ entered the story of the vineyard, he didn't become a better version of Ahab. He became Naboth. He was condemned on trumped-up charges. He was lynched. But his justice was to pray, "Father, forgive." And his resurrection showed that God's forgiveness really does make things better in a way that our justice cannot.

If only we were a people known by everyone for forgiveness. But we're not. We're known for being obsessed with the law. If only what we were renowned for was forgiveness. That's what Jesus is dying for. Because forgiveness is the justice of God.

CHAPTER 4

Learning to Read Again

The church doesn't need a theory of scriptural authority — or even a precise doctrine of revelation. It just needs to read the Bible, to gather around the Bible, to expect God to speak through the Bible, and to see the word "understand" as a synonym for "stand under." So what I offer here is not a complex theory of interpretation, with due deference to the circumstances of the writer, the location of the reader, and the reflective wisdom gained from seeking to perform the text. Instead I present six sections, each of which seeks to practice that process of reading, gathering, expecting, and understanding. The intent is to be not definitive but infectious.

The first section identifies themes that run throughout the chapter. It challenges the notion that the scriptural story is a fixed account that the detached reader can regard as an object of faith and study. It seeks to show how the reader cannot come away from the scriptural narrative unscathed. The subsequent parts address the diverse range of writings in the Bible — the Torah, the narratives of the kingdom of Israel, the "minor" prophets, the Gospels, and the book of Revelation. Each part demonstrates the way the Scriptures are never simply personal or simply political — but always both.

Reading the Bible and Letting the Bible Read You

I wonder if you've ever had the experience of realizing that you and another person have both been reading the same story but have been interpreting it in very different ways. Many years ago I saw the film *The Mission*.[1] The film is set in South America in the eighteenth century. It portrays a group of Spanish Jesuits who go into the Paraguayan rain forest to convert the local Guarani people. One of the Jesuits is a recent convert who goes as a penance for having killed his brother in a passionate duel over a woman they both love. The mission is a miraculous success: we're given an idyllic picture of Catholic teaching blended with indigenous culture. But a sinister treaty signed in Europe transfers sovereignty of the territory from Spanish to Portuguese hands. Suddenly, the mission is in serious danger. Unlike Spain, Portugal has no law against slavery. So there's nothing to stop a horde of rapacious Portuguese plantation owners who descend upon the mission, determined to enslave the population. The Jesuits are divided as to how to respond: some train the local people to take up the sword; others simply walk toward the attackers holding the blessed sacrament. The ruthless Portuguese slaughter both groups with equal vigor. The film ends with local children rescuing precious relics from the mission and taking them deeper into the jungle, and with the words of John's Gospel: "The light shines in the darkness, and the darkness has not overcome it" (John 1:5 ESV).

After I'd seen the movie, a friend asked if I liked it. I said, "It's beautiful and affecting and tragic, but I thought as a religious film it left a bit to be desired." "Oh," she replied, quite taken aback. "I never thought of it as a *religious* film." There was I, thinking it was all about repentance and evangelism and the sacraments and Christian nonviolence. And there was she, thinking it was about colonialism and slavery and popular struggles and injustice. I thought she was ridiculous. It was obviously a film about Christianity. But she thought I was ridiculous, because it was obviously a film about colonialism. In truth, we were both right.

---

1. *The Mission*, Warner Brothers, 1986, screenplay by Robert Bolt, directed by Roland Joffé.

I want to suggest that reading the Bible is very much like watching that film. Let's look at the opening verses of the book of Exodus and see what happens to us as we read them. Remember that this is the beginning of one of the most influential, formative, and explosive stories in the whole of world literature.

Let's read this awesome and electric story.

Now a new king arose over Egypt, who did not know Joseph. He said to his people, "Look, the Israelite people are more numerous and more powerful than we. Come, let us deal shrewdly with them, or they will increase and, in the event of war, join our enemies and fight against us and escape from the land." Therefore they set taskmasters over them to oppress them with forced labor. They built supply cities, Pithom and Rameses, for Pharaoh. But the more they were oppressed, the more they multiplied and spread, so that the Egyptians came to dread the Israelites. The Egyptians became ruthless in imposing tasks on the Israelites, and made their lives bitter with hard service in mortar and brick and in every kind of field labor. They were ruthless in all the tasks that they imposed on them.

The king of Egypt said to the Hebrew midwives, one of whom was named Shiphrah and the other Puah, "When you act as midwives to the Hebrew women, and see them on the birthstool, if it is a boy, kill him; but if it is a girl, she shall live." But the midwives feared God; they did not do as the king of Egypt commanded them, but they let the boys live. So the king of Egypt summoned the midwives and said to them, "Why have you done this, and allowed the boys to live?" The midwives said to Pharaoh, "Because the Hebrew women are not like the Egyptian women; for they are vigorous and give birth before the midwife comes to them." So God dealt well with the midwives; and the people multiplied and became very strong. And because the midwives feared God, he gave them families. Then Pharaoh commanded all his people, "Every boy that is born to the Hebrews you shall throw into the Nile, but you shall let every girl live."

Now a man from the house of Levi went and married a Levite

woman. The woman conceived and bore a son; and when she saw that he was a fine baby, she hid him three months. When she could hide him no longer she got a papyrus basket for him, and plastered it with bitumen and pitch; she put the child in it and placed it among the reeds on the bank of the river. His sister stood at a distance, to see what would happen to him.

The daughter of Pharaoh came down to bathe at the river, while her attendants walked beside the river. She saw the basket among the reeds and sent her maid to bring it. When she opened it, she saw the child. He was crying, and she took pity on him, "This must be one of the Hebrews' children," she said. Then his sister said to Pharaoh's daughter, "Shall I go and get you a nurse from the Hebrew women to nurse the child for you?" Pharaoh's daughter said to her, "Yes." So the girl went and called the child's mother. Pharaoh's daughter said to her, "Take this child and nurse it for me, and I will give you your wages." So the woman took the child and nursed it. When the child grew up, she brought him to Pharaoh's daughter, and she took him as her son. She named him Moses, "because," she said, "I drew him out of the water." (Exodus 1:8–2:10)

Pharaoh sets his heart against the Hebrew people and makes them slaves. Getting increasingly nervous, he determines to kill all the Hebrew males at birth. Thwarted by the local midwives, he orders his people to throw every Hebrew baby boy into the Nile. But one Hebrew woman floats her son down the river in a papyrus basket. Pharaoh's own daughter spots the baby, adopts him, and hires his real mother to be his nurse. She calls the child Moses.

Think about what's happening here. Life coming up out of the chaos of the waters. It's a new creation story. A little boat, floating on a dangerous piece of water, contains the destiny of God's promises. It's a new Noah story. One human being, through whom God plans the blessing and deliverance of a particular people. It's a new Abraham story. So already, by chapter 2, Exodus has woven together the themes of the book of Genesis – the beginning, the new beginning after the Fall, and the beginning of Israel. We're about to witness the fourth beginning. We've gathered for the breaking of the waters. We've come to see a birth.

Next, look at how the story of Moses and his basket is a microcosm of the story of the exodus as a whole. Moses and his mother are dangerous dwellers in Pharaoh's court just as the Hebrews are a threatening presence in the land of Egypt. Moses is set among reeds; later, he leads his people through the Sea of Reeds — the Red Sea. Moses comes up out of the water just as the children of Israel will later come up out of the water. Moses' unnamed sister plays a vital role in this watery rescue just as Moses' sister Miriam plays a vital role in the crossing of the Red Sea. The midwives of the Hebrew boys' deliverance anticipate the way Moses becomes the midwife of God's deliverance of Israel.

Finally, look at how many themes from this story reappear in the story of Jesus. King Herod becomes a latter-day Pharaoh, seeking to destroy every young boy in Bethlehem. Jesus' rescue involves Egypt, just like the Hebrews' rescue does. Jesus goes down into the place of death and emerges, miraculously, as the first of many to find new life, just as the baby Moses is lowered down into the watery place of danger and is drawn out to become the one who will lead his people to freedom.

This is how we read the Bible — noticing layer upon layer of repetition, correspondence, added significance, and extra dimensions. The closer you get to the story, the more you see, the richer the resonance of every phrase. You become practiced at discerning God's hand at work. How do you learn to do this? Well, think carefully about how you hold the Bible. When you open the Bible you always hold it in two hands. When you hold it in two hands, it's always an offering you're giving to God, and it's always, more importantly, a gift *from* God that you're receiving as carefully as you can. In other words, by holding the Bible in two hands you're always remembering that reading the Bible is an act of worship. Opening the Bible is opening your heart and life up to be touched and changed by God. It's saying to the Holy Spirit, "I'm expecting you to do something right now. Surprise me."

Think also about your left hand and your right hand. In your left hand you hold the Old Testament; in your right hand you hold the New. Christians read the New Testament in the light of the Old and the

Old Testament in the light of the New. In your left hand you carry Israel, the Jewish people; in your right hand you carry the church. Christians never read the Bible alone; they always read the Bible through the eyes of the Jews and in the company of the church.

But reading the Bible is only half the story. It takes time, and practice, and patience, and care — but it's still the easy part. I'm now going to tell you what the difficult part is. The difficult part is letting the Bible read *you*. What on earth could that mean?

Let's go back to the conversation I had with my friend all those years ago about the movie *The Mission*. We both thought carefully about the film. I thought it was about evangelism and she thought it was about colonialism, and earlier I said we were both right. In fact, we were both wrong. Why? Because we both pondered the plight of those wonderful Jesuits and how they should have responded to the rapacious Portuguese. In other words, we both *read* the story. But neither of us *let the story read us*. If we had, we'd have realized that in this story we two educated Westerners weren't the Jesuits and we weren't the Spanish and we certainly weren't the local people. *We were the Portuguese*. We were the exploiters, we were the slaveholders, we were the invaders, we were the ruthless murderers.

If you read between the lines of the movie, you see that the twentieth- and twenty-first-century rape of the rain forest in the same region of South America has been far more damaging and far-reaching than the actions of the eighteenth-century Portuguese. What seems at first to be a sad, poignant, beautiful film that leaves us moved and touched turns into an uncompromising, devastating exposé of the way we in the West make the rest of the world pay for us to maintain our comfortable lifestyle. We Westerners leave the cinema angry, defensive, searching for excuses and wishing we'd never been made to feel so uncomfortable and guilty. We are the Portuguese. Ouch. That's what happens if we allow the film to read us.

Let's get back to the exodus. When we Western Christians read the story of the exodus, of course we identify with the Hebrews. We've known hardship, we've known oppression, we've known despair. And God hears our cries, sees our distress, rages against injustice, and comes to set us free. Sure, there's bound to be a few Egyptian casualties, but this is a story of God meeting us in our experience of slavery and parting the Red Sea to give us freedom and joy.

That's what it's like to read this story. But what would it mean to let this story read you? By this time I hope you're beginning to feel angry and defensive. I trust you're beginning to feel the knot in your stomach and the fury that comes from seeing something you thought belonged to you being carried off by the bailiff or the burglar. I'm not surprised if you feel like that, because that's what it feels like to let the Bible read you. When we let the story of the exodus read us, we realize to our horror and dismay that in this story we're not the innocent Hebrews. We're the Egyptians.[2]

Notice what Pharaoh says in Exodus 1. "Look," he says. "Egypt is crawling with immigrants. There's too many of them. If we're not careful they'll outnumber us. They're un-Egyptian. They have too many children. They're at fault for everything that's wrong around here." That's the kind of thing *we* say. Pharaoh believes he's rich and powerful because he's worked hard, and he thinks, "I'm not going to let the weak, the immigrant, or the underclass take away my entitlement." That's the kind of thing *we* think. Pharaoh makes up a story, a story of fear and mistrust and suspicion. He says, "They might outnumber us; there might be a war; they might fight against us with our enemies; they might run away." That's the kind of story *we* make up, and then we run to politicians who stoke our fears and play on our mistrust.

That's what we discover when we begin to let the story read *us*. So you can see why we don't do it. We keep the story in a pious cocoon. Yes, it's about oppression and deliverance, and not many of us are actually slaves or suffer under merciless taskmasters. So we spiritualize the story and say it's really about deliverance from fear, or temptation, or loneliness, or illness. Don't get me wrong. These spiritual things are real and important. But put yourself in Paraguay right now, and see what it looks like when we middle-class Western Christians watch *The Mission* and it doesn't occur to us that we're the Portuguese. Put your-

2. See Laurel A. Dykstra, *Set Them Free: The Other Side of Exodus* (Maryknoll, N.Y.: Orbis, 2002), 59-63.

self on the Gaza Strip right now and see what it looks like that we Western Christians are reading the exodus story and yet it doesn't occur to us for one moment that *we're* the enslaving Egyptians — that *we're* the oppressive Pharaoh.

Of course, we don't want to read the story that way because it makes us feel miserable and embarrassed and guilty and wrong. And we quite happily tell everybody, "Oh, yes, *I* read my Bible" — until we come across someone whose life really does look like that of a Hebrew slave, who says to us, "I bet you do. But do you ever allow your Bible to read *you?*"

On the face of it this is terrible news. We read the Bible and we're inspired and liberated. And then we let the Bible read *us*, and we're exposed and full of guilt. But wait a moment. When we open the Bible, it's not just an enacted prayer that God may open our hearts; it's also a prayer that the Holy Spirit may tell us something we didn't already know, may show us someone we hadn't ever taken notice of, may give us what we need to live penitent, renewed lives as forgiven sinners. So let's now read this story a third time, sobered and humble as it's left us. It turns out we're Egyptians in this story, and we're feeling pretty sore about it.

Here's the surprising good news. Egyptians we are, but there's more than one way to be an Egyptian.

Look at Pharaoh's daughter. She's got privilege. She benefits from the policies of the oppressor. (He's her dad, after all.) But in her own flawed but beautiful way, she imitates God. She sees the child in the basket. She hears the cries of this infant in peril, just as God at the burning bush later tells Moses that he has seen the suffering of his people and heard their cries (Exodus 3:7). Pharaoh's daughter *incubates the exodus*. She's an Egyptian, sure, but she can still be on the side of the kingdom. Maybe, so can we. Could you incubate an exodus? Could you be an Egyptian on the side of the kingdom?[3]

And look at the midwives. It's not clear whether they're Hebrews or Egyptians. But they fear God, and they refuse to carry out their orders. Going against Pharaoh's instructions, they let the Hebrew boys

---

3. Dykstra, *Set Them Free*, 146-62.

live. This has been called the first recorded act of civil disobedience in world literature. The midwives may have been Egyptians, but they found a way to subvert the oppression they were ordered to be a part of. Maybe, so can we. Could you orchestrate divine disobedience? Is that what you're being called to do right now?[4]

Here's the beginning of the exodus, the pivotal story of the Old Testament, the template onto which the early church imprinted the death and resurrection of Christ. Read it, and enjoy all its dimensions of liberation. And then, if you dare, *let it read you*, and repent of where Christians in the West truly belong in this story. But don't despair. Find the humility to *read it one more time*, and let it show you how to be a subversive Christian in this Egyptian culture. Let it show you how to see suffering. Let it reveal how to hear the cry of the people Western Christians oppress. Let it show you how to incubate liberation in its infancy. Let it demonstrate how to fear God. And let it call you to exercise God's civil, but divine, disobedience.

I'm a Prophet, Get Me Out of Here

I was on a Christian radio show once, and the presenter was asking me about one of my books. He said, "I guess you found yourself asking these questions and having these wonderings, and you thought, 'I'll go look at the Bible and see what God wants to say about these things.'" I wasn't looking to be argumentative, but I replied, "In fact, it was the other way around. I was reading the Bible, and it made me ask all these questions and have all these wonderings." I quickly realized that was the wrong answer, and before I knew it I wasn't talking to the presenter but to the producer and she was thanking me for being on the show, and I was off air and gone.

There's a way of talking about the Bible that turns it into a self-help manual that's full of good advice about how to navigate all of life's problems. That approach was clearly what my radio interviewer was looking for. But that approach ends up looking silly when confronted

4. Dykstra, *Set Them Free*, 163-78.

by a story like the book of Jonah. The book of Jonah pushes us into a lot of questions and a lot of wonderings. It can't quickly be turned into a moral fable. It makes us laugh and it makes us cry. Somewhere along the way it makes us Christians.

I'm going to tell the story of Jonah four times, once for the bare bones of the narrative, a second time to see what the story means to Jews, a third time to see what this strange story meant to the early church, and a fourth time to see what it might mean to Christians today. So here we go with the bare bones.

Jonah's one of those tiny books tucked in between Ezekiel and the end of the Old Testament. Most of us have had that scary moment when someone says, "Could you just read to us from Jonah chapter 3?" And we've replied, "Ah, yes, Jonah, my favorite, errr, Jonah, yes, short book, errr . . . after Amos, isn't it? And, errr, oh no, that's Joel, . . . errr, after Joel, and Obadiah, but before Micah, errr . . . yes, obviously, before Micah — yes, of course, everyone knows that, ah, here we are — which chapter was it again?" So we come to these short books expecting them to be obscure and fearing they'll expose our ignorance. But we all know Jonah's a story about a whale. It's up there on the children's shelf next to Noah and the ark. So surely that must make it the easy one, right? Wrong.

God tells Jonah to go to Nineveh to cry out against its wickedness. Jonah's having none of it. He sets out in the opposite direction — gets on a boat heading across the Mediterranean. The Lord sends a hurricane upon the sea, and the boat is in all kinds of trouble. The sailors try to work out why this calamity has come upon them. Eventually Jonah admits that he's running away from the Lord. Jonah tells the sailors to throw him into the sea — which, reluctantly, they do. Immediately Jonah hits the water, the storm ceases. Jonah's swallowed by an outsized fish and takes up residence in the fish's belly. There he thanks God for being given a second chance. After three days and nights the fish vomits Jonah up on dry land.

The Lord hasn't finished with Jonah. The Lord tells Jonah a second time to go to Nineveh and tell the citizens to repent because God intends to destroy their city. This time the reluctant prophet does as he's told. Much to Jonah's astonishment, Nineveh does repent, and in no time not only the common people but even the king and the livestock are dressed in sackcloth and ashes. Now, that's prophecy. Way to go, Jonah. God's impressed, and decides not to destroy Nineveh after all. But Jonah isn't impressed. Jonah's furious. He doesn't want anything to do with this mercy nonsense. He'd be more than happy to see God destroy Nineveh.

This time, instead of sending a big fish, God sends a bush, and the bush, together with the little booth Jonah has made for himself, gives Jonah shade from the sun. But God sends a worm to attack the bush, and a hot east wind to make Jonah dehydrated. Jonah has totally had enough. He asks to die. The story ends with God saying, "If you care about the bush, how much more should I care about the people of Nineveh?"

If we wanted to make it a story with a simple moral point, a couple come immediately to hand. God can work through us, but if we don't cooperate, God can find another way to get the job done. That's one. And a second is, what really makes us angry isn't God's justice, it's God's mercy. There's nothing more infuriating than God loving our enemies. God's mercy is utterly outrageous.

But before we rush ahead to the moral, let's read the story again, this time with our Old Testament spectacles on. The key word is "Nineveh." Nineveh isn't just any old ancient city. Nineveh's the capital of the Assyrian Empire, today a huge archaeological site located in northern Iraq. And what is the Assyrian Empire? It's Israel's nemesis. David and Solomon's kingdom split around 900 B.C. into two kingdoms, northern and southern. Around 175 years later the Assyrians destroyed the northern kingdom and took its leaders into exile. They never returned. The northern kingdom was lost and gone forever. So Nineveh's a name that evokes being destroyed, being gobbled up, being digested and never seen again. Another 140 years later the Chaldeans invaded the southern kingdom and took its leaders off to Babylon. This is the crisis from which the whole of the Old Testament arises. Would the southern kingdom be wiped from the face of the earth like the northern kingdom was? This is the question lying behind most of the Bible, including the book of Jonah.

The secret of the book goes back to Genesis 12, and God's call to

Abraham to be one in whom all nations may find a blessing. Jonah, or we should say, Israel, forgets that his whole purpose is to be faithful to God and so be a blessing to the nations. The sailors on the boat with Jonah represent those nations. They are in peril because Jonah has lost the plot. Jonah's swallowed up by the big fish just as the northern kingdom is swallowed up by Assyria and the southern kingdom by Babylon. The key question is, what happens next? It turns out, unlike the northern kingdom, Jonah finds he can make himself quite at home in the belly of the big fish, and in its welfare find his own welfare. The time comes for the fish to spit him out, just as Babylon returns the Jews to Jerusalem.

And now Jonah gets a second chance. This, surely, is the moment when the book of Jonah is written. The book is telling the people of Jerusalem that, astonishingly, they've returned from Babylon – they've been spat out from the belly of the big fish. What are they going to do now? Run away again? Or be what they were always called to be – a blessing to the nations? Notice that Nineveh's so big that it takes three days to walk across it. That's a subtle nudge to see Nineveh as the equivalent of the big fish, in which Jonah spent three days. But Jonah misses the analogy. Once again he ignores his vocation. And in doing so he denies his heritage. Abraham argues with God as Jonah does, but Abraham argues to save the cities of Sodom and Gomorrah, not to destroy them. Moses, like Jonah, is given the task of saving a people, but Moses carries out the task rather than refusing it. Elijah tells God he wants to die just as Jonah does, but it's because his mission against Jezebel has failed, whereas the reason Jonah wants to die is because his mission has succeeded. Job tells God he can't live because God is so harsh. Jonah tells God he wants to die because God is so merciful.

All these parallels focus on the definitive nature of what Jonah is going to do. The bush that's killed by the worm at the end of the book represents the withering of the line of kings tracing back to David.[5] By the time this book was written, there was no more hope of a revival of that great 500-year line of kings. The restoration of God's people is go-

5. For this and several other insights, I am grateful to Phillip Cary, *Jonah*, Brazos Theological Commentary on the Bible (Grand Rapids: Brazos, 2008), 142-51, 153-55.

ing to have to come some other way. Somehow the whole crisis of the Old Testament focuses on this moment at the end of the book of Jonah. Not once but twice God has done something astonishing to preserve Israel for its vocation to be a blessing to the nations. Jonah was glad to be on the receiving end of grace, but he's disgusted at the idea of extending it to his enemies. So this is the question. God has abounded in mercy. What's Israel going to abound in?

And this, for Christians, is exactly the moment Jesus Christ walks into the story. Let's look at what the book of Jonah meant for the early church. Think about the contrast between the Noah story and the Jonah story. In the Noah story, the whole world dies but the godly man and his family are saved. In the Jonah story, Jonah is thrown off the boat so that the whole world, all the sailors, are saved. Jesus is like Jonah at this moment. He dies, so that all people might be saved. He's the scapegoat and the sacrifice that gives the world a second chance. In his death he saves Gentiles and brings them to faith in God. And then, what happens next? Jesus goes down into the tomb for three days just as Jonah goes down into the belly of the big fish for three days. If you bring in the Israel dimension, Jesus emerging from the tomb is as unlikely as Israel returning from Babylon or Jonah coming back out of the fish. But return is precisely what all three of them do. Jonah is vomited up on dry land; Israel finds its way back to Jerusalem; and Jesus rises from the tomb on the third day. This is what Jesus calls the sign of Jonah (Matthew 12:39-41; 16:4; Luke 11:29-32). And it's not the end of the story, because just as Jonah then goes and preaches to Nineveh, so Christians after the day of Pentecost go and preach to the whole world. For the early church, the book of Jonah wasn't just a mini–Old Testament. It was a mini–New Testament too.[6]

So finally, what is God telling us through Jonah today? The whole story begins with the Lord. We get so used to the term "Lord" that we forget what it means. It's the translation adopted for the holy name of God, so holy that Jews can't say it. It's not just the same as saying "God." A lot of religions and peoples, and even pledges of allegiance, speak of "God." But this is the Lord, gracious and merciful, and abounding in

6. Cary, *Jonah*, 17-22, 78-81.

steadfast love. It's this name that Jesus adopted; it's this identity that caused the early church to see Jesus as not just the epitome of the merciful God but as the very heart of that God. Jonah is saved by the Lord, but he keeps relating to God as if it's the same distant, arbitrary deity. The book of Jonah presents us with the three crucial characteristics of the God of Jesus Christ: the Lord is merciful beyond comprehension, the Lord does astonishing things, and the Lord will go to any length to save a people who will be a blessing to the whole earth.

Let me close with two examples, one global and one personal. Christians are hopelessly at sea about how to relate to Jews. It's partly confusion about whether Christianity is a new religion or whether it's best to think of it as a prodigal child of Judaism. It's partly guilt about the Holocaust and the way the Holocaust was the climax to centuries of Christian intolerance of the Jews. And it's partly misgivings about the state of Israel, and about whether, in a way that's hard to talk about, the relationship between America and Israel has become like a toxic marriage, damaging to the character of both parties. I suggest that Jonah is the book above all others that Christians and Jews should read together. That way both groups can say the blunt and brutally honest things they need to say to each another. Jews can say to Christians, "You're the Ninevites. You're our enemies. It's only because we love the Lord that we're learning to love you. We have no idea what the Lord sees in you. Your existence is the embodiment of God's exasperating grace." And Christians can say to Jews, "You're Jonah. You only exist to be a blessing to the nations, like us. That's what God keeps you in existence for. Is it possible you've forgotten that? How can we help you continue to be a blessing?"[7]

Here's the personal example. The story of Jonah is pushing us to identify who we're in the business of worshiping, serving, following, and loving: some faceless, arbitrary, coldhearted, and distant God, or the Lord, made known in Jesus Christ. Which is it? I'm going to ask you one question. When you look back on your life, do you feel, like Jonah, that at a certain stage, maybe more than once, you've been in the belly of a whale and somehow, astonishingly, the Lord has given

7. For a similar discussion of these issues, see Cary, *Jonah*, 163-74.

you another chance when it looked like you were swallowed up and gone? And now, like Jonah, you have the choice between continuing to see God as faceless, arbitrary, coldhearted, and distant, and resenting the Lord's mercy to those as undeserving as you, or worshiping, serving, following, and loving the Lord, the one who repays evil with good, mistrust with mercy, and fear with joy? Is this the moment when you say, "At last I've found out what my story means and what I'm here for. God made and preserved me for this one thing: that my life should be a blessing"?

Two Questions

The book of Genesis is always three stories. Story One is about everybody. Story Two is about Israel. And Story Three is about you. To read Genesis is to see it as everybody's story, as Israel's story, and as your story, all at the same time. I'm going to tell the story of Cain and Abel three times, once as everyone's story, once as Israel's story, and once as your story.

I grew up with a sister who was three years four months and eleven days older than me. When I was a boy there were two things I wanted more than anything else. One was to be an elephant. And the other was to be older than my sister. Maybe the two desires were really the same desire. It seemed in everything that mattered, like getting extra dessert and staying up late on weekends and becoming streetwise at elementary school, I was always second. And there's only so much coming in second a man can take — especially a seven-year-old man.

What *is* it about siblings? We can't live with them; we can't live without them. If someone attacks them we're first to step in, and if they're sick we can't sleep for worry; but leave us alone in a room with them, and in no time we find ourselves turning from wallflowers into firecrackers. I once had Christmas dinner with a friend who had his ninety-three-year-old and ninety-one-year-old great-aunts and his eighty-nine-year-old great-uncle join us for the festive occasion. The great-uncle said, "Pass the roast potatoes, would you?" — and proceeded to help himself to a generous portion. "Stop it — put those back,"

Edinburgh City Libraries
Central Lending Library
Tel: 0131 242 8020
central.lending.library@edinburgh.gov.uk

Borrowed Items 28/12/2016 12:50
XXXXXXX7788

Item Title	Due Date
Our return to the light : a new path to health	07/01/2017
* Gladys Aylward : the little woman	18/01/2017
* God's smuggler	18/01/2017
* Does my soul look big in this?	18/01/2017
* Learning to dream again : rediscovering th	18/01/2017

Amount Outstanding: £2.90

* Indicates items borrowed today

http://yourlibrary.edinburgh.gov.uk
Follow us on Twitter - @edcentrallib
www.facebook.com/edinburghcentrallibrary
Save time. Do it online
www.edinburgh.gov.uk

Holiday Opening Hours
The library will be closed on:
Monday 2nd January
Tuesday 3rd January
All other days - normal opening hours apply
Seasons Greetings to all our Customers

snapped his older sister. "Don't be so greedy." The younger sister pleaded, "But surely, it's Christmas Day!" The elder sister was not to be deterred. Looking imperiously at her eighty-nine-year-old brother, she said, "He *has* to learn!"

This is the soil out of which the story of Cain and Abel becomes the story of everybody. A great many politicians and religious leaders talk about safeguarding or promoting or focusing on the family — but you wonder if these people have ever lived in one. The book of Genesis isn't the slightest bit sentimental when it comes to the realities of growing up with a brother. Here are Cain and Abel, the first siblings in the Bible: the elder brother Cain is a tiller of the ground, and his little brother Abel is a keeper of sheep. Both brothers bring an offering to the Lord, but God has regard for Abel's offering and not for Cain's. Cain is furious — and straightaway Abel's blood is crying out from the ground.

In no time at all we have Noah pronouncing a curse on Ham's son Canaan and saying he shall be a slave to his brothers Shem and Japheth. See what happens when the favoritism of a parent is added to the Molotov cocktail of sibling rivalry. I wonder if you know exactly what that feels like. Maybe your parents paid for your brother or sister to go to the private high school but they never paid for you. Maybe you were the one who always got the good grades and your parents' affirmation, and your sister hated you for it.

Then a few chapters later in Genesis we have Abraham and Lot, who were cousins but in one place are called brothers. We have this resonant sentence, "Their possessions were so great that they could not live together" (Genesis 13:6). Ouch. Feel the quality of that for a moment. "Their possessions were so great that they could not live together." Have you ever tried sharing a room with a sibling? It's not the snoring, it's not the posters, it's not the talking while you're trying to sleep — it's *"I can't believe anyone in the world needs this many pairs of jeans!"* My sister and I became the best of friends only when she went away to college. I didn't realize we were living out the Abraham and Lot story.

Then there's Isaac and Ishmael. Imagine being a half brother. You're the older one and you're constantly told you should be nice to your little brother even though every time you look at him you think,

"It was your mother that ruined my parents' marriage. How can I not hate you? Why should I love someone who's taken away my dad's attention that used to be all mine?" Or you're the younger one and you think, "I didn't choose this domestic arrangement, so why do I get blamed for it? What do I have to do to be taken seriously in this house and not treated as a toy?"

And we haven't even thought yet about Jacob and Esau, and what happens when one parent starts using a child in her maneuverings against the other. That makes it even more complicated, when you're caught in the middle between your parents! Last of all, there's Joseph and his brothers; in that story every element in all the previous stories seems to come together in a volcano of fratricide and parental favoritism and an overinflated ego – and yet profound love. I'd be surprised if you didn't recognize yourself in at least one of these stories. If your life is a chaos of thinly veiled warfare, or a desperate struggle for recognition, or love you long for but dare not ask for, or long-festering resentment, or freshly minted fury – welcome to the land of the Bible. You'll be quite at home.

So the story of Cain and Abel is everybody's story. Not everybody's story ends in bloodshed. But we've all *thought* of it. Most of us find it a whole lot harder to live the gospel in the privacy of our birth family than anywhere else on earth. Sure, evangelize the people of western China. Sure, save desperate children in the slums of Calcutta. Anything to avoid having to go home and face living the gospel with your pigheaded sister or bigheaded brother. The Cain and Abel story is telling us, *live the forgiveness and reconciliation of the gospel at home or don't live it at all.* This could be the toughest part of the good news to deal with. But deal with it we have to. You know the phrase "Charity begins at home"? It usually sounds like selfishness. In this story it turns out to be an incredible challenge.

Now let's read the story of Cain and Abel again, this time as Israel's story. No one knows exactly when the books of the Old Testament came to be written down, but what's clear is that much or most of the Old Testament is a direct or coded reflection on two catastrophes. The first is the split between the southern kingdom of Judah and the northern kingdom of Israel, a split that occurred after the death of Solomon around 900 B.C. The second is the invasion of the southern kingdom and the destruction of the Jerusalem temple around 600 B.C. by the Chaldeans and the deportation of a great portion of the population to Babylon. The story of Cain and Abel foreshadows those two key events in significant ways.

We start with two brothers, one of whom is a keeper of sheep, while the other is a tiller of the ground. Abel is the sheep farmer, Cain the agriculturalist. Think about Israel's history. For a long time they were a wandering people, dependent on their animals for food and clothing and materials from which to make tents and shelters. They lived a hand-to-mouth existence, and the stories from that time are of a people very close to God — by no means always faithful, but nonetheless a people as wrapped up in God as his purpose was wrapped up in them.

But then we get a different period in Israel's history, a more settled, agricultural period. This was a time when Israel became open to the idolatry of the worship of the Baals, the local gods of Canaan, because the Baals seemed more in keeping with the agricultural rhythm of the year. Now Israel was liable to feel self-sufficient and to become like other nations and forget her God. So now it becomes a little less mysterious why God rejects the offering of Cain, the fruit of the ground, and favors Abel's fat portions from the firstlings of the flock. We can see this as a warning sign to be borne out in Israel's later history, that if she gives herself completely over to the rhythm of the agricultural year, she could lose sight of God.[8]

But Israel and Judah acrimoniously split apart, in around 900 B.C. Can we not see these two kingdoms as like the sequence of warring brothers portrayed in Genesis? All the deep distrust, endemic rivalry, scorn, fear, jealousy, murderous intent, and pent-up malevolence displayed in the Cain and Abel story spill out in the rivalry between Israel and Judah, a rivalry that sends both eventually to their doom.

Then we turn to Cain's bewilderment as "a fugitive and a wanderer on the earth" (Genesis 4:12). Here we have a prefiguration of the Jew-

8. Etienne Charpentier, *How to Read the Old Testament* (New York: Crossroad, 1982), 19-20, 47.

ish existence in exile in Babylon. And even Babylon itself is anticipated in Cain's journey to a land "east of Eden" (Genesis 4:16). Of course, we don't know where Eden was, but from the perspective of Jews in exile in Babylon in the sixth century B.C., Eden was the Promised Land of Israel from which their parents had been deported. They were now east of Eden, and in the story of Cain and Abel they found part of an explanation why. They'd grown fat on the land and lost sight of God. They'd fought with their brother against God's will. And they'd been sent wandering as a result. But they found in Babylon, as Cain found in the land of Nod, that they still bore God's mark and God's hand was still on their life.

Finally, let's read this story a third time as a story about you. You and God. I have an academic friend who goes to conferences all around the country. Every year at his field's annual meeting he shares a room with the same colleague from graduate student days. As soon as they are reunited, usually in the hotel room, they ask each other the same question. "Are you living well?" Somehow that question covers everything that matters. That's a question to ask one another regularly. "Are you living well?" Remember that what immediately precedes this story in Genesis is that of Adam and Eve. In the Adam and Eve story God calls to Adam, "Where are you?" (Genesis 3:9). *"Where are you?"* And here in the next chapter God calls to Cain, "Where is your brother?" (Genesis 4:9).

"Where *are* you?" "Where is your *brother?*" These are probably the two most important questions you will ever be asked. And the order is important. Remember the words of Paul in the letter to the Philippians: "Work out your own salvation with fear and trembling" (Philippians 2:12). Your first duty is to save your own soul. You have no greater responsibility in life than this: when God comes to you "walking in the garden at the time of the evening breeze" and says "Where are you?" do you make an eager answer, or are you skulking in the bushes hoping not to be seen? Can you answer that question: "Where *are* you?" Are you answering eagerly, or are you shrinking into the shadows?

Only when you've faced up to that first question are you ready for the second question, "Where is your brother?" Imagine you're standing before the Lord Jesus at his judgment seat in heaven, and he's looking at you with eyes of compassion and mercy and love like you've never seen or known before. Imagine he's saying to you the words God said to Cain: "Where is your brother?" And suddenly you realize you've got this whole salvation thing wrong. You thought it was about keeping your nose clean and hoping God overlooks your foolishness and pride. But Jesus is saying, "What about the others? Did you leave them behind? Where are they? Are they in Haiti? Are they in New Orleans? Are they on the Mexican border? Where is your brother?" Do you have an answer for him? Is your life drenched in ifs and buts and excuses and explanations? Are you standing there at the judgment seat asking for an extension as if salvation were some kind of end-of-semester assignment and if you had a couple more days you'd be ready? Where is your brother? What's your answer? There's only one answer Jesus wants. "Right here beside me."

You can live a hundred years, you can be the pinup in every dorm room in the whole of the state, you can be MVP in the Super Bowl a thousand times and find a cure to the ten most dangerous diseases on the planet. But in the end, all that matters is your answer to these two questions. "Where are you?" "Where is your brother?" If you're the kind of person who doesn't find it easy to pray long prayers or hasn't the technological wizardry to keep intercession lists on your iPhone or your roommate or spouse can't cope with you meditating at six in the morning, I suggest you just do this. Every single day at the same time, sit still and let God ask you these two questions. "Where are you?" "Where is your brother?" And then answer them. Your life and your salvation depend on this.

Dwelling in the Comma

"If you were put on trial for being a Christian, would there be enough evidence to convict you?" It's an old question, but it's still a good one. Of course, the answer rather depends on what you think being a Christian means. Let's look at three kinds of answers.

One answer says, "God comes to visit us when we're on our last dime, when we have nothing and no one to turn to." So being a Christian means saying, "I am naked before God. But I spend my life pretending otherwise. I want to be at home with those whose nakedness, fragility, and pain are no secret." Jesus' life is shaped around people whose tears have flowed for so long their eyes have run dry, around those who would scream out loud if they could find the voice or the words, around all whose prayer is simply, "Lord, give me strength to get through today."

It's a good answer. It speaks of the compassion of God. But what about the goodness of God?

And so a second answer says, "God wants us to be holy, and being a Christian means letting the Holy Spirit craft us in ways of righteousness and paths of purity." It tends to ask questions like, "Have you kept the Ten Commandments? Have you made room in your life for personal devotion, public worship, charitable giving, and civic service?"

It's a good answer. It speaks of the goodness of God. But what about the justice of God?

A third answer says, "God wants us to stand up for justice, to advocate for the disadvantaged, to witness for our faith, to turn words into actions and to put ourselves in places of danger." Being a Christian is about actively seeking to mirror and bring about the kingdom of God on earth. It asks, "Have you let your faith propel you into courageous deeds? Or have you let your inhibitions make you hesitate on grounds of fear or propriety or politeness?"

I wonder if you recognize yourself in any of these three answers. I wonder if you were profoundly shaped as a child or later in life to believe that one of these was right and the others were dubious or wrong. The church is more or less split around these different answers to the basic question, "What does it look like to be a Christian?"

So . . . which is it? Which one is right? Can we really settle for just one of the three?

The place to go for an answer to this question is to chapter 5 of Matthew's Gospel, where Jesus, like Moses before him, goes up on a mountain and utters the most significant words of his life. The Beatitudes are the most succinct account of what it means to be a Christian we have. One biblical scholar calls them the most significant words ever spoken.[9] How do these precious words answer our question? What, according to the Beatitudes, does it look like to be a Christian?

There are nine beatitudes, and I want to look at them with you as three groups of three. Let's start with the first group of three. "Blessed are the poor in spirit. . . . Blessed are those who mourn. . . . Blessed are the meek" (Matthew 5:3-5). Jesus is saying, "Christianity begins with the desperate. Are you miserable? Is your life in pieces? Are your plans for your career, your marriage, your degree, your health, or your very survival ruined? If so, here's the good news: you're right where the gospel takes root." But there's also a message here for you if you're bored, disillusioned, paralyzed by choice, jaded, or noncommittal, and you want to see what Christianity is really about. The message is, "Go hang out with someone whose stomach is empty, whose head is hurting, whose spirit is crushed, whose heart is heavy. Because that's where Jesus starts."

But it's more subtle than that. Look at the way Jesus gives us three kinds of misery. The first is being poor in spirit. What does that mean? It means to know you've done something wrong, maybe a lot of things wrong, maybe something very wrong, perhaps something really terrible. And then you lose confidence, and your pride makes you ashamed to show your face, frightened to reveal your true self to anyone, resentful of people's harsh standards and judgmental attitudes. You may not regret what you did, or what you're currently doing, but you know it puts you outside the camp. And so you self-segregate yourself from regular company, regular church, regular friendships, a regular relationship with God. You're poor in spirit.

Then there are those who mourn. Those who grieve because mortality and fragility and maybe sheer bad luck have deprived them of something or, more probably, someone who was their reason for living, who made their heart sing. Mourning means suffering by merely allowing your life to be deeply invested in the life of someone else. It means loving and losing. Those who mourn are those who suffer because they have loved.

---

9. Frederick Dale Bruner, *Matthew: A Commentary*, vol. 1, *The Christbook: Matthew 1–12* (Grand Rapids: Eerdmans, 2004), 157.

And then there are the meek. The meek are those who suffer through the fault of somebody else. The meek are the oppressed, the disadvantaged, the discriminated against, the voiceless, the faceless statistic, the dispossessed. In these first three beatitudes Jesus is saying that the gospel begins in the gutter, the ditch, regardless of whether someone put you there, bad luck put you there, or you put yourself there. Here Jesus echoes the first of our three answers. Being a Christian means dwelling in the naked place of tears.

But we've still got six beatitudes to go. This is what the next three beatitudes say. "Blessed are those who hunger and thirst for righteousness. . . . Blessed are the merciful. . . . Blessed are the pure in heart" (Matthew 5:6-8).

Imagine having such a longing, such an ache and yearning to imitate God, that it feels like hunger and thirst. Those who hunger and thirst for righteousness are so focused on God, so conscious of their shortcomings before God but so active in their steps to walk in God's ways and share God's heart, that this desire becomes their meat and drink, their daily sustenance. I once asked a young woman, "Why are you a Christian? What's it all about for you?" She replied, "I just want to be like Jesus — to think like him, act like him, love like him, live like him." That's what it means to hunger and thirst for righteousness.

Next are the merciful. This is the central beatitude of the nine. If righteousness is our regard for God, mercy is our attitude to one another. Later in Matthew Jesus says, "Treat others the way you want them to treat you" (Matthew 7:12, paraphrased). Here Jesus says, "Treat others the way God has already treated you." How would you like God to treat you on judgment day? Treat others that way today. Demonstrate to others the mercy you beg God for. Recognize God in others, and God will recognize himself in you.

Then we come to "Blessed are the pure in heart." The thirsting for righteousness is about God, being merciful is about others, and being pure in heart is about you. Søren Kierkegaard said, "Purity of heart is to will one thing."[10] Maybe you've been told that to hold down a re-

10. Søren Kierkegaard, *Purity of Heart Is to Will One Thing*, trans. Douglas V. Steere (New York: Harper, 1956).

sponsible job you need to distinguish between the urgent and the important, and to judge which things are urgent but not important, which things are important but not urgent, and which things are neither urgent nor important. Well, purity of heart is about knowing as a matter of habit and uncomplicated clarity which things are important. Not fashionable, not popular, not effective, not lucrative, not eye-catching, not relaxing, not clever, not witty, not dramatic, not necessarily urgent: but important. And then, in a crisis, when everyone else has lost his or her sense of perspective, you'll be able to see the one thing that no one else is able to see. Because you never stopped looking at it.

Here Jesus echoes the second of our three answers to the question of what being a Christian means. It's not about you changing the world, it's about letting God change you.

But there's more. The last three beatitudes are about what happens to us when we follow the logic of Jesus' life and teaching — when we put feet on the gospel. We start with "Blessed are the peacemakers" (Matthew 5:9). To be a peacemaker you need to understand the first group of beatitudes — how sin and unfairness and oppression and suffering lead to conflicts. But you also need to embody the second group of beatitudes, because peacemaking needs mercy, needs a healthy sense of perspective, and needs God. How do you become a peacemaker? Well, here's a question you can ask yourself when you get out of bed each morning: "How am I going to be a reconciling presence in the life of my neighbor?"

Then there are the last two: "Blessed are those who are persecuted for righteousness' sake. . . . Blessed are you when people revile you and persecute you and utter all kinds of evil against you falsely on my account" (Matthew 5:10-11). In both of these final beatitudes, Jesus is talking about those who love God so much that they don't care who knows, how much it costs, how unpopular it makes them, and how much it endangers their lives. This is a faith that follows through the implications of Christ's love to the very end, a faith that doesn't duck the logic of the gospel, a faith that never tires, even in the face of hostility, even in the face of hatred, even in the face of danger. Even in the face of death.

Jesus doesn't seem able to choose between our three answers. So why do we? Is it because we want Jesus but we don't want the cross?

Because, you see, Jesus doesn't just speak the gospel. He lives it. It turns out the Beatitudes are nothing less than the story of Jesus. Every single one of them anticipates a moment on Jesus' journey to and death on the cross. He's poor in spirit when he takes on the sin of the whole world (John 1:29; 2 Corinthians 5:21; Hebrews 9:28). He mourns when his heart is heavy in Gethsemane (Matthew 26:36-44; Mark 14:32-38; Luke 22:39-46). He's meek when he's falsely accused and yet never says a mumblin' word (Matthew 27:12-14; Mark 15:5-4; Luke 23:8-9; John 19:10). He's meek when he thirsts on the cross (John 19:28). He's merciful when he says, "Father, forgive them . . ." (Luke 23:34). He's pure in heart when he says, "Not my will but yours be done" (Luke 22:42; cf. Matthew 26:39; Mark 14:36). He's a peacemaker when he tells Peter to put down his sword during Jesus' arrest (John 18:10-11). He's persecuted and reviled by priests, scribes, soldiers, and bystanders at his trial and while he hangs on the cross (Matthew 26:67-68; 27:28-31, 39-44; Mark 14:65; 15:17-20, 29-32; Luke 22:63-65; 23:10-11, 35-39; John 18:22; 19:1-3). This is Jesus' autobiography. The beatitudes are Jesus saying, "This is who I am – and this is how to be like me – *this is how to be me, to be my body in the world.*"

To be a Christian is to live the Beatitudes. Let's look a bit more closely at what that means.

Every beatitude comes in three parts. There's the first part, which is really a description of the cross: poor, thirsty, meek, merciful, persecuted. Then there's the last part, which is a description of the resurrection; each beatitude has a resurrection promise. "They will be comforted." "They will inherit the earth." "They will be filled." "They will receive mercy." "They will be called children of God." "Theirs is the kingdom of heaven." The Beatitudes are a description of Jesus in his cross and in his resurrection. To be a Christian is to live in Jesus' cross and in his resurrection.

But wait. Between the cross and the resurrection lies a comma. Every beatitude has a comma in the middle. That comma is a kind of valley between the horror of the cross and the wonder of the resurrection. I want you to think about that comma. That pause – that place where the cross and the resurrection meet. *That comma is your life as a Christian.* To be a Christian is to *dwell in that comma* that lies between the first and second half of each beatitude. That comma is your home on earth. That comma represents the pathos and the joy of the Christian life. That comma is where you find Jesus.

What does it look like to be a Christian? Jesus is saying, the people who know are those who are closest to my cross. The closer you get to my cross, the closer you get to resurrection. If you're one of those people, happy are you. If you're not one of those people, start hanging around with those who are. That's what it means to dwell in the comma. Jesus is the place where cross and resurrection meet. So are you.

It's time to stop limiting yourself to just one third of the gospel. It's time to live the whole thing. It's time to dwell in the comma, where the cross meets the resurrection. This is where you meet Jesus. This is what Christianity is. This is where to find it. This is how to live it. This is blessedness. Blessed, blessed are you.

Five Smooth Stones

The story of David and Goliath is simple. God wanted to be Israel's only king. But Israel wanted its own king. So God gave Israel King Saul. But Saul lost his way and Israel started to become too much like other nations. So God chose David. 1 Samuel 17 shows a lot of what went wrong with Saul and a lot of what was different about David. The Philistines were dominating Israel in battle. Their commanders had their foot on Israel's neck. But rather than proceed with the mass slaughter of battle, they decided to settle matters with a duel between their champion and Israel's champion.

Their champion is the massive Goliath. Goliath is ten feet tall and has so much armor someone has to carry his shield for him. Israel's champion ought to be Saul, who is also, after all, very tall, and who has, as we discover in the course of this story, plenty of armor of his own. But Saul isn't interested. So David steps forth from obscurity. Using wit and wisdom rather than hustle and muscle, David defeats Goliath. The Philistines flee and the Israelite army is rejuvenated.

We like this story because it confirms something we believe is at the heart of our culture. Stand up for the little guy. There's nothing we love more than to see the small liberal arts college fight through to the Final Four of the NCAA basketball tournament to take on the big state school powerhouse. It makes everyone feel great. If you're the little guy, it makes you feel like you really could make it. If you're the big guy, it reassures you that with hard work, ingenuity, and a little luck, anyone can make it.

Everyone loves the movie where the small-town attorney takes on the sprawling multinational conglomerate that's poisoning the water in the local streams. Everyone cries in the final frame of the film when she clenches her fist in victory. But privately everyone knows the inspiring movie about the resilience of the little guy has been made by exactly the kind of giant faceless multimedia corporation the attorney in the movie is standing up against.

The figure of David before Goliath has captured the imagination of our public conversation. In most presidential elections both parties want to tell us they are on David's side. They're standing up for the honest little guy against the big heartless corporate world. Both parties love to present themselves as standing bravely for the fundamental rights that those dangerous other guys are poised to seize away at any moment. We somehow all like to see ourselves as David, with the odds stacked against us.

So why then do we spend so much time trying so hard to be Goliath? We think it's quaint and clever that David got by with five smooth stones and a sling, but we spend our energies building up our supply of swords and spears and javelins. We clad our car and our house and our country to look like Goliath, with so many safety and security features we can hardly move around in them.

Why is a degree from a prestigious college so coveted? Because it gives us a chance to be Goliath. It gives us the armor, it gives us the weapons, it gives us the respect, it gives us the acclaim. All the things Goliath had. All the things David didn't have.

Why are mainline denominations feeling such a creeping sense of panic in this country right now? Because they're facing numerical decline. Why is that a problem? After all, Christianity isn't any less true just because it is less widely believed. The reason it's a problem is that mainline denominations have assumed for as long as anyone can remember that they're supposed to be Goliaths. They're supposed to be huge, they're supposed to be important, they're supposed to be players on the national stage, they're supposed to be the acknowledged voice of the people. All the things Goliath was. All the things David wasn't.

There's a painful irony about what became of David after he put down the slingshot. If only David had stuck with the five smooth stones, history might have turned out a little differently. There he was, full of confidence, full of faith, full of hope, telling Saul he didn't need the heavy armor and telling Goliath he didn't need mighty power and bombastic big talk. David defeated Goliath. The people swung behind David. David became king. And gradually the terrible irony began to kick in. *David became Goliath.* David became the inflated, bullying, beached whale he had begun his career by destroying. Just like Elvis Presley, for whom fame and fortune turned gyrating hips into bloated cheeks. David became Goliath. What a tragedy that was.

But the poignancy doesn't end there. When we read the story of David and Goliath, we don't just see the contrast with David's later life. We also think of the one whom the Gospels often call the Son of David. When we think of Jesus as Son of David, are we thinking of the David who *became* Goliath or the David who *overcame* Goliath? The tragic irony is the same as before. We know that in walking the way of the cross, Jesus was the disarmed young David who walked slowly and calmly without armor to face the Goliath of empire and death. But we constantly fall back into celebrating Jesus as if he were the kingly David of power politics and conquest — the David who became Goliath. We take a long, lingering look at the God revealed in Jesus of Galilee, the God made known in touch, and word, and silence, and not in weapon, or wealth, or war . . . and we say, "No, thanks."

We say we like David but we choose Goliath. David started off with five smooth stones and a sling and ended up becoming Goliath. But Jesus didn't. We may turn Jesus into Goliath in our imaginations, in our politics, in our rhetoric, even sometimes in our worship. But Jesus never turned into Goliath. And Jesus never does. When we read the story of David and Goliath back through the lens of Jesus — when we realize that this story of the good shepherd from Bethlehem is an account of the choices facing Jesus as he set out on his ministry – we discover that this is a story about where power truly lies.

This is still a story for the little guy and for the big guy. In your life right now you may be feeling like a very small boat on a very big and rough sea. You may be feeling that you're surrounded by mountainous waves, or perhaps just facing one in particular, and you don't know whether to cry with despair or bury your face in the pillow and hope it will all go away. Or you may be wondering if you've become Goliath, if you've become the beached whale who's so busy and important and full of meetings and committees and task groups and action plans that you can't move. Either way, maybe you get up most mornings and think, "No, thanks." Maybe it's a good time to look at where this story says power really comes from.

David's power lies in his five smooth stones. And this story shows us five sources of power. Let's turn these five stones over in our hands together.

Stone number one for David is, he knows how to serve. He knows how to put his own needs and desires to one side for an extended period to do unregarded work. That's what David does in the first part of this story. He looks after his father's sheep at Bethlehem. And he takes provisions to and fro between the various soldiers and commanders of the army. There are some parts of every life, and every part of some lives, that are unrewarding, unregarded, and unattractive. Have you lost the art of the everyday, and lapsed into a sequence of thrills punctuated by hours and days of resentment? David finds a way to make the ordinary into a source of pride, a form of training, and a way to build relationships. That's where he gets his power. Is that where you get your power?

Stone number two for David is, he's close to the land. David doesn't rely on technology or physical advantage. He's spent his life outside. He knows how to keep sheep. He knows where to find smooth stones. He knows how to craft a sling. He knows how to snare an animal, even a lion or a bear. He knows the tricks of the forest and the wilds of the woods. If your life is feeling stuffy right now, ask yourself, "When was the last time I felt my created nature and sharpened my wily wits by spending some time in the fields, in the streams, in the mountains?

Have I so surrounded my life with gadgets and comforts that I've forgotten the exhilaration of the hillside breeze?" David learns from his outdoor life the wisdom of the owl, the cunning of the fox, the agility of the wildcat, the sharp eye of the eagle. That's where he gets his power. Is that where you get your power?

Stone number three for David is, he knows himself. Saul assumes David should be dressed up to look as much like Goliath as possible. So he gets out the full set of armor — bronze helmet, coat of mail, and hefty sword. But David knows he's not Goliath. And he knows he's not Saul. If your life is an uphill struggle right now, is it because you're wearing someone else's armor, trying to be someone you're not and never will be? Strive to be what only you can be. Don't be a second-rate version of someone else. David knows there's no point in putting on Saul's armor. Of course, Saul might think he was being disrespectful, taking unnecessary risks, letting him down. But David knows there's no point in trusting someone else's half-baked judgment. He knows his own weaknesses, and he knows his own strengths. That's where he gets his power. Is that where you get your power?

Stone number four for David is, he knows God is on his side. Once before Saul and once before Goliath he shows his confidence in where power really lies. To Saul he says, "The LORD, who saved me from the paw of the lion and from the paw of the bear, will save me from the hand of this Philistine" (1 Samuel 17:37). To Goliath he says, "You come to me with sword and spear and javelin; but I come to you in the name of the LORD of hosts" (1 Samuel 17:45). I once went through a dry season where I knew I was in the wrong place but I had no idea where the right place was. A friend I didn't know all that well noticed I wasn't myself and asked the right question in the right way. I poured out all the problems and difficulties and constraints that made me wonder how things could ever get better. When I had finished he just put his hand on my shoulder and looked in my eyes and said, "Sam, where's your faith?" David has the trust I so desperately needed that day. Maybe you need it just as much today. In the end, it's the only power that counts. That's where David gets his power. Is that where you get your power?

Finally, stone number five for David is, he knows how God exercises power. As we've seen, this is the hardest one of all. The other four

145

are all important. David has a servant heart. He understands his territory. He knows himself. He trusts God. These all matter. But unless he realizes who God is and how God works, the sling and stones become just a technique for becoming Goliath himself. The same applies to Jesus. Cross and resurrection aren't techniques for Jesus becoming a cosmic bully like Goliath. They're our windows into the heart of God.

God isn't interested in becoming Goliath. God transforms the world through the Son of David. God isn't interested in *us* becoming Goliath. In fact, our desire to become Goliath is a sign we've lost faith in God and lost sight of who God is. David did both, later on. Most of us do, for a season. Maybe you have, right now. If so, go back to where real power lies. Find joy in the ordinary, find the breath of life outdoors, come to know yourself, and trust God. But most of all, don't for a moment think God is Goliath. God is a shepherd, and all he's got in the face of violence and threats and fear are five smooth stones. But here's the good news. One of those stones is you.

The Healing of the Nations

Poetry is what happens when you put two words side by side that don't usually belong together, and then sit still and allow the sounds and resonances and associations to echo and conflict and spark and coalesce. I want to think with you about the poetry of the book of Revelation, and about two words we don't usually put together: "healing" and "politics."

Healing we usually think of as personal, private, and hidden. Politics we connect with Washington, elections, speeches, and backroom deals. Healing sounds wholesome. Politics sounds emotive, like what happens in the workplace when you don't understand what's going on at the staff meeting but your boss says he or she will tell you later. Healing might be something you come to church to find. Politics could be something you come to church to avoid.

But the book of Revelation is concerned with the healing of politics. And that healing is vividly portrayed in the final scenes of the book, where John sees a new heaven and a new earth, and the holy city, the new Jerusalem, coming down out of heaven from God. The city has

146

no temple, and is in perpetual light. Its gates are always open. A river runs through it, and on either side of the river is the tree of life, whose leaves are for the healing of the nations (Revelation 21:1-4, 22-27; 22:1-5). This picture sets out for us what politics is, what healing is, and what it might mean to talk about the healing of politics and the politics of healing.

Here are the three striking things about the way Revelation ends. First, there's a new earth. We're so familiar with the words "And then I saw a new heaven and a new earth" that we seldom pause and reflect on what they mean. They mean the earth is a *permanent* part of God's vision for our life. It's not that earth is finally destroyed and then we're all in heaven forever. This vision is telling us there will always be an earth, not necessarily exactly the same way it is now, but nonetheless there will always be an earth. God so loved the world that when the old one was worn out he didn't throw it out but made it new, and made a new heaven to match.

Think back to the tower of Babel, in Genesis 11. At Babel, humanity tried to become homogeneous and tried to reach heaven through its own ingenuity. God scattered the people and languages at Babel. God was making a clear statement that humanity was meant to enjoy diversity, not obliterate it, and that getting to heaven was God's gift, not humanity's achievement. Unlike Babel, which tried to take earth up to heaven, this picture in Revelation is of heaven coming to earth. We can't make salvation come. It comes to us. But salvation won't whisk us away. It will transform what's already here. God has healed the earth.

This is vitally important for the way we see our bodily existence, for the way we imagine politics, for the way we relate to the wider animal, vegetable, and mineral creation. The earth is not a means to an end. It's not the wrapping paper we toss away once we get to chew on the candy of heaven. Our embodied existence is the way it's always going to be. Relating to one another in all our diversity and relating to the earth in all its vibrant complexity are the way we're always going to live. This world isn't ghastly and irredeemable. God's plan for everlasting life is recognizably similar to what we already know. Politics isn't a waste of time, or a necessary evil. It's the way we're going to be spending eternity.

Second, what comes down from heaven is called "Jerusalem." In other words, God's plan for eternity is in continuity with the Jewish people, with the covenant, with the temple, with the whole story of the chosen people before God. God doesn't obliterate the earth to make a new world, and God doesn't obliterate Israel to make the church. This one gesture — calling the heavenly city "Jerusalem" — incorporates the politics of Israel into the politics of heaven. God has not forgotten the covenant. The way God's people drew together God's salvation, God's judgment, God's possession of the land, and the way they responded in praise and worship — these will be real and present in the politics of heaven. The Old and New Testaments provide the ingredients from which God concocts the recipe for heaven. But the new Jerusalem has no temple, because Jesus is present and worship is constant and reconciliation with God is complete and so there is no need for a temple. God has healed Jerusalem.

Third, Jerusalem is a city. The Bible is ambivalent about cities. Remember, the story begins in a garden. In the Garden of Eden human beings are at peace with one another, at peace with the animal, vegetable, and mineral creation, and at peace with God. What happens after the Fall is that divine abundance turns to human scarcity, and relationships among human beings, between human beings and the wider creation, and between human beings and God are suddenly all in jeopardy. This is represented by the symbolic journey from Adam and Eve's garden to Cain's city. The city is the living embodiment of humanity's failure to live in the garden.

The tension between city and garden runs through Jesus' story. Jesus enters the city in triumph on Palm Sunday, but four days later he's rejected in the city. His betrayer leaves the Last Supper in the city but kisses Jesus in the garden. On Good Friday Jesus is tried in the city but buried in the garden. On Easter Day he appears to Mary in the garden *and* to his disciples in the city. So for heaven to be portrayed as a city is a decisive form of redemption.

But notice, crucially, what finally happens to the garden. God doesn't finally make a choice between a city and a garden. God brings the garden into the city. There is a river and there is the tree of life and there are twelve kinds of fruit and there are leaves on the tree. God doesn't wipe out the history of human interaction in the city. The tension between city and garden that runs right through the Bible is finally resolved by the creation of a garden city. God has healed the city.

These three dimensions of the book of Revelation's picture of heaven describe for us the healing of politics. God does not destroy the earth: God makes the earth new. God does not reject Israel: God makes a new Jerusalem, but one that reflects the presence of Jesus. God does not choose between the garden and the city: God brings the garden into the city.

The crucial link between all these dimensions of the healing of politics is the tree. In the Garden of Eden, even though it was paradise, there was still politics. And that was because politics is as much about the best enjoyment of God's abundance as it is about the inadequate distribution of our scarcity. People still needed to balance various goods, address common issues, and get the best out of one another. The Fall of Adam and Eve focuses on the tree. After eating from the tree, trust is gone, innocence is gone, abundance is gone, and mutuality is gone. Politics is suddenly a problematic, conflictual game of resentments and suspicion and secrets and lies. The tree of Eden is healed in the tree of Calvary. The cross on Calvary is the definition of healing and the redefinition of politics. It exposes the profound horror of politics — that human interactions of power and authority could collaborate to execute the embodiment of God's abundance, trust, simplicity, joy, and truth. But in the resurrection God transforms and heals that politics, by offering the two things conventional politics finds so hard to grasp — the forgiveness of sins and eternal life.

The third tree, the tree of life in the book of Revelation, is about the politics of Eden and the healing of Calvary. The leaves of the tree are for the healing of the nations. What do we learn in Revelation that shapes our understanding of healing and reshapes our notion of politics?

Well, here's a little manifesto that applies equally well to your household, your workplace, your country, and your church.

Revelation's politics is one of abundance. There is no shortage of light, because God's light is permanent and sufficient. Is the politics of your household, workplace, country, or church obsessed by the items of scarcity that cause jealousy and resentment? Or does it constantly dwell on the things of God that never run out, the things that everyone can have?

Revelation's politics is one of diversity. The foundations of the wall of the city are adorned with every kind of jewel and all the nations are there. The tree of life produces twelve kinds of fruit. Is the politics of your household, workplace, country, or church bent on a fearful preservation of a narrow certainty or homogeneity or heritage or culture? Or does it see difference and variety of identity and practice and tradition and experience as fundamentally good and enriching and renewing and godly?

Revelation's politics is one of inclusion. The gates of the city are never shut. Is the politics of your household, workplace, country, or church one that sees every newcomer as a thief, every stranger as a swindler, every chance encounter as a threat? Or does your politics seek out the unusual person, enjoy the foreigner, study to speak to foreigners in their own language, and offer hospitality to the lost?

Revelation's politics is one of reuniting the garden and the city. Is the politics of your household, workplace, country, or church one that treats the mineral world as a disposable resource, vegetation as fuel for consumption, and the earth as an orange to be squeezed till the pips squeak? Or does your politics see harmony with the earth as all of a piece with peace with your neighbor and reconciliation with God?

Finally, Revelation's politics is one of continuing to enjoy rather than discarding or destroying. God doesn't discard or destroy the earth, but makes the earth new. God doesn't discard or destroy Jerusalem, but makes Jerusalem new. God doesn't discard or destroy the city, but makes the city new. And this is our fundamental resurrection hope. God doesn't discard or destroy you and me, but makes you and me new.

The word for making new is "healing." The other word for making new is "politics." This is what the politics of heaven is about: abundance, diversity, inclusion, reunion, healing. Politics begins the moment you realize discarding and destroying are not options available to you, and you have to work with and enjoy and celebrate and renew what you've got. That's what Revelation finally teaches us. In the kingdom of heaven, healing is what politics is finally about.

CHAPTER 5

Learning to Feel Again

The sections in this chapter take us closer to the gut than the forego-
ing part of the book. The first is a study in envy – one of the most
powerful, pervasive, and least-discussed forces at work in the church,
and in any human community. The second can be read as an exploration of depression, at least in a nonclinical way. It considers circumstances that seem beyond redemption. The third seeks to show how
deep is the significance of gratitude. The next is a consideration of
marriage, particularly in the light of contemporary awareness of how
fragile marriage can be, and of uncertainty about whether marital
love, if it is indeed for life, is yet forever. Then comes a discussion of
death, with particular reference to contemporary understandings of
widely discussed deaths. The chapter concludes with a reflection on
the difference between weakness and sin, recognizing how hard they
can sometimes be to tell apart, but how truly God wills to transform
both. The approach in each section is to speak to the deepest, often
least-articulated, places in our souls, in order to let the Scripture speak
in the places that count the most.

The Godfather

Some years ago I went for a long walk with a friend. She had a lot on
her mind. She wanted to talk about her mentor, who'd also been her

first boss. My friend said, "She's been really kind to me over the years, introducing me to all the leading people in the field, getting me openings and writing me references. But now, since her marriage broke up, she's become a bit strange. She's dressing as if she were my age, and she seems to want to get invited to all the events and parties I go to. She's always asking about my husband and the children. I'm beginning to find it a bit creepy."

I said, "It sounds to me like she wants to be you."

"What on earth do you mean?" my friend replied, incredulous. "She's quite famous, she's a very successful woman — I'm just a minnow in the pond."

I had to stop my friend and look straight at her, because I realized what I was about to say was a lot for her to take in and was going to unsettle much that she seemed to take for granted. "Look at your life. You have beautiful children, a good husband, and a healthy career. Who cares who's got the best CV and has the big salary? This woman doesn't care about those things deep down. She wants what you have, and in her misery she's somehow got it into her head that the closer she gets to you, emotionally and physically, the more she's going to become like you and have what you have."

My friend was horrified. She said, "I've never realized people thought like that."

I responded, "That's because you're different from most people. Your life isn't consumed by envy. A big organization like the one you work in is a huge chemical experiment in envy. Everybody's comparing themselves to each other all the time: everyone is constantly coveting the acclaim, or security, or recognition, or salary, or family life, or emotional balance, or office with windows, or title, or parking space, or annual award, or promotion, or anything else that someone else has. You seem to be oblivious of all of that, and that makes this woman envy you all the more."

My friend was totally bewildered. "What can I do about it?"

I said, "Absolutely nothing."

I wonder which person in this story you most closely relate to. I wonder if you think I was exaggerating when I talked about envy. As a pastor, I've come to think envy is the most widespread sin of all. Almost all of us look at one another and think, "If only I had her looks, or his brains, or her children, or his wife, or her job, or his house, or her poise, or his charm, or her courage, or his faith." The Gospel of Matthew invites us to read the story of Joseph and Mary through the lens of envy — wanting what you don't have — and jealousy — the desperate anxiety to keep what you do have.

I once invited a group of a dozen people to gather around a Christmas crèche scene. I asked each person to choose one figure out of the stable and explain the choice. One man chose the donkey. He said, "I know I'm not the brightest spark in the box, but I like to stay as close to Jesus as I can." One woman chose Balthasar, the first of the wise men, who brought the gold. She said, "I long to make beautiful things and give them to Jesus, even when he's not in much of a spot to use them. That's the way I worship." Another woman chose one of the shepherds. She said, "I feel I've spent most of my life out on the hillsides. Somehow church has felt like Bethlehem — too cozy and settled for me. My life is wild and outdoors. But every now and again I want to come close to the mystery, like the shepherds did that night, and like I'm doing now."

But then a man of few words and many noble actions stepped up. He picked out Joseph. He had some difficult things to say, so he didn't look at the rest of us while he was speaking — he looked at the small wooden figure in his hand instead. He said, "I've chosen Joseph, because for several years I felt like I was Joseph. My wife became a Christian a long time before me. All the while she kept talking about this 'Holy Spirit' character. She was a whole lot more interested in the Holy Spirit than she was in me, that's for sure. Later, I became a Christian myself, and I sort of understood. But I identify with Joseph. Mary's expecting a baby, and I'm supposed to believe this story about an angel and the Holy Spirit. I've heard of 'He made me do it,' and 'I don't know what came over me,' but this is ridiculous. I spent all those years envying the Holy Spirit, and looking jealously at my wife; and I kind of wonder whether maybe Joseph did too."

Joseph isn't center stage in the Christmas story. Well may he have felt jealous and envious. If you and I manage to conjure up envy in our

153

obscure and ordinary lives, how much more so Joseph, who's up against the Holy Spirit? But I want to look very closely at what he does, because I believe it gives us clues, jealous and envious as we are, on how to model our lives on his.

Matthew gives us the basics of the story without accompanying sentiment. "When his mother Mary had been engaged to Joseph, but before they lived together, she was found to be with child from the Holy Spirit" (Matthew 1:18). Now, an unexpected pregnancy is as deeply confusing today as it was back then. It opens the door to a whole bunch of things that occupy the imagination but about which it's hard to talk with almost anyone, and it trespasses into a host of sensitivities — from those who'd love to be pregnant but aren't, to those whose haste to judgment perhaps masks a more complex history of their own. All of which lead to the hesitant words, "Well . . . I guess it's congratulations!" But add to that the tiny problem that the betrothed husband is quite sure he's not the father of the child, and the death by stoning as the historic penalty for adultery, and this is a social catastrophe on a grand scale. No one has a clue what to say.

When we look at this story, we immediately see it from Mary's point of view. It's terrifying to think of the vulnerability of a teenage girl in a world that focuses so much of its fascination and anger on sexual transgression. Surely it's not just, not right, to make a young girl the focus of a society's pent-up fury.

We're right to see through the eyes of Mary. But I also want us to see through Joseph's eyes. I want to look at three stages in Joseph's response to Mary's startling news. The first thing Matthew tells us is that Joseph is "a righteous man" (Matthew 1:19). In other words, Joseph is a keeper of the law. Anyone concerned for justice has got to have a lot of sympathy for Joseph. He's done the right thing. He's gone through a formal betrothal; he's waited for this young girl of thirteen or fourteen to grow a year older; he's preparing for when she'll come to his home and be his wife. We talk a lot about justice in our society, but this is an illustration of where being just doesn't come close to dealing with the real problem. Justice suggests the young girl should be exposed and humiliated, Joseph be exonerated, and no doubt some financial accommodation made to recognize the damage to his well-being and reputation from this public disgrace.[1] But what if Joseph loved Mary? What if he was jealous for her, not as a piece of property, but as the love of his life? What if he didn't stop loving Mary whatever she might have been up to? No money or public humiliation could give him what he really wanted. What he wanted was her. Justice is an important word in our society. But I wonder how often, as for Joseph, all our striving for it still fails to give us what we really want.

Joseph knows this. And so he seeks a second word. That word is mercy. Matthew tells us Joseph was "unwilling to expose [Mary] to public disgrace," and so he "planned to dismiss her quietly." I don't think we should underestimate the tortured human emotions buried within this simple description. A lot of us quite happily sing songs that say that Jesus took the sins of the whole world on his shoulders on the cross — but we wouldn't dream of shouldering a single sin of someone else's ourselves. This is the hidden, unrewarded part of love — Joseph shoulders the social shame himself, and looks a fool, even though he's done absolutely nothing wrong. I wonder if you know what this feels like. Somebody has hurt you, wounded you, taken advantage of you — but for that person's sake and salvation, you carry the shame on yourself and never breathe a word about it, even when you endure the other's name being praised and honored by all and sundry. The second word Joseph seeks is mercy. For Joseph, mercy outweighs justice.

When you see or know a person facing public disgrace, does your heart jump to justice or to mercy? Do you eagerly devour the headlines that proclaim righteous indignation and groveling humiliation? Do you think, "Look, at least there's someone in the world who's worse than me," or do you think, "It's about time one of those cheats and scoundrels finally got his comeuppance"? I wonder whether the church has got so carried away with righteousness and justice that it's forgotten what Joseph shows it so vividly — that mercy outweighs justice. The truth is that any of us, if everything about our lives was exposed to public scrutiny, would be in for humiliation and disgrace, and begging for mercy and un-

1. R. T. France, *The Gospel of Matthew*, New International Commentary on the New Testament (Grand Rapids: Eerdmans, 2007), 51-52; cf. Douglas R. A. Hare, *Matthew*, Interpretation (Louisville: John Knox, 1993), 9.

derstanding. If only, like Joseph, mercy was our reflex rather than justice and even vengeance. If only we practiced the mercy we beg for.

Joseph takes a third step in his journey. Like any other person in distress, Joseph does the most sensible thing. He goes to sleep. But, like his namesake in the Genesis story, Joseph dreams. And, like the first Joseph, this Joseph trusts his dreams. In this dream the angel of the Lord tells him who the father of Mary's child truly is, and what this new baby will one day be and do. Our first reaction might be to say, "Oh, that's all right then. I was a bit worried for a moment there about how Mary was going to get out of that one and how Joseph was going to endure the exposure and embarrassment, let alone his jealousy over his betrothed and his envy at the true father. But now that I see it's all God's doing, and it's part of a big plan to save everyone and be with them forever, then that's obviously all in order. No problem. Carry on." But don't lose the human part of the story. Joseph has to revise everything he previously thought was normal. It's not like regular life is ever going to return for him. He'll never be a father — always a godfather.

This is the crucial moment in the story for Joseph. This is the crucial moment for us. This is the moment when we have to decide whether we're going to be a righteous person — a person of justice and perhaps even of mercy — or whether we're going to be a Christian. This is the moment when Joseph chooses which story he's going to be in. The jealousy story goes like this: "I want to be the only person in Mary's life — and whoever's at the root of this, I'm going to get him." The justice story goes like this: "I shouldn't have to pay for other people's mistakes — so this time I'm going to make someone else pay." The mercy story goes like this: "We all make mistakes, and I care deeply about Mary, and I've got nothing to gain from making a public spectacle of her — so let's just bring this episode to an end as generously and gently as we can."

But there's another story. It's called the grace story. It goes beyond justice, and beyond mercy. It goes like this: "I've realized that I was never the main character in this story. This was always a story about God and how God was being present and saving his people. It's just that I never realized all that until now. It's amazing. I get to be the godfather to this child whose father is God. I know my life will never be normal again. I know no one will ever fully understand my side of this story. I know Mary is one of the most special people there ever was and I'll always feel small beside her. But I want to live a life open to God's Spirit. I want to live a life that's always ready to be turned upside down by God. I want to be a person at whom others will point and say, 'That's what grace can do.'"

Joseph chose the grace story. The rest of the story is what we call the gospel. We don't all get to choose whether to be the godfather of the Son of God. But we all face moments of truth that challenge us to choose which story we're going to be in. Maybe you're at such a moment right now. Maybe you're facing injustice, illness, disappointment, betrayal, financial crisis, a big decision. Which story is going to be your story? Will it be envy and jealousy — you want what others have, and to keep tight hold of what you have? Will it be righteousness and justice, which do the proper thing, even if it's not going to give you what deep down you really want and need? Will it be mercy, taking on yourself the sins of others and recognizing the fragile humanity in us all?

Or will it possibly, just possibly, be grace — grace that lets God take over your story, grace that makes you realize you were always a small part in a story that was truly about God, grace that melts envy and heals jealousy and transcends justice and exudes mercy, grace that turns your whole life into worship of the God revealed in Jesus?

Joseph chose grace, and the rest of the story is what we call gospel. Now it's your turn.

Can These Dry Bones Live?

Some while ago I saw a picture of my own skull. Every now and again a physician decides he or she needs a new photograph for your file, so the doctor does a CT scan on you. And then you glance over at the screen — and there it is, your very own skull, ugly as hell. You start by thinking it's an idle thing, just a picture. But then you realize, "That's not a thing; it's me! It's a truer picture of me than any smiling photograph." And it stares at you, as if to say, "One day you'll be pared down to this; I'm what you really are, under the skin."

I wonder how you'd feel, coming face-to-face with your own skull.

It makes you shudder. It makes you protest and say, "That's not me — my life has texture, and tenderness, and beauty, and relationship, and sound, and flesh." But the skull says back, "Not for long." And you wonder if you hear a little chuckle.

This is what Ezekiel wants us to face up to. The prophet Ezekiel has a vision in which God shows him how things are and talks to him. The setting is a valley. Have you ever stood at the bottom of a deep ravine, and looked up at the cliffs on either side, high above, in front and behind, and thought, "There's no way out of here"? In chapter 37, Ezekiel's thinking the same thing. "There's no way out of here. I'm in the valley. The valley of death. There are bones everywhere. This is the wreckage of the once mighty people of Israel" (Ezekiel 37:1-14).

At the Battle of Balaclava, in 1854, during the Crimean War, the six hundred members of the Light Brigade mounted a cavalry charge into a precipitous valley. There was only one problem. The valley was over-looked on three sides by enemy guns. It was a catastrophic mistake. What ensued was a grotesque and wholesale massacre. Alfred Tennyson described the scene in these words:

> Theirs not to reason why,
> Theirs but to do and die:
> Into the valley of Death
>   Rode the six hundred.
> Cannon to right of them,
> Cannon to left of them,
> Cannon in front of them
>   Volleyed and thundered;
> Stormed at with shot and shell,
> Boldly they rode and well,
> Into the jaws of Death,
> Into the mouth of Hell
>   Rode the six hundred.[2]

2. Alfred Lord Tennyson, "The Charge of the Light Brigade," in *The Oxford Anthology of English Poetry*, vol. 2, *Blake to Heaney* (Oxford: Oxford University Press, 1986), 392.

Ezekiel is transported into the valley of horror, into the jaws of death. But it's even more chilling, because the bones he sees there are *dry*. That means they've been there a while. Israel's dead; it's been dead for a long time; and there's no escape. That's what the valley of the dry bones means. And God asks Ezekiel an absurd question — a question that sums up the Old Testament, the story of the heart of God being yoked to the children of Israel, and the folly of those children and the breaking of that heart. This is the question: "Can these bones live?" (Ezekiel 37:3). Israel's bones. Humanity's bones. Creation's bones. Your bones. This is the knife-edge question at the heart of the Bible: "Can these dry bones live?"

The 2004 Swedish film *As It Is in Heaven* portrays a gifted orchestral conductor named Daniel.[3] Bullied at his elementary school in northern Sweden, Daniel blossoms in adolescence as a famous and acclaimed musical protégé. But his adult professional career becomes hugely demanding, and he develops debilitating stress-related nasal hemorrhages, resulting in a heart attack on stage while in his thirties. Forced to retire, he buys the old elementary school in his native village in snowy northern Sweden, and takes up a simple life. He eavesdrops on the local church choir rehearsal, and finds himself persuaded into becoming their conductor.

In no time his genius galvanizes the choir, and he seeks to give them a whole new outlook on music and on life. At the same time, the members of the choir, as they begin to dream, expose all their fragilities. One is enraged by a lifetime of being teased about his weight. Another can't find a love with her husband that transcends his inhibitions. A middle-aged man finds that perfectionism cripples his ability to relate to others. A young woman is left heartbroken following a two-year romance with a man she discovers is already married. An innocent boy fails to understand why his learning disability means he can't join the choir. And one woman with an angel's voice has a husband who beats her brutally.

The violent husband, Conny, turns out to be the same bully who

---

3. *As It Is in Heaven*, originally released as *Så som i himmelen*, directed by Kay Pollak (Lorber Films, 2004).

tortured Daniel when they were both growing up. In his jealousy of what's happening to his wife, Conny tries to drown Daniel. Meanwhile Stig, the local Lutheran pastor, is equally enraged by the charismatic conductor, and closes down the church choir – only for its members as one body to march down the street to Daniel's house and reinvent themselves as Daniel's choir.

Daniel believes music opens people's hearts. He's alarmed when the choir enters a major international competition at Innsbruck in Austria, because he believes music isn't about winners and losers. But he can see how the prospect inspires the singers, so eventually he agrees to the long journey. He teaches each of the choristers to sing from his or her soul in a way the judges will never have heard before. In Innsbruck, just before the performance, Daniel has another heart attack and hemorrhage. The choristers, unaware of where he is, carry on without their conductor, singing wordless music from the depths of their being and electrifying the whole auditorium. Judges, other choristers, audience, and everyone present are on their feet, joining in and applauding wildly. Daniel hears the theater erupt with joy as he dies, alone, in a rest room below.

The story displays how dry bones live. The Swedish village is a valley of dry bones. Each member of the choir is a fragile mass of washed-up humanity. Daniel is exhausted, body and soul, a valley of dry bones all in himself. This isn't a story of a village or a choir or a conductor coming *back* to life. This is about the infusion and discovery of life that was never there before. The song the choir sings at the Austrian festival is a kind of music no one, not they themselves, not Daniel, not the audience or judges, had ever previously heard. The iron grip of the violent Conny and the small-minded Stig had impoverished the village for as long as anyone could remember. Now the people had a song in their soul, and that song brought their bodies to life. The dry bones at first clumsily banged against one another; but gradually they found their sinews and muscles and cartilage and flesh and skin and worked out how to live like never before.

Look at yourself. Is what you see a valley of dry bones? Are parts of you dry – really dry, neglected, abandoned, left for dead? Is your heart a place of carnage and destruction, a valley that's given up reasoning why, but just riding on to do and die, because it's the path of least resistance, because that's what keeps the peace, because you haven't got the strength to imagine anything beyond the valley? Have you given up believing God will ever bring you to life?

Perhaps you have friends, associates, colleagues, peers, like the choristers in the movie had one another. But maybe, like the choir, you're only living a half-life with one another. Maybe you're a singer without a song, with tired lungs and a weary throat, without trust in those around you, or hope in yourself, or true direction to look up to.

The movie disturbs us. If we're going to allow ourselves to become such a choir, to be galvanized, transformed, harmonized, and converted, we're going to face others' scorn, envy, and violence, we're going to have to confront our fears and our enemies, we're going to be launched on a journey whose final destination we don't know and can't control. If we say no to the siren call of the choir, the film gives us two options: we can try to suppress it by machination and manipulation, like the pastor, or we can try to destroy it by aggression and intimidation, like the abusive husband. In one of the movie's defining moments, the furious husband comes to reclaim his terrified wife from a rehearsal and stop her from getting on the bus to Austria, only to find that the choir closes around and enfolds her, leaving him powerless and speechless. The dry bones have found their muscle.

But before we condemn the husband and the pastor, let's recognize that what they're saying is, "Leave those dry bones right where they are." This is a life-or-death struggle, fought from the gut. Joining this choir is a decision made at the core of our being, and it's bound to shake each of us in ways that make our bones chatter and shiver and rattle. Every member of the choir faces three questions. (1) Am I prepared, at this weary, tired, and worn-out moment in my life, to discover a new way of singing, to learn a new song, to let this conductor into my heart, to let music into the depths of my being? (2) Am I prepared to relearn the disciplines of working together; to face and name the limitations and rejections and profound anger I see in the other choristers, and they see in me; to participate in making something beautiful not according to the textbook but out of the ugly dry bones that lie in my valley and theirs? And (3) Am I prepared to face the embarrassment, hostility, failure, frustration, and anxiety all of this is going to provoke?

In John 11 when Jesus gets the news that Lazarus is dead, he says, "Let us go to Judea again" (John 11:7). The disciples say, "But Judea's full of people who want to kill you." Let's call them Romans and religious leaders — let's call them Conny the husband and Stig the pastor. Thomas is the only one who realizes what Jesus is really saying to the disciples. Thomas knows that the disciples have to ask themselves the same questions in the face of Jesus that the choristers have to ask themselves in the face of Daniel, their conductor. Can I learn a new song? Can I face the truth about myself and my companions? Can I face the hostility this is going to provoke in others? Thomas knows his answer. He declares, "Let us also go, that we may die with him" (John 11:16).

And quickly we realize that the story of Daniel and the choir is the story of Jesus and the disciples. The conductor harmonizes a motley crowd of fragile failures into something beautiful and courageous and inspiring. So does Jesus. Daniel faces conflict and opposition, but brings forgiveness and healing. So does Jesus. At Innsbruck, Daniel goes back to the concert auditorium, the place of danger he knows so well and fears so deeply because it gave him a heart attack last time he was there. Innsbruck is Daniel's Jerusalem. The members of the choir have no idea what going to Innsbruck really represents for him. But Daniel goes to Innsbruck and gladly lays down his life so the dry bones of the choir may be infused with the glorious new music of the Spirit. It's the story of Jesus translated into Swedish.

At this point everything fuses into one picture. We've witnessed that the story of Ezekiel and the valley of the dry bones is the story of the Old Testament, because it's about whether God can make the dead Israel live again. We've discovered that the Swedish story of Daniel and the choir is the story of Ezekiel and the dry bones, because it's about how dry bones, through the music of the Spirit, come slowly, clumsily, but ultimately thrillingly to life. We've realized that the story of the Swedish choir is the story of Jesus and the disciples, because they're both about the conductor so loving the choir that he goes to the place of greatest danger and lays down his life to let loose the Spirit of new music and new joy that transfigures not just them but the whole world.

Now, finally, we can see what this all means: the story of Ezekiel and the valley of the dry bones is the story not just of the Old Testament but also of the New, because Jesus is the one who finally enters the deepest valley, and prophesies to our bodies and our spirits with his body and his Spirit, and makes these bones shake and rattle and roll. And this same question, the question at the heart of the Old Testament and the New Testament, is the question facing us today more than any other. Can these dry bones live?

Look at your life. Look at that valley of dry bones. Feel the hand of the Lord come upon you. Hear the Spirit of the Lord whisper in your ear. Listen to this question the Lord is asking you: "Beloved child, can these dry bones live?" Recognize in yourself the violent Conny and the manipulative Stig that make you shrug your shoulders and say, "I dunno. Don't ask *me*." Look at your life again. Are you looking at a valley of dry bones? Have you been dragging this sack of dry bones through the valley for longer than you can remember? Why pretend any longer?

Ask yourself these three questions:

Am I truly willing to learn new music?
Am I willing to let the Spirit make music out of my dry, fragile flesh?
Am I willing to face scorn and shame as I start to sing this new song?

Just as the Lord whispered to Ezekiel, he's whispering to you: "I am going to open your grave, and bring you up from your grave. I will put my spirit within you, and you shall live."

Maybe it's time to join that choir.

The Power of Saying Thank You

One of the things I like best about living in America, or at least North Carolina, is that almost everyone is up for a conversation, almost all the time. I'm walking down the street, or to my office, and the stranger I walk past says, "Hi, how are ya?" I've learned that the correct answer is, "I'm good, how are you?" After that the conversation can go off in any number of directions, or it can simply stop with a cheerful sense of well-being. In England it doesn't work like that. Instead, you say, with your mouth half shut, "Mor*ning*." To which there are two answers. You can either say, "Nice day for it." Or you can say, "Shocking weather again." Usually you give the second reply and the conversation's over.

Even better than greeting is the American way of saying thank you. Here whenever one says "Thank you," there's always a reply, "You're welcome" — which turns a simple social grace into a real relationship, a real act of shared pleasure and hospitality. I've discovered there are two ways of saying "You're welcome." If you stress the first word and almost sing the second word, there's a hint of affectionate criticism, as if to say, "Didn't you realize I loved you?": "*You're* welcome." If, on the other hand, you really stress the second word, that means you want the gesture to be taken as the beginning of a friendship, or at least as a simple expression of the joy of finding that one has been genuinely helpful: "You're <u>wel</u>come." Again, in England, we almost always get this wrong. When someone says thank you, the best we can manage in reply is, "Don't mention it" — which is really an outright criticism making the person wonder whether to ever say thank you again; or, "The pleasure is all mine" — which is also a correction and leaves you feeling pretty miserable; or "Not at all" — which is the worst of the lot because it suggests the person saying thank you is just plain wrong.

I want to suggest that "thank you" is one of the most significant and powerful things one can say. Of course, the marketing experts already know this. Browse a bookshelf of business best sellers and you'll find books telling you that a timely thank you letter is the perfect way to get ahead and influence people, to leave a good impression and acquire a new client. True as this may be, I'm not talking about this kind of cynical manipulation. I'm talking about what you discover and who you become when you develop the habit of saying thank you.

Luke 17:11-19 starts out looking like a story about healing. Ten lepers approach Jesus, saying, "Jesus, Master, have mercy on us!" Jesus sends them to the priests, and as they go they are made clean. Up to this point in the story we've already learned a lot about healing. We've learned that God in Christ listens to those who call out to him for mercy. We've learned that the way to respond to Jesus and to find healing is simple obedience.

The same things are true in the story of Naaman's healing by the prophet Elisha in 2 Kings 5. Naaman, the commander of the army of the king of Aram, shows up at Elisha's house hoping to be cured of his leprosy. Naaman is outraged that Elisha doesn't put on a big show but instead simply asks him to wash seven times in the river Jordan. But then Naaman's servants utter some of the most poignant words about discipleship in all of Scripture: "If the prophet had commanded you to do something difficult, would you not have done it? How much more, when all he said to you was, 'Wash, and be clean'?" (2 Kings 5:13). The small fidelities are sometimes more significant than the grand gestures. Healing doesn't have to be difficult. Sometimes it's just about obedience. We've also learned that healing sometimes takes time. In Luke's story about the healing of the lepers, Jesus is on the borderlands of Galilee and Samaria, and he tells the lepers to go and see the priests, who almost all lived down near Jerusalem. That's a long journey. It says they were healed on the way, not straightaway.

So we've already learned a lot about healing by the time we get to the second part of the story: that only one of the lepers, a Samaritan, comes back to say thank you. When he does, Jesus tells him, "Your faith has made you well" – or, "your faith has saved you" (Luke 17:19). This part of the story tells us one more thing about healing – there's a difference between healing and salvation. All ten of the lepers are healed; only one of them is saved. All ten of the lepers get to live their lives free from social stigma, discrimination, and exclusion. Only one of them gets to enter the company of Jesus. For nine of the lepers Jesus is a means to an end. For only one of them is Jesus an end in himself. And the key to the difference between that one leper and the other nine lies in those two simple words: thank you.

By saying thank you, that one leper was saying, "This is not fundamentally a story about me; this is fundamentally a story about God. I have been healed not because I trained, or I researched, or I dieted, or even because I prayed; I have been healed because God chose to reveal his power in me." Remember Jesus' words about the man born blind in

John 9: "[This man] was born blind so that God's works might be revealed in him" — in other words, so that God's glory could be revealed in him (John 9:3). When we are reflecting on our lives — past, present, or future — do we judge them on how much we have achieved, how many people love us, or how much stuff we possess? Or do we judge our lives on whether they are the kinds of lives in which the glory of God has been revealed? The curious thing is that the glory of God isn't merely or even mostly revealed in lives of accomplishment and success. The glory of God tends mostly to be revealed in lives that are broken and have big holes in them. As one contemporary songwriter puts it, "There is a crack in everything, that's how the light gets in."[4] So when we say thank you to God, it isn't something we do when we've been given lots of success, lots of love, or lots of stuff; it's to recognize that we have been given lives in which the glory of God can be revealed. The Samaritan leper had such a life. So can we.

And if we have been given lives in which the glory of God can be revealed, that means we have been given a part to play in God's story. Just imagine the Samaritan leper waking up one morning and being told, "Good news! Jesus is coming by here later and if you play your cards right, you could end up appearing in the Gospel of Luke and being talked about by Christians thousands of years from now and living with God forever." That's quite a wake-up call. But just think for a moment. How is it different from the wake-up call you and I get every single day? You and I have been invited into this story too. You and I have lives in which the glory of God can be revealed, any day. And the way to play your cards right and get to be part of the story is quite simple, simpler even than Naaman's (eventual) response to Elisha. It's to praise God and say thank you. When we praise God and say thank you, we recognize that life may not have been this way at all. It may have been very different. God might not have created the world. God might not have created human beings. God might not have come in Jesus and saved us from our sins. God might not have sent his Holy Spirit to empower the church. God might not have created you and me. It might all

---

4. Leonard Cohen, "Anthem," from the album *The Future*, Columbia Records, 1992.

have been a very different story. There might not have been a place for you. There might not have been a place for any of us. And the way we recognize that things might have been very different lies in saying those two words: thank you.

Of course, we tend to forget the big picture and focus on the minor details. We take the world and our existence, even Jesus, for granted, and we concentrate on the parts that seem to go wrong. We discover our family isn't as happy or straightforward as other families, and we look for someone to blame, one of our parents perhaps. We find ourselves isolated from the way other people are woven into God's story, and so we take to imagining that we have a level of pain or hurt that is so much greater than anyone else's, and until that pain is heard and listened to and understood and affirmed, we refuse to trust or engage or enjoy the bigger story at all. To a life that is mired in resentment, gratitude is a stranger. But the only medicine for a life turned in on itself is rediscovering the art of saying thank you.

When he said thank you, the Samaritan leper entered a whole new community. Luke's Gospel is all about God bringing his people out of the exile of political oppression, physical sickness, spiritual blindness, and communal exclusion by forming a new community around the crucified and risen Jesus. Four times in Luke's Gospel Jesus says the words "Your faith has made you well."[5] The first is to the woman in the house of Simon the Pharisee, whom everyone knew to be a sinner (Luke 7:50). The second is to the woman with the twelve years of hemorrhages (8:48). The third is to the Samaritan leper (17:19), and the fourth is to a blind beggar (18:42). In other words, Jesus makes a new community out of the sinner, the sick, the second-class, the disabled, the foreigner, and the socially excluded. And they are all astonished and joyful and full of thanks for being made part of God's story in Jesus. They turn out to be people in whom the glory of God is revealed.

You can become one of those people by learning to say the words

---

5. The Greek phrase is the same in all four occurrences (ἡ πίστις σου σέσωκέν σε), but the NRSV translates two as "Your faith has saved you" and the other two as "Your faith has made you well."

"thank you." It's an interesting company to join of course. Our society typically expends a lot of energy to stay away from the sinner, the sick, the second-class, the disabled, the foreigner, and the socially excluded. But that's certainly not the reason you come to church. You come to church to join the company of people in whom the glory of God is revealed. And it turns out that first among them are the sinner, the sick, the second-class, the disabled, the foreigner, and the socially excluded. It's a wonderful company, so long as one never makes the mistake of thinking it's a limited company. And it's a company you enter when you say thank you.

When you say thank you to the person who serves you food, to the person who holds the door open for you, to the person who notices you're limping, to the person who handles your groceries through the checkout line, in this small way you're recognizing that, like God, this person has made you a part of a bigger story, a story in which people are overwhelmed not by what they've suffered but by what they've received. To say thank you is to recognize your dependence on another person, to say "You make my life possible." And to say thank you is slowly, gradually, to become the most powerful person in the world, the person who is so filled with awe and wonder with the life and grace he or she has been given by God that no suffering or cruelty or manipulation or misunderstanding or disease or tragedy can break that person's spirit. The most powerful person in the world is the one who in the face of horror and scarcity can only see beyond it to glory and abundance. Nothing can destroy such a person.

Such a person was Martin Rinkart. He became pastor in the small German town of Eilenberg in 1618, just as the slaughter and chaos of the Thirty Years' War were beginning. This was a period so catastrophic that the population of Germany fell by around a third over thirty years. Eilenberg was a walled city. It became a crowded haven for political and military refugees. This left the city vulnerable to disease and famine. In 1637 there was terrible plague. Martin Rinkart was the only pastor remaining in Eilenberg. He conducted 4,000 funerals in that year, including up to 50 funerals a day. By the time the signs of peace began to appear and the tide of slaughter, famine, and plague began to recede in the 1640s, Martin Rinkart had lost half his household, including his wife, and could have been forgiven for feeling resentful, angry, and unforgiving. But instead he sat down and wrote one of the most famous hymns in the German language, *Nun danket alle Gott*, which we know in English as "Now Thank We All Our God." Viewing the wreckage of war, and the folly of his fellow human beings, he nonetheless still saw the ultimate grace of God, which had given him life, had given him Jesus, had given him hope, had given him unlikely friends, and still gave him faith. Like Naaman, he did the simple thing and just said thank you. It's difficult to imagine what it might have meant for Martin Rinkart to be healed. But it's hard to doubt that he was saved. And in writing this hymn he displayed the same lesson discovered by Naaman the Syrian and the Samaritan leper: the power of saying thank you.

Martin Rinkart was a person in whom the glory of God was revealed. It was revealed through his ability and willingness, even amid untold suffering, to say thank you to the God of wonder and glory, who created us all, who suffers in our suffering, and who alone can raise us to new life. May we too learn to say thank you, in great ways and small, and may we too become people in whom the glory of God is revealed.

Like the Angels

The actor Tom Baker tells the story of how he was once at a party. He was being his gregarious self, regaling anyone who'd listen with tales from his days on stage, in the movies, and especially on TV. He felt a tap on his shoulder, and turned around to see a woman about his own age whom he vaguely recognized. Her eyes contained a depth of emotion he couldn't immediately account for. She said, "Tom!" He paused, feeling something deep and personal was required of him — but not able to tell quite what. He replied, searching the outer reaches of his thespian memory, "Were we *in* something together?" The woman said, "We used to be married."

It's easy to dismiss this story as the far-fetched anecdote of a celebrity living a Bohemian lifestyle. But if we let it pierce our conscience for a moment, we quickly become deeply uncomfortable. Uncomfortable, because it portrays perhaps our worst nightmare about marriage. Sure, violent marriages are a living hell for those many who endure them. Sure, betrayal is devastating. Sure, spouses and former spouses can make us unspeakably angry, and it's possible to build up an unassailable wall of resentment at how it seems we shape our whole life to accommodate or advance our spouse's well-being or reputation. But Tom Baker's story displays an even greater nightmare: imagine giving your body and soul to another person, showing that person the heart of your being and walking beside him or her in sunshine and rain – and then finding some years later that the person has completely forgotten you. You had become utterly invisible to your former spouse. You didn't even register in his or her social memory. It's hard to think of a more deflating experience, not just for the ego, but for one's whole trust in the power of human relationship.

If you think Tom Baker is too upsetting to your sense of love and permanence and real relationship, you might not want to pay too much attention to Jesus. Like Tom Baker, in Luke 20 Jesus is in a busy place, surrounded by people, in this case in the Jerusalem temple; and like Tom Baker's former wife, the Sadducees tap Jesus on the shoulder and say something that's supposed to knock him sideways (Luke 20:27-38). The two things you need to know about the Sadducees are that they only recognized the first five books of the Bible and they didn't believe in the resurrection of the dead, which they took to be a doctrine revealed only by later writings. So they try to expose Jesus' lack of scriptural faithfulness by showing the absurdity of belief in life after death. If a woman marries a man, they propose, and after his death marries his brother, and on and on as many as seven times, which one will she be married to in the resurrection?

What's Jesus going to say? His reply knocks *us* sideways and makes Tom Baker's dialogue with his former wife seem small fry. Why? Because Jesus blows away our conventional notions of both marriage and life after death. First of all he talks about "those who are considered worthy of a place in that age and in the resurrection from the dead" (Luke 20:35). That's a bit of a shock to any who might imagine life after death as some kind of guaranteed shoo-in. Jesus isn't talking about the immortality of the soul. He's talking about God raising people from the dead. But not everybody, apparently. And then look at what he says about them. "Those who are considered worthy of a place in that age and in the resurrection from the dead neither marry nor are given in marriage" (20:35). So, no wedding bells in heaven, then. Jesus cites Moses as his authority about the resurrection, which silences the Sadducees because the passage he refers to lies at the heart of the first five books of the Bible. That's all very well for the Sadducees, but what about us? We've just had our soft-focused ideals about marriage and life after death blown away — and we're supposed to be happy about it? How do Jesus' words qualify as good news?

Let's start by asking, What is marriage for? In the Sadducees' world there is one thing above all else that marriage is for. Marriage is for perpetuating the male line through the controlled production and rearing of male heirs. Marriage has other social purposes. In a patriarchal world marriage protects a woman from isolation, vulnerability, and exploitation in a society in which she can't be an independent earner and property owner. But there's no pretending marriage exists mainly for women in this story of the bride and the seven brothers. She becomes the property of one brother after another, and she's never more than a means to an end, that end being to produce a son.

But Jesus is saying that this isn't what resurrection looks like. Resurrection isn't something we can bring about by conceiving and rearing children and grandchildren. Resurrection is something only God can give, and by giving it, God transforms marriage, because marriage and the bearing of children are no longer necessary for human survival. There is no human survival after death. Instead there are real death and astonishing resurrection. And in every case that resurrection is not our human achievement but the gift of a gracious God. This means women don't exist to bear children. It means children don't exist simply to fulfill the frustrated dreams and projections of their thwarted parents. It means human beings don't exist simply to propagate themselves.

This is good news because it is news of liberation. Women's lives need no longer be defined by their degree of usefulness to men. Having children becomes a vocation for some, rather than an obligation or a necessity for everyone.

Throughout the history of the church, marriage has always been a social reality that church authorities have to different degrees sought to bless, commend, encourage, or control. In recent generations a number of factors have clustered together to change the context of marriage considerably. There was a time when people lived much shorter lives, and a long marriage was twenty or twenty-five years. There was a time when one pregnancy in five could end in the mother's death. There was a time when sexual relations led sooner or later to the conception of children, and so sex before or outside marriage was dangerous and socially subversive. There was a time when no woman could contemplate owning property or having an independent life or career. There was a time when the household was the primary center of economic activity and the welfare of the vulnerable. These things cemented marriages, for good or ill.

Those times are largely gone in the West. And few genuinely lament their passing. But that means the social and cultural scaffolding that used to support marriage has been more or less dismantled. When a friend calls you up and says, "You know, Sandy and I have been going through a rough time, and we're living apart just now," of course you say the usual things like, "I'm very sorry," and "You must both be really hurting right now," and "I guess this has been coming for a long time and none of us ever realized it," and "Thank you for having the courage to call me up and tell me," and "Is there anything I can do to help?" But do you always hope and earnestly pray that they will find a way to get back together? I'm not sure that you always do. Friends and advisers tend to polarize between the duty-bound and idealistic, who say marriage is for life and once you're one flesh you can't ever become two again, and the pragmatic and protective, for whom it's all about the well-being of children and the cost of therapy and the construction of support networks. When a friend says to us, "I'm sorry. I've tried, really I have, but I just can't do it anymore," do we really have it in us to say, "Yes, you can"? More often than not, I rather doubt it.

Christians in every state of life — single, married, separated, divorced, married again, lay, monastic, ordained — are struggling to come to terms with today's reality that marriage isn't the necessity it once was, and so it has to be a constant choice. Couples need to make a constant choice to stay married, and to foster the conditions that help them thrive in marriage, rather than expect social gravity to do it for them. We live in a different era from that of the Sadducees, and the bride with the seven brothers.

And yet the curious thing is that marriage has just as powerful a hold on our imaginations as ever. It turns out there *is* a contemporary analogy through which Jesus' words speak as powerfully today as they did to the Sadducees. The Sadducees had constructed a world where having heirs meant you could transcend your own mortality and attain a kind of life after death. We have constructed a not wholly different world. We've made a world where we believe that if you wrap up all your feelings and desires and longings and joys and ecstasies into one yearning and project it all upon one person, you can break through to a level of human experience that goes beyond the mundane and the mortal and the temporal. That's the epitome of the advertiser's pitch, and the college freshman's dream, and the grandmother's tears at the reception dinner: that somehow a single relationship can break through the fragile, the failed, and the ordinary to a higher plane of perpetual peak experience. It's the closest thing our culture gets to a conception of eternal life. Marriage becomes our passport to eternal life, for different reasons from those of the Sadducees — but to the same extent. It's somehow supposed to take us onto a higher level of existence, emotionally, sexually, relationally. And when we focus all that expectation on one single relationship, it's not altogether surprising that, in a lot of cases, the relationship can't take it. And today, without the buttressing of cultural norms and socioeconomic necessities to hold things together, a lot of people are calling a friend to say, "I'm sorry. Sandy and I aren't going to make it."

Just because the whole of society doesn't come crashing down when a marriage comes to an end, that doesn't mean it's any less devastating for the parties involved. Remember Tom Baker's former wife's reaction when he said, lamely, "Were we in something together?" It's a sense of not just your ego but of everything you dream of and still want to aspire to being utterly crushed. If you focus every emotional atom in your being on one other person and your relationship, divorce is bound to feel like rejection, failure, and the death of hope — or, as one person

173

described it, like being in a car crash every day for two years. But see this: if we invest marriage with all our understandings of eternal life, then its failure literally means the end of the world.

And so hear again Jesus' words, "Those who are considered worthy of a place in that age and in the resurrection from the dead neither marry nor are given in marriage . . . because they are like angels and are children of God." Hear these words for the first time — perhaps the first time ever — as tender and compassionate good news — possibly counterintuitive, but nonetheless genuinely good news. Gently detach from marriage the freight it can't finally bear. Don't expect it to provide you with immortality, either through multiplying descendants or through transcendent emotional experience. Look to God for what only God can give. Only God can give eternal life, only God can give transcendence, only God offers love that lasts forever. Treasure marriage not because it lasts forever — but *precisely because it doesn't*, and so it needs to be cherished and enjoyed and nurtured all the more.

Then, when we've stopped trying to make marriage a route to immortality, we can let it be what it truly can be. When Jesus describes everlasting life in this exchange with the Sadducees, he calls it being present to God. He says Abraham, Isaac, and Jacob are present to God — so they must be living beyond death. Being present has two connotations — it means being in God's presence, and it means existing in the present tense. Both of these apply. That's what eternal life is: being in God's presence, and staying in the present tense — not just a past memory or a future hope.

And that's what marriage can truly be. Marriage means saying to one person, "We are going to be *present* to one another — emotionally, physically, mentally, in sorrow and joy, in sunshine and in rain. We are going to be present even though marriage reveals to us the worst in each other and prevents us from any longer hiding from the worst in ourselves. We together are going to live our lives in *God's* presence, always knowing that each of us belongs fundamentally first and forever to God. We are going to live together in the presence of those God may bring into our lives, as children or friends or dependents. And we are going to try to live in the present *tense* — not nostalgic or bitter or wistful about the past, nor naïve or overinvested or controlling about the future." All these intentions are crystallized in the most important word in the wedding ceremony, "cherish." It's not ecstasy. It's not easy. It's not heaven. But it is a worthy life project. It is a beautiful thing. And it is one significant way in which we can learn to be present to God.

Marriage may often not be heaven. It turns out Jesus says it was never supposed to be. But it can still be a training ground for heaven – a training ground for living life in God's presence, for being in the present tense, all the time. Because this is the gospel. Whatever we are – married, single, single again, married again – God in Jesus taps us, his beloved people, on the shoulder. And we, mystified and vaguely remembering something, mutter in reply, "Were we in something together?" And God, without a trace of self-pity, but with loving eyes, meets us in our failure and feckless forgetfulness. He could say, in lament and bitterness, "We used to be married." But God doesn't say that. Instead, with a twinkle in the eye, God says, "Yes, we *are* in something together. And always will be. Forever."

I May Not Get There with You

The death of Steve Jobs, the man who gave the apple the most attention it's received since the Garden of Eden, and the inventor of sleek devices modeled around the letter *i*, brought renewed attention to a famous commencement address he made about his own illness. The speech included these words: "No one wants to die. Even people who want to go to heaven don't want to die to get there. And yet death is the destination we all share. No one has ever escaped it. And that is as it should be, because Death is very likely the single best invention of Life. It is Life's change agent. It clears out the old to make way for the new."[6]

What makes these words compelling is that the man speaking them found a technological solution to almost everything one can imagine, and did a corporate resurrection by becoming CEO of a company that ousted him only a few years before – and here he is in the

6. Steve Jobs, Stanford commencement address, June 12, 2005. Full text available at http://news.stanford.edu/news/2005/june15/jobs-061505.html.

role of dispenser of wisdom, appearing to say that even death can be managed if you go about it the right way. He's so engaging, and he's touching on such a raw nerve, that you desperately want to believe him. And you almost do. This is a man who's found a gadget to fix everything. Maybe, just maybe, he's offering us the greatest gadget of them all. Maybe it's called the iDeath.

But if you've lived through real bereavement and profound loss, I suspect you won't be taken in. Because when you've truly loved someone, and that person is uprooted from existence, and you're left with a gaping hole and an aching soul, there's no wise words or helpful gadgets that can replace the lifeblood you shared or assuage the dizzying dismay of grief. It's like having your lungs taken out so you can't breathe, or your stomach removed so you can't eat. It's as if a bomb blast had created a huge crater in your midriff. This is how W. H. Auden describes the harrowing emptiness of losing the companion he'd shaped his life around.

> He was my North, my South, my East and West,
> My working week and my Sunday rest,
> My noon, my midnight, my talk, my song;
> I thought that love would last for ever: I was wrong.[7]

To be a Christian and to contemplate death is to locate yourself somewhere in the yawning gap between Steve Jobs and W. H. Auden. Auden's words are cathartic because they plead that death empties life of all meaning, and they furiously and bitterly throw themselves against the cruel doors of death like a storm wave crashing relentlessly, savagely, but fruitlessly against a seawall. And yet Auden's words are cleansing, because he pushes us to restore a sense of balance. It's as if he makes death the only thing he knows, and subjects all other truth to merciless dismemberment in the face of mortality. Sure, death is real, we want to reply: but death isn't all of reality, and it doesn't obliterate all that is good and true.

7. W. H. Auden, "Stop All the Clocks," in *The English Auden* (London: Faber and Faber, 1977), 163.

Meanwhile there's something hubristically grating about Steve Jobs's brisk and businesslike approach to death that again makes us look for a sense of balance and yearn for Auden's melancholy. And yet surely Jobs is right at least in this, that maybe death, while sad, is yet not altogether bad. Maybe most of the things that are truly good about life wouldn't be so good if there were no sense of limitation to make them so rare and precious.

The death of a Christian is never *just* a tragedy, because there's always that element of hope tucked within it. And yet it *is* always a tragedy, and no amount of faith and trust and wise words and consoling gestures can take away feelings of aching loss and blinding grief. It's the same when we contemplate our own death. We approach death with fear and sometimes panicked resistance, a mixture of denial and paralysis — all of which are features of tragedy. But we also approach death with hope, with the sense that this life has been the foretaste for the real thing yet to come, with the anticipation of having finished the appetizer and preparing our palates for the main dish, with the trust that the God who had the ingenuity to bring about this present existence must have something pretty special in store for the next. Tragedy and hope. Cross and resurrection. This is how we face death.

Deuteronomy chapter 34 completes the Torah, the first five books of the Bible, with the death of Moses inches short of Israel's long-awaited entry into the Promised Land. Let's see what wisdom we can discover from Moses as he faces up to the tragedy and hope of his own death. Moses' achievements are beyond comparison. Here is the man who went to Pharaoh and said, "Let my people go," and when Pharaoh said no, he brought his people out of slavery, took them across the Red Sea, led them in peril and strife through the wilderness, and received the covenant from God at Mount Sinai. Here is the man who taught his people, interceded on their behalf, was furious with them and berated them, forgave them and loved them until the end. The book of Deuteronomy espouses a simple philosophy based around a straightforward equation: if you keep my commandments, you'll live long in the land I am giving you. It's confident that good deeds bring healthy rewards. And so it's constantly struggling with one great mystery: How come Moses, who had done such great and mighty things, doesn't get to enter the Promised Land?

Deuteronomy tries several times in different ways to make sense of why Moses doesn't get to lead his people into the Promised Land. It's not at all clear whether the reason is that Moses is being punished for the sin of his people or whether he's being denied entry to the land on his own account. The point for us is, every death is like this. Every death leaves us with questions about how things might have been different or why life is so ironic and unfair. Every death is a failure, because no life attains the kind of completeness we long for and find truly satisfying, and every death leaves unfinished business. If we suffer, it's seldom entirely clear if it's because of someone else's failure, because of our own, or because that's just life and there is no discernible reason. We're bound to struggle for a meaning in our failures and disappointments and sufferings, but like Deuteronomy, our certainty that there must be a reason doesn't mean we're going to find one.

Here are some famous words of a man torn between tragedy and hope, speaking on the night before his own death. "Like anybody, I would like to live a long life. Longevity has its place. But I'm not concerned about that now. I just want to do God's will. And he's allowed me to go up to the mountain. And I've looked over. And I've seen the Promised Land. I may not get there with you. But I want you to know tonight, that we, as a people, will get to the Promised Land!"[8] Those words were spoken by Martin Luther King Jr., in Memphis, Tennessee, hours before his life was ended by a bullet to the cheek. King identifies with Moses. They both go to the mountaintop. They both look over into the abundant land of Gilead and Dan and Manasseh and Jericho — the land of milk and honey. They both trust that their descendants will enjoy that land. But neither of them gets there himself. They're both poised between tragedy and hope.

What is our hope in the face of death? The language of hope is especially difficult to articulate today. This is because educated Western cultures are infused with several trends that dismantle the notion of hope. There's a philosophical skepticism that we can ever know any-

8. Martin Luther King Jr., "I've Been to the Mountaintop" (speech at Bishop Charles Mason Temple, April 3, 1968). Full text available at http://mlk-kpp01.stanford.edu/index.php/encyclopedia/documentsentry/ive_been_to_the_mountaintop/.

thing for certain. There's a sociological suspicion that any widespread opinion is likely to be a way for powerful voices to impose their perspective on vulnerable minorities. There's a cultural relativism that's reluctant to suggest any one conviction is better than any other. And there's a political pragmatism that's almost wholly concerned with achieving a limited set of this-worldly common goals. These forces are each healthy in their own way, but together they constitute a corrosive force that makes it very hard to envisage a shared human hope, and instead limits our imagination to each person trying to construct a life that can only be measured in its quantity of activity and its degree of experiential satisfaction.

In such a culture, two possible forms of hope present themselves. The first is to conform to the consensus that experiential satisfaction is all there is to hope for. Hope becomes the fulfillment of desire — for visible, tangible possession, for deep, evocative feeling, and for abiding, gratifying comfort. The trouble is, death utterly destroys all these hopes. So the only remedy is to make these desires and their fulfillment so all-consuming that we're able to forget or at least ignore death until the last possible moment. That's why funerals can be so bewildering today. We've evacuated the language of mortality from our shared vocabulary, such that death has become a baffling anomaly.

The second form of hope is to displace a vision for one's own survival and diffuse it into the well-being of all. This is what soldiers do in laying down their lives for their country or for its perception of the greater good. This is what victims' families do when they express an aspiration that the lessons learned from their loved one's death will alleviate suffering or prevent accidents or eliminate malpractice and thus enhance the lives of those to come. Even if most of us live by the privatized experiential satisfaction criteria, when it comes to public statements, this is the language we tend to adopt. One wit noted, "We're always doing things for posterity, but what has posterity ever done for us?"[9]

9. The saying is typically attributed to Groucho Marx, and traced back to Joseph Addison, who wrote, "We are always doing something for posterity, but I would fain see posterity do something for us." See Gillian Beer, "Imagining Posterity, Then and Now," *International Literary Quarterly* 5 (November 2008); available at http://interlitq.org/issue5/gillian_beer/job.php.

There's a significant point here, which exposes the false pride of our attempts to leave a mark on the world. Percy Shelley characterizes this pitiful self-importance in his poem "Ozymandias," where he describes a traveler coming upon a set of vast ruins lying in a windswept desert. On the ruins there's an inscription exhorting the reader to look on these mighty works and despair, for this is surely the mark of the king of kings. And yet here they are now, great trunkless legs of stone, adrift in the trackless desert, a withering symbol of human vainglory.[10] Those shapeless, amorphous, devouring sands are a telling metaphor for the ultimate destiny of a life without God.

Perhaps most of us fuse these two forms of hope, seeking in work, and family, and a network of friendships some kind of a blend of the experiential satisfaction of the self and the sense of contributing to a greater and one-day-achievable social good. But is this real hope? Is this really much more than an effort of will and imagination and a collective determination to make human endeavor attain a permanence it can never realize? Haven't you walked away from many a memorial service thinking, deep down, "That was all very well, but was it really much more than deeply felt and eloquently expressed rage against the dying of the light?" Doesn't our coldhearted truthful sobriety realize that the candle burned out long ago, and the legend pretty soon will?

There is no hope outside God. That's a bleak realization. But flip the coin over, and we find that there is limitless hope *in* God. Truly limitless. Literally infinite. How much time and thought and effort and energy we expend trying to find hope elsewhere! But there is none. When we become a Christian we enter a realm of boundless hope in God. But there's no going back. Leave that realm, and we realize how empty and fabricated and sentimental and hubristic and futile all other grounds for hope are. There's nowhere else to go. Nowhere else, that is, to find hope. The cross of Christ tells us that our hope is not without tragedy, not without indescribable cost to God. And many of our lives confirm it. But the resurrection of Christ promises us that out of fear and suffering and tragedy and death arises never-ending, overwhelm-

---

10. Percy Shelley, "Ozymandias," in *Percy Bysshe Shelley: The Major Works*, ed. Zachary Leader and Michael O'Neill (Oxford: Oxford University Press, 2003), 198.

ing, beyond-describing, ever-flowing life in God. The invitation of hope is, Are you ready to enter this life at your moment of death? The challenge of hope is, If so, *why not start living it now?*

I want to describe two men who together give us a picture of the cross and resurrection, the tragedy and the hope, of facing death in God. Poet and hymn writer Joachim Neander was a seventeenth-century German Calvinist. Like Moses and Martin Luther King Jr., he stood at the edge of his own death, looked into the unknown, and chose to hope in God. At the tender age of thirty, just before he died from tuberculosis, Neander wrote these words: "All my hope on God is founded;/He doth still my trust renew,/me through change and chance He guideth,/only good and only true./God unknown, He alone/calls my heart to be His own."[11]

Two hundred fifty years later, Neander's hymn was sent to the famous composer Herbert Howells. Howells was deep in grief after the death from spinal meningitis of his nine-year-old son Michael. Legend has it that Howells received the hymn text at breakfast time and didn't move from his chair until he'd composed the tune. Howells was profoundly moved by what these words said about the interplay of tragedy and hope, of cross and resurrection, in the face of death. He was overwhelmed by how these words described his grief and yet faith in the face of the death of his son. And so, looking into the unknown, like Moses on the mountaintop, in gratitude to the faithfulness of Joachim Neander, in tribute to his nine-year-old son, and in praise of the God on whom all his hope was founded, Howells named the tune "Michael."

Are You Tired?

Picture the scene. It's Sunday night. You're at home with your loved ones — except just tonight, they don't really feel like loved ones: they

---

11. Neander's original hymn was *Meine Hoffnung stehet feste* (1680). This quotation is from Robert Bridges' hymn, "All My Hope on God Is Founded" (1899), which is loosely based on Neander's hymn text.

feel like dull, ordinary, hang-around ones, the people who leave their laundry on the ground for you to pick up, the companions who leave their dishes in the sink for you miraculously to beautify, the house-mates who never in a million years remember what day the garbage truck comes along your street at six o'clock in the morning and think to put the trash out the night before — those kind of take-for-granted, been-years-since-you've-really-looked-me-in-the-eye-or-gave-me-flowers loved ones. Bodies are splayed out over sofas, as if to say "I'm so tired I can hardly face Monday morning, and there's nothing that could raise my body from horizontal," and even the idea of feeding the eyes on TV candy or a mindless computer game seems too demanding. If this apocalyptic scene were a cartoon, the caption would read, "The night that energy levels finally plummeted below zero."

And then . . . the telephone rings. And in this digitized age, it's that rare thing — a caller whose number is not recognized by any of the technology your household has assembled for the purpose. Your companion answers the call. Suddenly the whole ecosphere changes. Your companion starts laughing and agreeing with everything the caller says, rocking back and forth on the sofa with breathless intensity and jumping up to fetch a document from another room and answer whatever it was that occasioned the call. Your companion's found a reserve of energy that's convulsed him or her, as dramatically as a computer screen booting up from hibernation mode to full activity. You immediately wonder, "Who *is* this person on the other end of the line? What *precisely* is so exciting about this caller that suddenly turns a sack of potatoes into a dancing ballerina?" And it's almost impossible to avoid a paroxysm of envy. "Where did that burst of energy come from? Why do *I* never see that kind of energy? Maybe Sunday nights aren't about being tired of work or tired of life. Maybe they're about being tired of me."

Do you know what that Sunday night feels like? Do you know what it means to wonder if your head can think anymore, if your limbs can move anymore, if your mouth can speak anymore, if your heart can beat anymore, if your soul can breathe anymore? Are you tired? Are you so tired that it's like looking to the bottom of a very deep well and finding there's no water there — it's completely dry, and sending a bucket down there will do no more than churn up the bare earth?

Maybe there's a good reason why you're tired. Maybe you're tired because you've tried so hard for so long. On December 1, 1955, the Cleveland Avenue bus in Montgomery, Alabama, was filling up. Rosa Parks was asked to give up her seat to prevent a white person having to stand. But Rosa Parks was tired. She was tired of giving in. She was tired of being humiliated. She was tired of being invisible. Four days later, on the day of her trial, the day the yearlong Montgomery Bus Boycott began, fifty clergy and community leaders gathered together. They had one thing in common. They were tired. But like that companion on Sunday night who received the phone call that elicited previously inconceivable energy, these leaders found something they'd never contemplated before. They elected as their president a young pastor, who spoke to them these famous words:

> There comes a time when people get tired of being trampled over by the iron feet of oppression. There comes a time, my friends, when people get tired of being plunged across the abyss of humiliation, where they experience the bleakness of nagging despair. There comes a time when people get tired of being pushed out of the glittering sunlight of life's July and left standing amid the piercing chill of an alpine November. There comes a time.[12]

Are you tired? Are you tired of "being plunged across the abyss of humiliation," and experiencing "the bleakness of nagging despair"? I'm not saying everyone knows what it means to be on the receiving end of the poison of racism and segregation. But maybe you've given your life to enhancing the public schools, maybe you've tried your hardest to heal our health system, maybe you've spent your days trying to change laws or practices that grieve your soul and shame our country, or working on our prisons or on torture or on capital punishment or on care for those with chronic mental illness. Or maybe your struggle is behind the

12. Martin Luther King Jr., Address to First Montgomery Improvement Association (MIA) Mass Meeting, at Holt Street Baptist Church, December 5, 1955. Full speech available at http://mlk-kpp01.stanford.edu/index.php/encyclopedia/documentsentry/the_addres_to_the_first_montgomery_improvement_association_mia_mass_meeting/.

closed doors of the home, and you have a child who's broken your heart and you don't know how to unwind the spiral of pain and mistrust, or you have a sibling you can never look in the eye, or a spouse you've covered up for and colluded with for decades, or a parent who undermines you by the tiniest gesture or the subtlest silence. Or perhaps your struggle is with your own place in the world, your studies, your career, your future, and you feel like you're in a lobby and all the doors leading from it are locked and you've been beating on them with your fists for too long and all you can think to do is to place your forehead against one of the doors and slowly sink down to your knees and weep.

There comes a time when people get tired of being trampled on. There comes a time, my friends, when people get tired of being plunged across the abyss of despair. There comes a time when people get tired of the piercing chill of a damp and chilly February day in a seemingly endless winter. There comes a time. I wonder if that time has come for you. Are you tired?

But there's more than one kind of tired. Let me tell you about another kind of tired. A bad kind of tired. The 2011 film *The Help* portrays the interactions of a number of African American maids in a 1960s Mississippi neighborhood with the white mistresses of the households in which they work.[13] A key figure in the story is Hilly Holbrook, a young woman who successfully found a husband at college, successfully brought into the world a couple of designer children, and is now successfully devoting her time to promoting the "Home Help Sanitation Initiative." Through this initiative Miss Hilly sets out on the brave but vital quest to provide, in every home, separate bathrooms for the "black help" because, as Miss Hilly puts it, "They carry different diseases to us." The more absurd and unsustainable this cause gets, the more fierce and desperate become Hilly Holbrook's efforts to promote it.

Miss Hilly is a symbol for the whole culture of segregation. Hilly Holbrook cannot tolerate having an African American maid who won't play a submissive role in Hilly's increasingly ridiculous attempt

13. Kathryn Stockett, *The Help* (New York: Berkley Trade, 2011). Adapted for film in the movie *The Help*, directed by Tate Taylor, Dreamworks, 2011. All quotations from the film.

to provide a rationale for her prejudice and practice of subjugation. Miss Hilly becomes exasperated with a classmate from college days who resists the stereotypical lifestyle of a Southern belle with the desire for husband, children, maids, and segregated causes. She detests a woman whom she regards as white trash, who stole Hilly's college boyfriend and treats her African American maid much more humanely and respectfully. She falls out even with her mother's generation of women who themselves are ceasing to believe in the moribund social structure Hilly is trying so hard to promote. By the end of the story, Miss Hilly has lost all her allies and is isolated and exasperated. In an effort to banish her latest insubordinate "help," Hilly invents a story about her maid stealing some silverware. The slander is simply a pretext for banishing yet another person who won't fit into her mistress's game. But this time Aibileen, the maid, resolves not to go quietly. Aibileen is like Rosa Parks. She's not going to take it any longer. She strides up to Miss Hilly, stands nose to nose before her, and says, "Mrs. Holbrook, you're a godless woman." Aibileen then pauses, and says, more inquiringly and reflectively, "Ain't you tired, Mrs. Holbrook? Ain't you tired?"

It's a great question. Miss Hilly's world is caving in around her, as fast as a clapboard house collapsing in on itself. Like a totalitarian dictator striving to prop up a disintegrating regime, Hilly Holbrook is trying with all her might to save her disappearing universe. But Aibileen's question catches her off guard. Because of course Aibileen's right. Hilly Holbrook *is* tired. If she stopped for one moment to admit how insane her life was, how hard she was working and how fast she was running to protect a kind of honor that enriches no one and impoverishes many, she'd collapse in humiliation and shame. So she doesn't. She goes faster and more furiously because she's so tired and can't afford to admit it.

Is that you? Are you tired? Are you tired the way Hilly Holbrook is tired? Do you look at your life and see a state of delayed collapse, postponed only by your increasingly frantic and desperate attempts to keep the whole system functioning? It's painful to look in the mirror, because you're frightened of what you might see; it's terrifying to stop running, because the truth may catch up with you; it's too risky genuinely to catch someone's eye, because that person may see into your soul and say those paralyzing words, "Ain't you tired? Ain't you tired?"

Many of us are tired. Some of us are "Rosa Parks tired" — tired of being humiliated and tired of giving our all and having nothing to show for it. Some of us are "Hilly Holbrook tired" — tired of pretending and lying and upholding a life or a culture that's built on falsehood and pride and cruelty. Do you know what? There ought to be a whole lot of other kinds of tired, but I'm actually not sure there are. It more or less comes down to these two. Tired of being trodden down. And tired of pretending. Of course, most of us are a mixture of the two. But I doubt we're an even mixture. I'm guessing that you're tired. And I'm sure you are a mixture of tired, but I'm just as sure that one or the other kind is the real one. And when I ask, "Are you tired?" you know which kind of tired you are.

Well, I've got news for you. The prophet Isaiah's got something to tell you, tired as you are, whether your name's Hilly or Rosa. It's the simplest and best news in the world, better than a warm bath after a long day, better than a feather pillow to rest your weary head. Here's the best news in the world. God's not tired.

Isaiah writes,

Have you not known? Have you not heard?
The LORD is the everlasting God,
    the Creator of the ends of the earth.
He does not faint or grow weary. (Isaiah 40:28)

God's not tired. The Lord is the everlasting God, the Creator of the ends of the earth. God's not tired. Are you listening, Rosa? Are you hearing me, Hilly? God doesn't faint or grow weary. God's not tired. God

gives power to the faint,
    and strengthens the powerless. (Isaiah 40:29)

God's not tired.

Listen up, Rosa. You feel you can't take any more criticism, you can't take any more grief, you can't take any more humiliation, you can't take any more shame. But here's the good news: God can. In Jesus God took all your criticism and pain and humiliation and shame. And he still does. You may be stretched out on the sofa on a Sunday night because you know the next week holds more conflict, more harsh words, more being undermined, and more being afraid than you can face even thinking about, and you're tired just imagining it, more tired than you can say. But God's not tired. God's not tired of justice. God's not tired of truth. God's not tired of the struggle.

> Even youths will faint and be weary,
>   and the young will fall exhausted;
> but those who wait for the LORD shall renew their strength,
>   they shall mount up with wings like eagles,
> they shall run and not be weary,
>   they shall walk and not faint. (Isaiah 40:30-31)

You may be all out of your energy, but just like that companion sprawled out on a Sunday night who gets the phone call that releases a source of energy no one in the household knew was there, you won't be running on your own tank, you won't be living in your own strength, you won't be flying with your own wings.

And Hilly, yes you, Hilly, you listen up too. Isaiah's news for you is just as good. You may be tired — it's a good thing you *are* tired, because it shows you know you're running, and maybe you're just beginning to admit who you're really running from. You may well be tired from all that running. *But God's not tired of you.* You may be trampling on God, wounding God, neglecting God, forgetting God, hurting God. But God's not tired of you. God keeps coming back to you, Hilly, even though you've constructed more and more elaborate devices to keep God away. All you need to say is, "I want to become the kind of person God knows I really am, the person God made me to be, the person God's making me if I would just let it happen." And then suddenly it's like you're curled up in that fetal position on the Sunday night sofa and the phone call comes and you find a rush of energy and life that you haven't known for months or years — perhaps ever. You can walk: after all those years of hobbling and stumbling, you can walk and not faint.

You can run: after all that time running away, you now find the joy of running toward – and when you're running toward God, you don't get weary. You can mount up with wings, because when you're filled with the wind of the Holy Spirit, you won't be needing your legs anymore; you'll be like an eagle, banking and swooping and soaring and diving like you could fly forever.

It's Sunday night. You're tired. You're tired as hell. But God's not tired. And God's certainly not tired of you. It's the best news in the whole world. Isaiah's calling – on a new number. The call is for you.

CHAPTER 6

Learning to Dream Again

This final chapter is intended as the climax of the book because it seeks to draw together themes of head, gut, heart, and hand in the notion of dreaming. The first section engages with the resonance of the word "again" by turning over and over the word "restore." It explores the notion of restoration and offers an alternative that is more firmly grounded in Christian hope. I then move to a meditation on failure. I see failure as having a particular historical location, in that it becomes very much more significant once the public theological imagination has ceased seriously contemplating the reality of hell. Fear of failure is at the bottom of so much contemporary anxiety, but a theological account of failure renarrates that anxiety. One subject where gut and head have been profoundly separated in much of recent American history is 9/11. In the third part of this chapter I seek to keep gut and head in close conversation and find resources for dreaming again after even so great a catastrophe. The central place where head and gut and heart are transformed is the Easter mystery: so I follow my accounts of suffering, failure, and catastrophe with an attempt to listen to the Easter accounts speaking on all these levels.

I complete the chapter, and the book, with a consideration of the dream – the dream of a vocation not etched in stone or formed on a template for all disciples, but emerging from community, suffering, and setback, a dream ever evolving but comprised of features bestowed by the scriptural story, a dream that is forever both anew and again.

Restoring the Years

The American South is a very noisy place. Sit out on your front porch on a summer evening and you're overwhelmed by the intensity of the sound of cicadas. Add the sweat of tropical heat, and you have the perpetual sense of anticipation, the constant sense that something powerful is about to happen, which makes this part of the country such an absorbing place.

Another small creature leaves its mark in a different way. That's the locust. When the desert locust is around, there's always the chance something dangerous is going to happen. Locusts like to get together. A desert locust swarm can pack 60 million locusts into less than half a square mile and stretch to 460 square miles in size. When the book of Joel talks about "the swarming locust . . . the hopper, the destroyer, and the cutter," and how they've ripped the heart out of the people of Judah, you know it's describing every farmer's worst nightmare (Joel 2:25). Each locust can eat its weight in plants in twenty-four hours, so a full-size locust swarm could eat 423 million pounds of plants a day.[1] A whole year of crops, a whole community's livelihood, a whole nation's survival can be destroyed in minutes. There's something about a locust attack – in its swarming, in its insatiable appetite, in its savage obliteration of the crops – that evokes a horror movie. There's nothing to be done other than to grab the shoulder of the person next to you, sink your fingernails into that person's forearm, and scream.

Stay with that locust storm for a moment. I wonder if you know what it means to experience the devastation of the swarming locust. I'm not thinking necessarily of the kind that destroys crops and petrifies farmers. I'm thinking of a young man who told me about a college prank that went badly wrong and left his brother in prison for a terrible, fixed-tariff, bunch of years, stretching out before his family's future like a yawning gap in their collective vision. He said, "My brother didn't mean it, but now . . . all those years until he comes out of jail. All those wasted years." I'm thinking of a friend who felt her rights had been painfully and criminally infringed and took the case through the

1. http://animals.nationalgeographic.com/animals/bugs/locust.html.

courts and faced year after year of uncertainty and expense and antagonism and grief and heartache until she recognized that the case had completely taken over her life. She said, "It feels like so many lost years. All those years." I'm thinking of a man who grew up with a father who was periodically and unpredictably a danger to himself and those around him in such a way that their home became a place of fear in which no one felt comfortable going to sleep, and the whole family developed habits of denial and distrust that infused all their relationships in later life. He said, "I'll never get those years back. My childhood was a gaping hole of lost years."

I wonder if any of these stories feels like your story. What they have in common is that the affected persons felt they'd been robbed of a whole section of their life. They felt, looking back, that all those years had disappeared into a hole. It wasn't just that they had no good memories of those times. It was that there was, even now, nothing to be said about those times — those years were so covered in shame and shrouded in regret and ring-fenced with grief and misery that they could be shared only with their most trusted confidante. I wonder if your personal history contains a chapter like that. Maybe you're in one right now.

There may well have been a locust swarm in Judah in the fifth century B.C. that destroyed livelihoods and ruined farmers and left the people starving. But for the prophet Joel, the swarm of locusts is a metaphor for the invading armies that had swarmed into the land of Israel in the preceding centuries, laying waste to the cities and plundering the countryside and leaving the children of God in utter despair. And this is where the power of the metaphor really kicks in. God visits every part of the suffering land and reawakens it, starting with the soil, and moving on to the animals of the field, and the trees, and finally the rain clouds (Joel 2:19-24). Then, when everything has come back to life, God delivers his promise that the people will eat in plenty and be satisfied; that he, the Lord, will dwell in the midst of them; and that they will never again be put to shame (2:26-27).

This is wonderful and welcome news, and the people are bound to hear it metaphorically as well as literally, in other words, as a promise that the long years of subjection to foreign rule are coming to an end and there will be good times for Israel once more. But think back to what this means for you, on a personal level. Your long nightmare is more or less over, and there's hope of good things to come. That's great. But where does that put those lost years? What joy does that bring to the time you still struggle to put into words, the period you can find no sense in and can infuse no meaning into? What about those moments when an event occurs that evokes a wave of memories from that buried era, and you hope that no one close to you says a tender word or places a hand on yours because you know if that happens you'll crumple into undisguisable sobbing?

Here's where God speaks right into the heart of your bewilderment and despair. *"I will restore the years the swarming locust has eaten"* (Joel 2:25 ESV). Listen to that. Not just a promise about the future. Not just a determination that the good times will roll and you can put the past behind you. No. Something more and different. A promise of healing the past. "I will restore the years the swarming locust has eaten." That's something extraordinary. Think of the young man whose brother spent all those years in prison. "I will *restore* those years." Think of the woman who spent all that time going to and fro between attorneys and judges and never getting any further with her legal case. "I will *restore* those years." Think of the young man who grew up in a house of unpredictable and violent danger. "I will *restore* those years." "I will restore the years the swarming locust has eaten."

Think about your own story. Let those words speak to you. Hear God's promise about abundant food, and an end to shame, and dwelling with the Lord in your midst. I understand if you've heard such promises and you've built up resistances to letting them reach the raw parts of you that cry out for understanding and hope and renewal. But now hear a new word. "I will restore the years." Which years? Come on, you don't need to pretend any longer. You know which years. God knows which years. You know which years. Let yourself hear this new promise, beyond anything you had dared to hope. "I will restore the years the swarming locust has eaten." Let these words seep into your soul.

This isn't about blame, it's not about anger, it's not a question of bitterness. There's a time for all those things, and a time when they can be named and spoken about and not hidden from and recognized and healed. But talking about the locust takes away the distraction of culpability. Swarming locusts aren't evil. They're just being locusts. They do terrible damage, but they're part of creation like the rest of us. The point is, finding who's to blame for those lost years isn't the answer. The years are still lost, whoever's to blame. This isn't about vindication. This is about something more wonderful. This is about *restoration*. This is about something that was lost becoming found, something that was a burden and a curse and a plague becoming a gift.

How can that happen? How can the unspeakable and the unmentionable and the constantly threatening source of loss and pain and degradation be restored as something that brings hope? Restore can mean replace. Well, on the surface, it looks like that's what God is offering. He's offering grain and wine and oil to replace what was taken by the locusts. But replacing is not restoring. When a friend has a precious possession and you break it and you get the money together and buy a new one and take it to the friend, the friend pretends and you pretend that the replacement is just the same; but it never is. Restore can also mean reimburse. When something's lost you can try to make up for it by compensating for its monetary value; but things that are really valuable are worth a whole lot more than money. More often than not, you'd take the money, but you never for a moment think the reimbursement is the same as restoration.

"I will restore the years." Those years can't be replaced and you can't be reimbursed for them. So how can they be restored? Well, they can be reincorporated. That's to say, they can come to shape your future in unexpected and beautiful ways. Experience is simply the name we give to our mistakes, and when experience does no more than take you back to the locust years that you remember like a bad migraine, there's not much to be said for it. But when experience is given time, and understanding, and discernment, and gentleness, and when you later find yourself in a situation that calls for all the resources you can draw on, then experience can be distilled into wisdom. We'd all like to imagine we walk forward into our future, but the truth is, we walk backward into our future, composing our reactions and behavior in unforeseen circumstances out of the discarded elements in our own personal histories.[2] If you're thinking to yourself, "I can't imagine any circumstances in which those locust years could come to offer any kind of blessing," the answer may be, "Perhaps not yet. But there could be something ahead of you where you'll think differently, and where you'll find yourself drawing on that troubling time in ways you could never have predicted." And at the very least, those years will inform your compassion, because you'll come to realize that, if *you* have in your past the years the swarming locust has eaten, maybe others you meet do *too*, however slick and put-together and smart and assured they seem. In fact, you come to *expect* that others have this, unless they truly insist that they don't, and even then you half wonder if really they do protest too much and the truth is they don't yet trust you enough to tell you.

Listen to those words once more. "I will restore the years the swarming locust has eaten." Just imagine you no longer had to try so hard to forget the past, artfully changing the subject every time a conversation got close to locust territory, always wondering, in every relationship, what the other person would think if he or she really knew the truth about you. Just imagine you were promised a future that didn't just replace what the locust had eaten, didn't just reimburse you for it, but truly grafted those years back into your destiny, no longer now as burden and curse but instead as wisdom and compassion. Just imagine, in other words, that you were being given the gospel — the gospel that restores your past and opens out your future. That's what the gospel does. And what's the word that describes succinctly the heart of this gospel? The word is "resurrection."

More than "replacement," more than "reimbursement," more than "reincorporation," more than "restoration": the word is *"resurrection."* The locusts scorched the earth until there was no life in it. Jesus too was buried in that scorched earth and there was no life in him. But he was brought back into the story, he was restored, so that all those years the locust had eaten, the ministry in Nazareth and Galilee that seems

---

2. The concepts of reincorporation and of walking backward into our future are explained in more depth in Samuel Wells, *Improvisation: The Drama of Christian Ethics* (Grand Rapids: Brazos, 2004), 143-53.

obliterated by the cross, and before that the years of God's companionship with Israel over many centuries and glories and tragedies that seems obliterated by the exile, all those locust years are restored to us — and we call them the Bible, our source of wisdom and compassion, our joy and our gift, the gift that comes from the restoration of those years. It is *resurrection* that finally heals the locust years, resurrection that gives us back our past as a gift, resurrection that begins to create our hopeful future out of the ruins of our wasted histories.

"I will restore the years the swarming locust has eaten." Think one last time about your wasted years, your locust years. Is it really beyond God to restore even them? Are you happy to let the swarming locust have the last word? The God who transformed the greatest waste of all, the ruthless slaying of his Son — can he not restore your years? Can he not resurrect even you?

The Word We Don't Mention

I'm thinking right now of a young man who left college ten years ago. He went into consulting work on the East Coast. He spent a bit of time on Wall Street, and had a spell out west learning how companies work. Three or four years ago he and a couple of others set up their own company. It was tough at first but soon it became quite a success. He had a chance to sell it to his original employer, but it meant too much to him to sell so soon. That company was his life, his identity, his pride, his joy. And then very suddenly it all went wrong. The company slid into bankruptcy like a sand castle engulfed by the incoming tide. The young man saw his dream disappear and his security, prestige, and self-esteem melt away with it. Years later, his mother and sister have yet to find a way even gently to refer to the subject with him. His life is shrouded in silence and dominated by the F-word: failure.

Of course, we have sophisticated strategies for calling failure something else. We call it broadening our experience. We call it a learning curve. We call it a blind alley. We mutter things like "If it doesn't kill you, it'll make you stronger." We quote Kipling and say, "If you can meet with Triumph and Disaster/And treat those two impostors just the same"[3] — even though we know that's nonsense and triumph and disaster are not impostors at all. In fact, they're as real as anything we can imagine.

Another approach is to adjust our sights and aim so low that we can't fail. When a person appears to be lazy, it's often a mask for a fear of failure. Being lazy means we can go on saying "Just you watch me when I go" — in other words, if I really *did* try, I really *would* succeed. An Irish humorist once said, "There's only one thing worse than not getting what you want — and that's getting it." In the film *Chariots of Fire*, Harold Abrahams is a young Jewish man with a fantastic ability to run.[4] He has to overcome various kinds of prejudice, but he nonetheless spends years preparing for the 100 meters at the 1924 Olympics in Paris. There's a poignant scene shortly after he's won the race. Abrahams is sitting in the changing room, nursing his precious gold medal. His teammates crash into the room to congratulate him, but his trainer holds them back. Looking at the static, oblivious figure of Abrahams, the trainer says to the teammates, "Hold on, wait, stand back, give him a bit more time and space. You don't know how difficult it is to win."

What I take him to mean is, even when we *do* achieve our ambition, we then have to face the rest of our days, and realize how small our life projects really are. Failure protects us in some ways, because we can remain obsessed by our unfulfilled goal. We only notice its insignificance if and when we attain it. It's difficult to win, because then the striving is over and all the fantasies truly threaten to unravel. I've had the privilege to know a few Nobel Prize winners. You'd think they'd be a proud and arrogant bunch, but they're quite the opposite. They tend to mumble self-effacingly about only getting the award because it was a bad year. It's as if genuine achievement is even more humbling than failure, because it makes you realize how small you really are.

The Bible is full of stories of failure. I want to look at two of them.

3. Rudyard Kipling, "If — ," in *Rudyard Kipling*, ed. Daniel Karlin (Oxford: Oxford University Press, 1999), 496.

4. *Chariots of Fire* (1981), directed by Hugh Hudson, original screenplay by Colin Welland, produced by Allied Stars Ltd. and Enigma Productions, distributed by 20th Century Fox.

The first comes from the book of Ruth. Naomi has a husband and two sons, and both sons take wives from outside the land of Israel. But Naomi's husband and two sons die, and she says to her two daughters-in-law, "Our situation is hopeless — go back to your own people." One daughter-in-law heads home, but the other, Ruth, clings to Naomi and says,

> "Do not press me to leave you
>   or to turn back from following you!
> Where you go, I will go;
>   where you lodge, I will lodge;
> your people shall be my people,
>   and your God my God." (Ruth 1:16)

It's a heartbreaking scene, in which Ruth, in the face of poverty and possible death, says that, for her, there's something that means more than self-preservation and survival. That something is loyalty and love. In showing such steadfast love against all expectations, she shows us the face of God in a way we might never have seen if she'd been lucky and successful.

The second story comes from John's Gospel. Jesus is finding that a lot of people who hung around him early on are turning away from him. He looks at his closest friends, the twelve disciples, and says, "So, are you going to go away too?" (John 6:67, paraphrased). It's as if the whole of the future of Jesus' ministry hangs on this one question. Maybe the whole of the future of Christianity rests in the balance. Is it over, then? Peter is the one who answers. Like Ruth, Peter says there's something more important than popularity and circumstances. And that's love and loyalty. He says, "To whom can we go? You have the words of eternal life" (John 6:68). It's almost like he's saying, Jesus, even if you've failed, your failure is still more important than anyone else's success. Again, Peter shows us the face of God, because God sticks with us even when no one else does, even when it looks like there's nothing in us that's worth sticking with.

The story of Ruth is a story of bad luck. The story from John's Gospel is a story of rejection. But they're both stories of failure. Failure isn't just attributable to our own weakness — it's often attributable to simple bad luck or unaccountable rejection. Why do we fear failure so much? I'm going to suggest why. About 150 years ago, in Western societies, belief in hell started to go out of fashion. It's hard to exaggerate the importance of this gradual cultural change. When people believe in a final judgment and in everlasting heaven and eternal hell, there's only one judgment that matters and that's God's judgment, and there's only one failure that counts and that's the failure to enter heaven. But when you gradually take hell out of the picture, all sorts of judgments become sought after and relevant, and correspondingly there become a thousand ways to fail. We come to fear earthly failure in the same way we fear death — in fact, failure becomes a kind of equivalent of death — which is why the young man's mother and sister found they couldn't even mention the subject to him. Our earthly successes become our quest for immortality, and if we fail, it's like a double dose of death. We crave success, and the reason we crave success is that success appears to be the way we transcend our contingent mortality.

But in different ways, religious faith is built on the insights of failure. The history of Islam begins in earnest when Muhammad the Prophet is virtually thrown out of Mecca and makes his way to Medina to look for more fertile soil for his message. A key to understanding Judaism is to see the despair of the Jews when they were dragged into exile after the invasion of the southern kingdom by the Chaldeans. When they left Jerusalem they thought they were leaving God behind, but when they got to Babylon they discovered God was there too. And failure is also at the heart of Christianity. After all, the symbol of Christianity is a man dying alone in agony, rejected by the great many and abandoned by the close few. Christianity is founded above all on the forgiveness of sins, which is something you only get to discover the day you have the courage and the humility to say "I realize I've been wrong and I've failed and I'm sorry." Christianity is like a twelve-step program: you only get to be part of it if you're prepared to say the terrifying words "I have failed."

The terrifying truth is, we all fail in the end. Life begins the moment you fail, and the moment you admit you've failed. Until then you're living in a fantasy bubble, and if it hasn't been burst yet, it's less likely because people think you're immortal and more likely because they're not optimistic you could cope with living outside it. Of all the moments of insight and self-knowledge in my own life, one of the most significant was probably at the age of about seven when I realized I wasn't going to be a professional soccer player. The rest of my friends took another five years or so to make the same discovery. I've always felt that gave me a head start, because I spent five early years not living in the fantasyland that surrounded my friends. I was quicker to realize I was a failure than they were.

A friend of mine was lamenting the demise of the nonprofit he'd been running and got into a conversation with an army commander. "Failed, did it?" said the commander, abruptly. "Your fault, or someone else's? Learn anything from it? Still lose sleep about it? Do anything differently next time?" The commander kept barking out the questions, but as each one cascaded down it felt not like criticism but liberation, because there was no shame or blame, just an exhilarating sense that life is seldom about much more than making honest mistakes. Finally the commander said, "My biggest failure was in Iraq. Got a lot wrong there. Felt a fool for a long time. Funny thing is, it's only since then that I've really enjoyed my job. Maybe it's because I'm no longer obsessed about meeting people's expectations."

If you want to learn how to transcend failure, if you want to discover how to live with your own failures and those of others, without resentment, you need to spend time with people dealing with long-term conflict and crisis, with problems that can't just be fixed. One such place is Northern Ireland. One priest in Northern Ireland taught me a lesson I've never forgotten. Reflecting on decades of disappointment and destruction and devastation and failure, he gently said, "It's better to fail in a cause that will finally succeed than to succeed in a cause that will finally fail."[5] Think again about Ruth's words to Naomi, and Peter's words to Jesus in John's Gospel. That's what makes them so powerful. "It's better to fail in a cause that will finally succeed than to succeed in a cause that will finally fail."

---

5. I owe this quotation to the late Reverend Bill Arlow, a priest of the Church of Ireland, who was active in the peace movement during the Northern Irish Troubles.

When you've succeeded, has it been in a cause that will finally fail? And when you've failed, has it been in a cause that will finally succeed? In the end the quality of your life will not be measured by the quantity of your successes or the extent of your achievements or your salary or your awards or promotions. It will come down to this: Have you identified and committed yourself to a cause in the light of which all successes and failures will be evaluated, a cause that will indeed finally succeed because of its truth, because of its beauty, because of its goodness? If not, you'll have no real way of knowing whether anything that lies ahead of you is really success or failure. But if you *have* discovered and embraced such a cause, if you've been claimed in such a way that you know who you are and whose you are, then you won't be destroyed by failure or ruined by success, because you'll know that any success of yours is just an embellishment to an already breathtaking picture, and no failure of yours can ruin a wondrous story.

This is my dream for you. That you have already found or will find that cause, or be found by it. That you're not dazzled by your own success, but that you are a hospitable place where others can recognize their own needs and fragility and not pretend success is everything or success makes you immortal. And most of all, that you let your life begin the day you really, seriously fail, and let that day be the day you discover who you truly are and whether that failure is really in a cause that will finally succeed. The most powerful person in the world is the one who isn't paralyzed by the fear of his or her own failure. My dream is that that person is you.

Starting from Zero

The term "Ground Zero" is not an ancient phrase that goes back to America's founding fathers. But neither did it enter the English language on 9/11. The term was first used during the Manhattan Project that planned the deadly bombing of Japan. The fearsome weapons dropped on Hiroshima and Nagasaki in 1945 killed around 200,000 civilians. After the Manhattan Project and its apocalyptic climax, "Ground Zero" came to mean that part of the ground situated immediately under an exploding bomb. Since 9/11 "Ground Zero" has come to refer to the site in New York City where a rather different Manhattan project turned airplanes into guided missiles and left over two and a half thousand people dead.

All of us know exactly where we were when we heard or saw the news. All of us experienced shudders of disbelief, panic, bewilderment, and horror — a sense of something new, and mesmerizing, and terrifying. Of all the distressing outcomes of that terrible day, one of the most poignant and disturbing is the quantity of dust that was generated. When you see the towers collapse, the first thing you see is an upsurge of dust and ash coming out of the descending buildings. That dust remained in the air for days and weeks, even years, afterward, and residents of New York City couldn't avoid it in the air they breathed. When you appreciate that around half of those who died in the Twin Towers were not afterward in any way identifiable in the remains, you realize with horror the incinerated lives that made up so much of that dust.

The original Manhattan Project went out into the desert of New Mexico in June 1945 and tested the world's first nuclear weapon. The code name for the spot chosen for the explosion was "Zero." Out of the dust of the desert, out of Zero, came the project of death. The Manhattan Project, and the obliteration of Hiroshima and Nagasaki that resulted, put an end to the War in the Pacific. That war had begun with the Japanese attack on Pearl Harbor in 1941.

Responding to Pearl Harbor led, four years later, to Zero, to the dust of the New Mexico desert, and to the use of nuclear weapons. Nuclear weapons were a new development in the history of warfare. They changed everything. They opened the door to the killing of defenseless civilians in almost unimaginable numbers. For the four and a half decades of the Cold War, the NATO powers pointed such weapons in the direction of the Soviet Union and Eastern Europe. They did so because it was believed Communism posed a fundamental threat to the identity and integrity of the West in general and America in particular. So great was the fear of the Soviet Union that there was a consensus behind going to almost any lengths to withstand its advance. Ronald Reagan called his adversary the "Evil Empire" — a designation that elevated political rivalry to the status of religious zeal. Reagan also maintained that Communism would soon be consigned to the "ash heap of history" – a claim that seemed to have come true a few years later, when the Soviet Union imploded and the Cold War came to an end.

But out of the dust and ashes of the Cold War, two things happened without many Westerners noticing. One was that the nature of warfare quietly changed. The one war that everyone was obsessed with for fifty years, and that never finally happened, was a war between nation-states: the Soviet Union on one side, and the United States on the other. In the fifteen years following the end of the Cold War, there were no fewer than 118 armed conflicts worldwide, and yet only 7 of them were the old-fashioned kind in which one state fought against another. The rules of war changed almost overnight. War is no longer something fought by soldiers on a foreign field; in the last generation the casualties of war have been mostly civilians, and their killers have usually been citizens of their own country. Part of the outrage of terrorism is that it seems terrorists are taking cruel advantage of democratic freedoms and not playing by the rules of warfare; but the reality is that the rules of warfare themselves have changed and almost no one is playing by the old rules anymore. People who say "9/11 changed everything" are simply naming the moment they stumbled upon this new reality.

The second thing that happened was that a significant body of people in different places around the globe, but especially in the Muslim world, came to regard America very much as America had once regarded the Soviet Union. America had set the precedent for describing its adversary as an evil empire, for arming itself with terrifying and indiscriminate weapons, and for going to almost any lengths to undermine a culture that seemed so deeply to threaten and challenge its own. It turned out that more than one party could play that game. Part of America's strategy had been to support and advance the *mujahideen* who fought against the Soviet Union in Afghanistan in the 1980s. Among those who rose to prominence in the Afghan guerilla war was a young Osama bin Laden.

For bin Laden and many people like him, the demise of the Soviet Union didn't dismantle the notion that there was an evil empire that was to blame for all the world's ills. The notion remained, but the name of the culprit simply became America. As America found itself, somewhat unexpectedly, to be alone as the world's only superpower, it inherited the mantle of being the source of all the world's woes. And this view of America appealed especially to those who saw the world's evils as lying principally in the global political decline of Islam since the seventeenth century — epitomized by the creation of the state of Israel and the long-term presence of American troops in the dusty desert of Arabia, not far from the holy sites of Mecca and Medina. Such people plotted to consign America to the ash heap of history. The zeal with which they did so produced a phenomenon almost unprecedented in American history: the attacker who knew that his attack would instantly cost his own life. And not just one, lone, perhaps possessed, confused, or unstable attacker: no fewer than nineteen hijackers, of one unwavering heart and one unswerving mind. It wasn't Islam that attacked America on 9/11: it was nineteen single-minded people who'd turned being anti-American into a whole new religion.

America is a country constructed around the idea that it is a wondrous thing for any person, however humble or eccentric, to fulfill his or her dreams. But what if the dreams are violent, murderous, and destructive on an unprecedented scale? The reality is, it's very difficult indeed to stop such people. Every step we make to stop them gives us less freedom, less to be proud of about our country, and less space in which to dream. You can't cultivate a freedom worth having without the danger that someone will abuse it. That's the risk of articulating a dream: someone, sooner or later, will trample on it and reduce it to dust.

Painful as it is, it's important today to recognize that the 9/11 hijackers achieved almost exactly what they set out to do. They showed vividly, and in a way no one could ever forget, how profoundly some people in the world resent, detest, and reject American global power and cultural influence. They used the definitive weapon of the new kind of war — a shocking attack upon unwary civilians — so as to achieve maximum casualties. They provoked the leadership of the United States to drastic responses, in the dusty heat of Afghanistan but even more so in the desert dust of Iraq, in internal security but even

more so in the use of torture and indiscriminate imprisonment abroad
– and these responses replicated and expanded precisely the kind of arbitrary and overbearing use of power that they had accused America of
in the first place. They concocted a blood-curdling potion that has poi-
soned the last ten years of American history, a dizzying cocktail of terror and incomprehension that has induced the most powerful economic and military power in history to adopt the mentality of a
wounded and half-crazed lion, breathing vengeance and losing sight of
proportionate response, resolved to do whatever it takes to obliterate
terror from the earth and thus assuage the memory and the pain of its
horrifying scar. And, most of all, the 9/11 hijackers left a series of searing visual images that continue to populate America's worst nightmares, images of sudden horror, hideous carnage, and terrifying destruction, the infinite might of America reduced to zero, an icon of the
demise of an "evil empire," all Ronald Reagan's evocative imagery
turned on its head, the most famous ash heap in history, tower and
temple turned to dust.[6]

In the book of Genesis, we are told, "Then the LORD God formed
man from the dust of the ground, and breathed into his nostrils the
breath of life" (Genesis 2:7). One chapter later, the Lord tells Adam and
Eve,

"You are dust,
  and to dust you shall return." (3:19)

Look carefully at those words. Dust – the dust of the earth, the dust of
the desert, the dust of trampled dreams, the dust of destroyed buildings, the dust of fire-ravaged bodies, the dust of dead skin, the dust
that filled the nostrils of Manhattan on 9/11: this is death, shocking,
earthy, unavoidable, overwhelming, mundane. Dust is death. *But this
is where God began.* God made humanity out of this dust. This is

6. This alludes to a line from Robert Bridges's hymn, "All My Hope on God Is
Founded" (1899): "Pride of man and earthly glory,/sword and crown betray his trust;/
what with care and toil he buildeth,/tower and temple fall to dust./But God's power,/
hour by hour,/is my temple and my tower."

Ground Zero. This is the epicenter of dust. This is where the good news begins. This is where God makes humanity. God formed us from the dust of the earth. God started from zero.

When Christ walked the way of the cross, three times he fell under its weight. The freedom God had given the world was abused so badly that it turned to the ultimate perversity of consigning Christ to Calvary. Three times the weight of the world's folly and foolishness and cold-blooded hatred made Christ implode and plummet to the ground. Three times Christ fell into the ash heap of history. Three times Christ bit the dust. But on Easter Day, God remade Christ out of the dust of the earth. Just as on the day of creation, God turned dust and ashes into flesh and blood. God started from zero and built something that truly would last forever.

God did not send 9/11. God does not condone the atrocity of 9/11. God does not make us for violence or suicide attacks or mass murder and destruction. But hear the words of God, speaking out of the rubble of that dreadful day, whispering to us from the ash heap of history: "You are dust, and to dust you shall return." In other words, "Go back to the beginning. Start from zero." We feel the terror of those poor people on the hijacked planes, facing their imminent death, powerless and panicked. But the truth is, *we're all on those planes*. We're all going to die, we're all ignorant of our destiny and powerless to prolong our life. We shall all be dust. We live in a beautiful country, flowing with milk and honey. Let's leave aside the fantasies about it being the greatest country or having the most spacious skies. Let's concentrate on being a good country, a faithful country, a country where the poor are respected, the stranger is made welcome, the enemy is treated like a human being, the victim can find justice, and the criminal can find restoration and forgiveness. We feel the horror of that pile of dust at Ground Zero. But the truth is, we shall all be part of that pile of dust one day. Sixty-five years ago we had the temerity to create Zero, to create destruction so overwhelming that we could reduce a whole metropolitan area to dust at a stroke. More than fifty years later we saw with horror that we too could become Zero, very suddenly, very cruelly, very painfully. We saw that we too are dust, and to dust we will return.

Towers and temples do turn to dust. Our lives will turn to dust.

There is no freedom that can ultimately prevent the devious, the determined, and the deranged from creating terror and turning goodness and pretension alike into dust. But all our hope lies in the God who makes beautiful things out of dust — who made us out of dust, called Abraham out of the dust of the desert, remade Christ from the dust of the tomb, will remake Manhattan from the dust of Ground Zero, and will finally make all things new — the God who abides in the dust of Afghanistan, the dust of Iraq, and the dust of Arabia, the God who transforms the dust of our trampled dreams, the God who restores those who repent in dust and ashes, the God who breathes life into nostrils cloyed by dust, the God who lifts us up like a firefighter and carries us home like a shepherd — if only, if only amid all our anger and self-justification and sadness, if only we can find the humility and the humanity, slowly and painfully, to start from zero and let God make something beautiful out of even this.

The Rolling Stones

Earthquake. The very word conjures up our deepest, primal fears. We build strong towers, secure walls, formidable foundations — but something up near the top of the Richter scale turns them all into dust and fragments. Whether it's Haiti, or China, or Chile, or Japan, or one day San Francisco again, we have these images of major highways and buildings in crumpled heaps of twisted metal and shattered rock. And, more than anything, we imagine being buried alive, scarcely able to move, with a massive mountain of concrete lying across our chest, asking, "Who will roll away this stone?"

Put yourself back on Good Friday night, A.D. 33. Jesus' body is safely tucked away in Joseph of Arimathea's tomb. And covering the tomb is one enormous stone. Focus on that stone for a moment. It's huge. It's solid. It's very, very heavy. It's utterly immovable. It's inanimate nature at its most unforgiving. It has probably existed for about as long as the earth itself has. It is not the kind of thing that dies. It's just always been there, from the beginning of time, through mollusks, bacteria, invertebrates, dinosaurs, mammoths, Neanderthals — it's seen them all. You can't negotiate with it. It's covering the tomb. It is the final statement on Jesus' death. And it's not going anywhere.

I want you to imagine that stone, and the power it represents, through the eyes of the different participants in the Easter story. Think first of the three women who run to the tomb early on this Sunday morning – Mary Magdalene, Mary the mother of James, and Salome – asking one another, "Who will roll away the stone for us?" (Mark 16:3). For these three women the stone represents the depths of grief. They'd loved, and they'd lost. They had dared to hope, and the object of that hope had been captured, cruelly beaten, unjustly tried, mercilessly ridiculed, and ruthlessly executed. The stone was the barrier between them and their past, a past in which they had believed in Jesus, believed in God, believed in themselves, believed in the power of love, believed in gentleness, and generosity, and forgiveness, and healing, and grace, and gladness, and truthfulness, and joy.

Yes – they'd believed in joy. They really had. Just for a moment there they'd found a life that they'd never known, a hope that they'd never imagined, a love that could never die. But it had died. Life, hope, love – they had all died. They were all squashed and squelched behind that stone. Getting up early to anoint Jesus' body with spices was a way of preserving this wondrous memory, of keeping alive something they couldn't accept was really dead, of honoring a legacy they could never, for one second, forget. It was an act of gratitude and beauty and dignity in the face of gruesome, calamitous, and final defeat. And the incontrovertible evidence of that defeat was that massive, immovable stone.

Now change perspective and think about how the Roman and Judean authorities thought about the stone. For the people running Jerusalem in A.D. 33, that huge, heavy, immovable stone represented their power, their authority, their being in control. They knew their rule was based on a lie. The Judean leaders like Caiaphas the high priest were Roman appointees. They lived with daily humiliation and its crushing compromises. The Romans themselves proclaimed the peace of the *Pax Romana* – a peace that was, in truth, no more than a slogan masking the dominance of one army over another. But such lies seemed a small price to pay for the social, economic, and political privileges of being the ruling elite. Jesus had been a serious threat to these cozy arrangements. By healing on the Sabbath, forgiving sins, cleansing the temple, and being called king, he clustered together all the authorities' worst fears. Having Jesus safely dead, and silencing the voices seeking religious renewal and social revolution – this was what the stone represented to the Jerusalem authorities. Their power was lodged uneasily in the present, not likely to last long; but this execution meant it was safe for another day. The great immovable stone was a bold statement that anyone who got in their way would be squashed like a fly.

But what of Jesus, the figure at the center of the story? What did the stone mean to him? On Palm Sunday Jesus is where God and humanity meet in perfect harmony. Jesus on a donkey epitomizes the renewal of God's people and the coming of the Lord. But five days later everything unravels. The people turn their back on their leader. And, on the cross on Good Friday, the Son discovers he's forsaken by his Father too (Mark 15:34). He dies utterly alone, disowned by humanity and apparently deserted by divinity. That's what the stone represents to Jesus: his separation from humanity and his separation from the Father. The antithesis of everything he is and came to bring about. Jesus is utterly with the Father and the Spirit in the unity of the Trinity, and he came to restore humanity to companionship with God by being utterly with humanity too. The stone is the sign of contradiction, the symbol of everything that separates the Father from the Son and the Son from humanity and all creation.

But here's the crucial point. The stone is part of God's good creation. The bondedness of Christ and the Father, together with the Holy Spirit, is the most fundamental truth there is. The coming of Christ among us shows that God's determination to make us companions in the life of the Trinity is as true and permanent as the life of the Trinity itself. Nothing, nothing whatsoever, neither death, nor life, nor angels, nor rulers, nor things present, nor things to come, nor powers, nor height, nor depth, nor anything else in all creation – and certainly not a large, cumbersome, solid stone – can separate Christ from the Father, or us from Christ (Romans 8:38-40). So, mighty stone, you may have been here since time began, but I guess it's time for you to roll on by. There's a force greater than gravity at work right now.

For the two Marys and Salome the stone represented the past — the glorious but failed memory of a dream that died. For the Jerusalem authorities, the stone represented the present — the compromised but merciless control they exerted while it lasted. But for Jesus, the stone represented the future. It was the symbol that nothing can separate the Father from him or him from us. Every permanent, immovable, unshakeable obstacle you could possibly think of, between us and God, between death and life, between this life and the life to come — every single one of them is going to find itself going the same way as that stone: rolling, rolling, rolling.

And what about your stone? What does the stone represent for you? Reflect for a moment on what is standing, heavy, unshakeable, immovable, between you and life, between you and love, between you and healing, between you and God. Think again about that image of the earthquake: you, scarcely able to move, with a huge slab of concrete lying across your chest, asking yourself, "Who will roll away this stone?" Is that where you are right now? Is that where you've been for a long time? Are you paralyzed, with a great weight across your body, buried under cynicism or sloth or suffering or sadness?

We're all like the three women — we all ache for a glimpse of glory, a taste of joy, a hint of a dream, a vision of hope. But we're all, a little more than we care to admit, like the Jerusalem authorities, full of the compromises that promise to secure control, full of the broken promises made fragile by our anxiety and reluctance to live with uncertainty, full of lies and secrets and half-truths and shabby pretenses. The stone seems unshiftable, but we know it's there partly because we haven't got the courage or the faith or the imagination to see that it could really be any different.

Don't forget that when Jesus' friend Lazarus had been four days in the tomb, and Jesus tells Mary and Martha to take away the stone, Martha's having none of it. Jesus' response is uncomplicated. "Do you want to see the glory of God or don't you?" (John 11:40, paraphrased). He's asking us the same question at Easter. Easter's going to unravel your habitual grief; Easter's going to dismantle your grubby compromises; Easter's going to unsettle your lingering sadness about the past and your half-baked ways of negotiating the present. Because Easter's asking you the same, simple question: "Do you want to see the glory of God or don't you?"

Just for a moment, imagine. Just for a moment, hear the whisper of wonder. Just for a moment, lift your hearts and open your eyes. It's Easter morning. What might it be like if that stone rolled away?

Easter's about something more powerful than an earthquake. An earthquake is when deep in the bowels of the earth something shifts, and the effects are felt on the earth's surface. Easter's about a heavenquake. A heavenquake is when deep in the heart of heaven something shifts, and the earth is never the same again. Here comes the heavenquake. Keep your eyes on that massive stone. It's starting to move. It's rolling. Watch it roll.

Watch that heavenquake roll away the stone of your past. Yes, there's sadness back there; yes, there are shattered dreams and fragile hearts; yes, there are missed opportunities and failed hopes; yes, there are bitterness and resentment, old wounds and broken promises; yes, there are hurts you can't forget and blessings you can't remember. But the stone's rolling from the tomb of your past. It's rolling. Watch it roll, and ask yourself, "Do I want to see the glory of God or don't I?"

Watch that heavenquake roll away the stone of your present. Yes, there are compromises; yes, there are ways you've sold out that would have horrified your youthful idealistic self; yes, there are ways you've domesticated Jesus and kept the church at arm's length and turned dreams into busyness and programmed your life so much there wasn't space to imagine; yes, you read the Beatitudes and don't recognize yourself in any of them; yes, you count the fruits of the Spirit and realize you haven't felt joy or peace or gentleness or kindness for years; yes, your heart is dominated by fears about money and the fragility of love and the anxiety of your own mortality and the sense of your own worthlessness — but the stone's rolling from the tomb of your present. It's rolling. Watch it roll, and ask yourself, "Do I want to see the glory of God or don't I?"

Watch that heavenquake roll away the stone of your future. Yes, I know, you've had this massive slab of concrete across your chest, weighing you down, as long as you can remember. It's hard to imagine the future without it. But the stone's rolling. It's rolling away your past. It's rolling away your present. Now it's coming for your future. Yes, you've always felt others were closer to God than you; yes, you've always feared that the hope of God was a fantasy; yes, you've always found prayer difficult; yes, you think the church is full of hypocrites even worse than yourself; yes, you feel paralyzed in the face of your own death, and the expectations of your culture and family, and the limitations of your own energies and resources; yes, you're terrified to entrust your body and soul to the everlasting arms of the crucified Savior — but the train's left the station, the ship's sailed, the stone has rolled. Watch it roll, and ask yourself, "Do I want to see the glory of God or don't I?"

The stone has rolled. Let it roll. Feel the joy of all your grief and folly and fragility and failure rolling with it. Let it roll. Feel your heart burst with the wonder of resurrection. Let it roll, let it roll, let it roll. This is a heavenquake. Jesus is risen. The stone of death and grief, the stone of sin and control, the stone of fear and paralysis — they couldn't hold steady. They've rolled — and your past and your present have rolled with them. But your future's still open. The stone has rolled away and the future is exposed to the fresh air of early morning and new life. Do you want to see the glory of God or don't you?

It's Easter. It's a heavenquake. It's the day of the rolling stones.

Learning to Dream Again

I once taught a class to a group of trainee youth workers. I was asked to speak on the Ten Commandments. I asked each person in the class to suggest an eleventh commandment. Most of the class came up with something involving the word "respect." As ever, one wise guy said, "Don't get caught." But one student offered something completely different. He said, "Live the dream." I regret to say I laughed, breaking all the rules of Teaching 101. I said, "Er, do you mind me asking which dream that might be exactly?" He said, "I'm not sure, but I still think we should all live the dream."

Jeremiah 32 is set against the backdrop not of a contemporary classroom but of war and despair. The year is 587 B.C., and the Babylo-

211

nians have been besieging Jerusalem for some time. The Promised Land is in enemy hands; the people of God are about to be transported a thousand miles east into exile; and the dream of everlasting life for Israel under God is about to die. Jeremiah is in prison for saying that the city is doomed. But he gets a word from the Lord to go and buy a field in his hometown of Anathoth, a few miles to the north of Jerusalem. And so he does. The story underlines the care with which he completes the transaction, bizarre as his doing so may appear. By almost any standards it's a crazy thing to do. What use is real estate when you've already been invaded and you're about to be exiled? It's like watching the weather forecast the day before Katrina hit and then buying uninsured property in New Orleans.

The punch line comes midway through the chapter: "For thus says the LORD of hosts, the God of Israel: Houses and fields and vineyards shall again be bought in this land" (Jeremiah 32:15). This appears to be a story of the eccentricity of a prophet who's gone off his rocker, or a man obsessed with hoarding the family's landholdings even when they are no good to him. But it turns out to be an astonishing story of hope. While everyone is in denial about today and in despair about tomorrow, seeing only the tidal wave of Babylonian power coming hurtling toward them, Jeremiah is making plans for fifty years' time, when the exile will be over, and a title deed could be mighty handy. Buying a field is a gesture that says, "I believe God will one day bring us home, and when that day comes, I want to be ready and waiting."

Sometimes the world of the Bible seems so far away that we struggle to relate it to our own. But I learned something important from a friend who has the gift of articulating things simply. This friend once said to me, the Bible tells us how God has done unbelievable things, most of all in Jesus.[7] And the way we show our belief in Jesus is to do unbelievable things too. The way to follow the God of the Bible is to do unbelievable things.

Leo Baeck was a man who did unbelievable things. He was one of the leaders of the Jewish community in Germany during Hitler's rise to power. The Jews of course had little idea of the absolute horror that

7. I am grateful to David Hollis for this phrase.

was to come, but Rabbi Leo Baeck was a key figure in organizing the various ways that Jewish people envisaged life beyond the growing terror. Perhaps his story is particularly precious to me because my mother was born in Berlin in 1930 into a family that had only recently converted from Judaism to Christianity. She came to Britain in 1938 as an eight-year-old girl. If it hadn't been for people like Leo Baeck, she never would have left Germany, and probably would not have survived the Holocaust. In the summer of 1939 Leo Baeck brought a trainload of schoolchildren like my mother to safety in Britain. One friend begged him to stay, but he refused. He said, "I will go when I am the last Jew alive in Germany."[8] He went back to Germany, just a short time before Germany invaded Poland and the war began, because he believed God had not finished with his people. It was an unbelievable thing to do.

Leo Baeck's journey back to Germany in 1939 is like Jeremiah's purchase of the field at Anathoth, because in the immediate circumstances of the time it made no sense at all. Just as you'd think any resident of Jerusalem in 587 B.C. would be trying to realize assets as fast as possible, not acquiring more real estate, so you'd think any Jew in 1939 wouldn't be traveling back to Germany but would be hurrying to get as far away from Germany as possible. But Leo Baeck's journey doesn't just imitate Jeremiah's field; it reminds us of the journey of Jesus Christ, from heaven to earth, from Galilee to Jerusalem. Jesus' journey from the heart of the triune God to the heart of human rejection of God was an unbelievable thing for God to do. Jesus' journey up to Jerusalem, to the place of danger, betrayal, and death, was an unbelievable thing to do. But just as Jeremiah's gesture only makes sense in the light of his conviction that Israel would return from exile, so Jesus' march down the way of the cross only makes sense in the light of his conviction that God would raise him from the dead. Even so, it was still an unbelievable thing to do.

When we place ourselves in relation to Christ, or even great figures of faith like the prophet Jeremiah and Rabbi Leo Baeck, we can think of our own efforts as insignificant. But think for a moment of

8. Leonard Baker, *Days of Sorrow and Pain: Leo Baeck and the Berlin Jews* (New York: Macmillan; London: Collier Macmillan, 1978), 238, 246-47.

the kinds of people who founded our great universities. When the to-bacco magnate James Buchanan Duke and the college president William Preston Few dreamed the dream of Duke University in the early 1920s, they planned a grand chapel to crown the edifice. Building Duke's West Campus and transforming what had been the small and provincial Trinity College into Duke's East Campus was a pretty re-markable thing to do. But building on Duke Chapel didn't begin until 1930, by which time America was plunged into the deepest and most notorious economic depression in its history. No one in 1930 was talk-ing about the depression being simply a passing crisis. It was an over-whelming catastrophe. No one would have been surprised if Duke's West Campus had been left incomplete and the building of the chapel left for another day. But the founders of Duke University had a dream. At a time when everyone around them had lost all hope, they pressed on and built the dazzling chapel, completing the construction in 1932 and the fine details in 1935. They did it, like Jeremiah, in the belief that the night of doubt and sorrow would not last forever, and that fields and vineyards would again be exchanged in the land. It was an unbe-lievable thing to do.

They built that chapel because they had a dream. And at root I be-lieve their dream was the same dream that Jeremiah had. I believe there is one fundamental dream that unites the dream of Jeremiah with the more famous dreams of Joseph before him and Daniel after him. And that is, the dream that God will yet bring his children out of exile, out of the place where their sin or the sin of others has placed them, and bring them to a true home, a home of friendship with God, with the knowledge of what it has taken to get there, and the deeper knowledge that, if it cost us something, it cost God so much more. Of course, the most famous dreamer in recent American history is Dr. Martin Luther King Jr., and I believe his dream was this same dream, not for the restoration of some imagined past, but for the bringing of the African American people out from the internal exile in which they had walked for so long. His dream included the vital insight that as long as some of her children walked in exile, none of America's people could regard themselves as genuinely at home or call themselves truly free. You don't need me to tell you that Martin Luther King had a dream. And you don't need me to tell you that Martin Luther King did unbelievable things.

But perhaps you do need me to tell you that a number of years ago I had a very painful experience in ministry. I was the pastor of a small and struggling congregation on the edge of a not very glamorous English city. A few short years earlier the diocese had erected a new church building on a housing project where few people had ever been churchgoers. It was a surprising, remarkable, perhaps an unbelievable thing to do. Sadly, many local people didn't take well to the new building, and a number of local children took to smashing the windows and even, on occasion, throwing stones at church members as they left worship services. Three years after I came to the church things were a little more stable, some of the programs of the church were growing rapidly, and we began to believe that we maybe, just possibly, could do unbelievable things. We used some leftover money from the building fund to install two stained glass windows on the first floor of the very same building where not four years previously every single window had been broken several times. It felt like Jeremiah buying a field at Anathoth. We were saying, one day all the people of this place will find in this church a blessing, and all the fear and antagonism will be gone. Everyone thought the stained glass windows idea was crazy. It was an unbelievable thing to do. But then some things started to go wrong and one or two of the programs of the church started to unravel and what had been a gathering joy started to feel like a nightmare of human frailty. And I didn't know what to do. So I did what Anglican priests are trained to do — I went to see my bishop.

My bishop listened gently as I told him the story. Finally he said, "What was the worst thing about it all for you?" And I said, "D'you know what, I think maybe for the first time in my life, I'd dared to dream." And I wept, there in his study. The reason for my telling you this story is what he then said. He looked at me tenderly and said, "You're going to need time — but you need to learn to dream again." I've never forgotten those words. "You need to learn to dream again."

I want to suggest to you, just as someone once said to me, that maybe it's time to learn to dream again.

Maybe I was wrong to laugh at that trainee youth worker. Maybe he was right about the eleventh commandment. Maybe the eleventh commandment really is "Live the dream." I laughed at what the youth worker said because I thought he was talking about an empty fantasy of facile desire, or he was parroting some kind of cheap advertising slogan. But if the dream is Jeremiah's dream of a return from exile, if the dream is Leo Baeck's dream of preserving his people for their future, if the dream is Martin Luther King's dream of bringing his people out of the exile of racism and into a true home of freedom, then there is only one way to walk in their footsteps — and that is *to live that dream.* Listen to Jeremiah, listen to Leo Baeck, listen to Martin Luther King — and *live their dream.* Live it. Don't just dream it — live it. Live the dream of Jeremiah that God will bring the exile to an end. Live the dream of Leo Baeck that not even a Holocaust can quench the fire of God's love. Live the dream of Martin Luther King that there is a place in this world for all God's children. Don't just dream that dream — live that dream. And may God use you to do unbelievable things.

Acknowledgments

All quotations from the Bible are from the NRSV unless otherwise noted.

Some of the material in this book has appeared in print before, in earlier versions. An amended version of "Our Tortured State" appeared as "Torture Undermines American Character," *Winston-Salem Journal*, January 27, 2012. "The Word We Don't Mention" originally appeared in *Journal for Preachers* 33, no. 4 (Pentecost 2010): 39-42. "The Rolling Stones" was a part of "The Challenge and Opportunity of Easter Preaching," *Journal for Preachers* 35, no. 3 (Easter 2012): 26-32.

Subject Index

Subject Index

Scripture Reference Index